GLOBALIZATION, CULTURAL IDENTITIES, and MEDIA REPRESENTATIONS

SUNY series, Explorations in Postcolonial Studies

Emmanuel C. Eze and Arif Dirlik, *editors*

NATASCHA GENTZ and STEFAN KRAMER
editors

GLOBALIZATION, CULTURAL IDENTITIES, and MEDIA REPRESENTATIONS

STATE UNIVERSITY OF NEW YORK PRESS

Published by

STATE UNIVERSITY OF NEW YORK PRESS

Albany

© 2006 State University of New York

For information, address
State University of New York Press.
194 Washington Avenue, Suite 305, Albany, NY 12210-2384

Production, Laurie Searl
Marketing, Michael Campochiaro

Library of Congress Cataloging-in-Publication Data

Globalization and media studies : cultural identity and media representations / edited by Stefan Kramer and Natascha Vittinghoff.
    p. cm. -- (SUNY series, explorations in postcolonial studies)
    Includes bibliographical references and index.
    ISBN 0-7914-6683-3 (hardcover : alk. paper) -- ISBN 0-7914-6684-1 (pbk. : alk. paper)
    1. Culture.   2. Mass media and culture.   3. Mass media--Social aspects.   4. Civilization, Modern--1950–   5. Ethnology.   6. Globalization. I. Kramer, Stefan, 1966–   II. Vittinghoff, Natascha.   III. Series.
HM621.G59 2006
302.23'09--dc22   2005014023
ISBN-13: 978-0-7914-6683-4 (hardcover : alk. paper)
ISBN-13: 978-0-7914-6684-1 (pbk. : alk. paper)

10   9   8   7   6   5   4   3   2   1

Contents

Acknowledgments

This volume is a selection of contributions from the international conference "Cultural Identities and Media Representations," held at the University of Constance in September 2001. Our first thanks goes to the members of the Collaborative Research Center 511, Literature and Anthropology, of the University of Constance, who generously sponsored this project and made it possible to bring together scholars from the most distant parts of the world.

The final outcome of this volume is, of course, to the credit of the participants of the conference themselves, and we owe them profound thanks for their stimulating papers and their friendly and, most of all, patient cooperation. We also wish to express a special word of gratitude to those whose papers are, for one reason or another, not included in this volume, for their contributions and inspiring comments, which have greatly enhanced the general intellectual spirit of the conference and this volume. These include Kayo Adachi-Rabe, Chris Berry, Greg Dimitriadis, Dorle Dracklé, Stefan Rieger, Nie Xinru, Nina Zimnik, and Zhu Jianhua. Finally, we would also like to thank the editors of SUNY Press for their meticulous editorial work and most friendly cooperation.

Natascha Gentz
Stefan Kramer

Constance and Frankfurt, November 2004

GLOBALIZATION,
CULTURAL IDENTITIES,
and
MEDIA
REPRESENTATIONS

Introduction:
Media of Culture and
the Culture of the Media

NATASCHA GENTZ, STEFAN KRAMER

This volume presents a range of explorations in the field of transcultural media studies, which aim to open up new paths for understanding the role of media in the construction of cultural identities. This collection highlights new methodological approaches to the field of transcultural media studies and engages in a transdisciplinary discourse, which is not harmonized, but, in its function as an intriguing dispute, may be characterized as dynamic and hybrid—a discourse that acknowledges differences and examines different cultural systems by disrupting and questioning the normative character and universalist pretensions of one's own view. Therefore, this volume does not privilege a specific culture or media genre, nor a specific academic discipline or methodological approach. Instead, it presents a wide range of topics from different geographical areas, historical periods, and media genres, such as the internet, film, TV, music, and the print industry, and combines historical, textual, and anthropological methodologies. By this, it tests the possibilities of a transcultural and transdisciplinary dialogue in order to map out new territories, borders, and limits for negotiating cultural identities. Two parallel approaches that engage in a dialogue with each other provide the starting point. On the one hand, the focus of the individual essays is on the role of the media in the process of identity construction. Here, the issue is how modern and late modern or postmodern communication media design collective identities and the cultural self-perception of individuals and impart them as, to use Benedict Anderson's term, "imagined communities" (Anderson 1991). On the other hand, the focus is on representations of identities in the media with regard to their sources of authorization, wherever these may come from. The notion of identity, which is omnipresent in cultural studies, is thus not perceived as a monolithic entity; rather, the participants' interests lie in the various forms of production of cultural knowledge and in the process of constructing cultural identities through discursive formations and cultural symbols.

Emerging from various disciplinary and cultural perspectives, the use of concepts such as interculturalism and transculturation in academic discourse attempts to provide universalist explanations for current developments and, thus, to clarify its own scientific position. Since the 1970s, the phenomena and processes of media societies have increasingly gained significance, both as domains of cultural appropriation and as communication parameters of knowledge and meaning. In this way, they have conformed to the post-Fordist developments in the culture industry. Subsequently, the traditional disciplines have begun to deal with the problems arising from such processes—starting with the studies of the Frankfurt School, followed by the research conducted at the Birmingham Centre for Contemporary Cultural Studies, and resulting in the now numerous institutes for media studies, intercultural communication, gender, queer, and native studies. This process has been attended by an increasing receptivity to such empirical sciences as economics and empirical sociology.

Numerous studies on intercultural media appropriation or forms of communication have demonstrated that the disciplines have entered into a lively, sometimes controversial, dialogue. But in the process, they have only rarely been able to diminish or dissolve the conventional methodological and epistemological limits of their own fields of research. Increasing disciplinary disputes over authority make the question of a possible transdisciplinary method (proclaimed by every participant in these discourses) ever more salient. Such an approach would have to position itself in relation to the methods of the numerous individual disciplines and would constantly have to take recourse in them.

The concentration on the question of localizing the observer of cultures, on the other hand, has opened the way for a transculturation, or, at least, an intercultural orientation of the sciences—emerging parallel to transdisciplinarity and practically inseparable from it (if one wishes to avoid the trap of an academic colonialism). The issue is even more salient when dealing with "foreign" or "alien" cultural systems, as anyone doing research on ostensibly alien cultures or cultural constructs has to confront the problem that one's own practices of perceiving and recording data become a subject of discourse. His or her rigid cultural ascriptions always also result in a lack of insight, as recent events and developments in world politics seem to tragically confirm. The mediation and representation of this standpoint constantly signify a further cultural ascription that has more to do with the claim to one's own authority than with that of the self-conception of the object observed. The concept of "travelling cultures" described by James Clifford (Clifford 1997) thus not only refers to the cultures being studied, but also to the observer's own standpoint and his or her methodological premises.

Accordingly, a focus on culture or corresponding phenomena is more the product of the culturally specific perspective of the observer than of some scientifically comprehensible "truth" about the object observed, which, in reality, largely defies any definition imposed on it from the outside. This not only brings into question the ontological status of "culture," but also of the subject of culture, if this is subjected to a permanent process of contested constructions. Thus, if the subject and the object of cultural analysis are indissolubly intertwined with one another, then universalist definitions of the cultural system must be replaced by a consideration of specific cultural systems. Current processes of global and local cultural circulation may thus be best described as the sum of the various cultural systems and meanings produced from their communicative processes, a sum going far beyond the simple addition of its components. What is needed, then, is a situated analysis of specific transcultural configurations, which takes into account both the complex interplay of social experience and the discoursive construction of its reception as well as the observer's specific point of view in interpreting these data.

A media-oriented cultural anthropology that defines itself as an ethnography of communication, regards culture as a process of mediating and staging the nature of man or of that which human beings in their particular socially-influenced discourses consider to be such. This entails taking into account both the specific everyday processes of the people and communities involved and the material and *dispositif* aspects of their communication in specific situated analysis. The price for this procedure may be the acknowledgment that no system of culture exists at all and that the search for human (or technological) universals, and thus for a unified "nature of human culture," still the aim of much research in this field (and in any case underlying the strategies of the transcultural culture industry), must yield to an inquiry into the specific constructions and representations of cultural identities. An interculturally oriented examination of specific cultural phenomena focuses not only on dichotomies, but primarily on what Homi K. Bhabha termed the "in-between" (Bhabha 1994), exploring the inherent power structures and political economies at work within this third space.

A fundamental problem lies in the mere perception of cultural units, construed by the agents in their cultural environments themselves or from an external perspective. In this respect, the general issue articulated in Bhabha's expression of "the location of culture" arises again (Bhabha 1994). Moreover, regarding its cultural origin and use, even the concept of culture is ideological and presumes a certain epistemological conception, which it also helps put into effect. In numerous societies and language communities there was no equivalent expression for culture until this term inscribed itself medially as a cultural project in most of the cultures of the world. Mass media communication and the transnational flux of knowledge and meaning, with its apparatus-oriented, technological, and *dispositif* conditions, infused all of its cultural and ideological characteristics into the self-concept of most of the people and societies in the world (e.g. one-point perspective in perception and representation, the formation of differences necessary for constructing the identities of individuals and communities, or implicit ideas of linear development). Yet, if the terminological statement of discourse parameters tends to disband or to absorb in advance any alternative conceptions, both the object and the method of conventional inquiry in the field of cultural studies largely exclude any capacity for insights transcending one's own particular cultural horizon.

This dilemma has been solved by the attempt to approach "the other" in a "hermeneutical dialogue." Interculturalism, within this context, cannot simply be defined as an attempt at communication between two otherwise hermetic societies and most certainly not solely as a dialogue between a colonial subject and a colonial object. On the contrary, it expresses itself primarily within the conflict of every society with itself and of every individual with himself or herself and with the multiple internal and external influences from which identity or identities, but also the terminology and the apprehension of the concept of identity, are construed.

On the epistemological level, as German systems theorist Dirk Baecker maintains, the consciousness constitutive of culture always includes an encounter with the imagined Other (Baecker 2000, 16ff). At the same time experience of the Other always determines the perception of self, which is derived from its differentiation from its Other. At the moment of this experience, then, the Other has become an inherent component of the self. At this moment of contact, it has inscribed itself into the latter's internal processes and changed these in an irreversible way. Thus, the Other cannot really be alien, and the unfamiliar media of representation, whether they are based on systems of writing, performances, audio or audiovisual apparatuses, with their respective culturally specific *dispositifs,* inevitably become an appropriated part of the self from the instant of their perception and utilization. This also means that the Other, by means of which the self is defined as self, is no longer alien, but has become a part of the self. The product and the source of cultural self-determination become, again according to Baecker, inextricably intertwined with one another in the *dispositifs* of real or virtual, immediate or mediated perception. Cultural processes do not become an inescapable part of a confrontation with culture, and thus, with some inherently colonialist other. On the contrary, these processes become a dialogue, above all, with the self, whose view of the Other is equally motivated and informed by colonialism.

In light of migration and the globalization of economic, political, and cultural processes, and the transnational character of media representation, no community can now effectively protect itself from coming into contact with alien influences. Yet, this globalization process perceived as a diffuse human experience of the present, needs to be clarified in relation to its specific effects on forms of local agency. Under the conditions of media culture as described by Douglas Kellner (Kellner 1995), every observer is also an object of observation for the observed. Moreover, if, according to Jacques Lacan, the media themselves always return the gaze of the observer, the media apparatuses and *dispositifs* and the intermedia aspects of the representation of culture have to become the center of attention. Culture that mediates itself and communicates itself through media to a public is also inevitably intercultural and an object, if not even in the first place, a product of comparative analysis. Even someone academically trained to interpret culture and cultures must present himself or herself as colonialist in order to maintain one's own claim to culture, from which the authority of the academic inquiry is derived. Yet, in the final analysis, self and Other do actually resist any sort of cultural colonization if these discourses on the respective Other emerge in the same media and are thus possibly able to appropriate the Other in some way and integrate it into the discourses of the self.

It is common sense that the overall presence of media in media societies change and shape individual experiences in a number of ways in terms of cognitive processes of perception, aesthetic representations, narrative strategies, institutional and social networks, and collective or private memory and authorization, aspects which are dealt with in special areas of media studies such as Media Epistemology, Media Semiotics, Media History, Media Anthropology, and so on. The contributions of this volume address these phenomena and methodological problems from divergent perspectives focusing on different geographical areas and media genres, in order to reveal, as a whole, the complexity and connectedness of all these issues. On the other hand, the detailed case study approach of each contribution allows for a deeper insight into the complexity of each single cultural subsystem as part of a—perhaps also imagined—whole media culture system.

Aleida Assmann opens this volume with her essay "The Printing Press and the Internet: From a Culture of Memory to a Culture of Attention," addressing the question of different perceptions of changes in communication cultures through new media in a historical perspective. Juxtaposing discourses reflecting upon the possibilities of new media from the distant past of the Gutenberg era with those from the present, Assmann's specific focus is on the nature of the transformation of the written culture in the new digital era. After comparing the remote discourses on the effects of the invention of printing with those contemporary discourses on the internet and establishing their common assumption of a possible restoration of an oral culture of the past, she identifies a major difference in their ideological frames: the former one being based in a "culture of memory," the latter in a "culture of attention." The different utopian visions behind these ideological frames aimed at different objects, transcending time in the material writing culture, transcending space in the electronic age. A historical perspective on these utopian visions reveals how the formerly religious concept of transcendence was displaced by the concept of secular intellectual transcendence of time, which, according to Aleida Assmann, is now displaced by a cybernetic transcendence of space.

In his essay "Globalization and the Experience of Culture: The Resilience of Nationhood," Wimal Dissanyake continues these reflections upon the individual experience of transcending space in a globalized, digitalized world by focusing on the complex interplay between localism and globalism. Globalism, understood in Raymond Williams's term as a new structure of feeling produced by intersecting narratives on the global and the local, offers an approach to new sensibilities in the experience of culture. As globalism cannot be understood in isolation from localism and also nationhood, Dissanayakee argues against a hasty abandonment of the idea of the nation, which is still so powerfully present in the formulations and constructions of cultural identities, albeit produced in a globalized context. Against this backdrop he discusses modern world cinema as a media which most powerfully articulates how cultural experiences and nations define and shape each other. The Indian and Hong Kong cinemas reveal how different resources of cultural authority are actualized within specific genres. His examples show that cultures cannot be contained within bounded spaces, on the one hand, and that forces of culture are no longer unidirectional, but multidirectional and disconnected, on the other.

How the Other is integrated into one's own culture is the topic of Stefan Kramer's contribution "Transcultural Narrations of the Local: Taiwanese Cinema Between Utopia and Heterotopia" on the cinematic narrations in contemporary Taiwanese cinema. Kramer discusses discourses of "Taiwanese identity" or "Chinese culture" as represented in contemporary Taiwanese cinema by elaborating on the concept of "heterotopia." In Taiwan, the societies must define their own cultural positions especially in relation to local traditionalism, Chinese hegemony, European and Japanese colonial traditions, the protectionism of the U.S., and, not least, the globalism that inevitably invaded the Southeast Chinese island republic in the midst of the "economic miracle," and in relation to the numerous relocalizations following in its wake. Taking Stan Lai's film *The Peach Blossom Land (Anlian Taohuayuan)* as an example, Kramer identifies numerous referential levels to major cultural discourses in Taiwan and shows how the heterotopias of the Taiwanese self-concept are results equally of cultural translation and intermedia transmission.

The circulation of cultural capital in a globalized music economy is situated in a broader perspective by Michael Stone's contribution "Garifuna Song, Groove Locale and 'World-Music' Mediation," which deals with the history and international travel routes of the originally African, Armenian, and later Carribean "Garifuna Music." Discussing the ideological and normative statements behind the label "world music," and its positive and negative evaluations, Stone sets out to situate this music genre in its relation to local authenticity and global marketability in a historical perspective. As he observes, Garifuna expressive traditions enact a dynamic performance strategy long versed in the cultural artistry of subaltern endurance, which can be described as an act of "strategic antiessentialism." Characterizing the operations involved in this process as "groove locale," he argues that the interactive field of commodified popular reception creates the intangible cultural allure (and thus the commercial viability) of sonic otherness, which can be described as a dialectical process wherein dominant and subordinate subjects, influences, forms, and forces converge and act upon one another to create a covariable (and accordingly unstable) field of musical dialogue. Thus, world music encompasses multiple subject positions, aesthetic perspectives, and political dispositions with far richer political potential than a crude mass culture critique is capable of rendering.

In "The Thousand Faces of Xena: Transculturality through Multi-Identity," Miriam Butt and Kyle Wohlmut approach the topic of globalizing images of model identities by analyzing the TV series *Xena: Warrior Princess*, which began its run in 1995 and became an extremely popular TV program. Taking the specific features of the construction of a multi-identity of the figure Xena (transcending heroism, sexuality, and geography) as a role model for identity construction detached from space and historical time, the authors discuss the different components that cater to an enthusiastic fan community in the U.S. Moreover, they draw attention to the intermedia relations in the process of the creation of this heroine figure in magazines and the internet in order to show the public participation in the process of construction of a figure that, in their view, transcends essentialist constructions of identity.

With Arif Dirlik's explorations into the field of narrative strategies for identity construction in "transnational literatures" in his essay "Literature/Identity: Transnationalism, Narrative and Representation," the topic of the close relationship between the global and the local is taken up again. Dirlik poses fundamental questions about the nature of ethnic literature versus historical writing, of which the latter has been placed at the service of exploring ethnic and transnational identities by both the recipients of this literature and their writers. As Dirlik shows in his analysis of contemporary critiques of Asian diaspora literature, national claims on literature have not disappeared with the emergence of transnational writers. Instead the racialization and culturalization of these ethnic writers derived additional force through the emergence of multiculturalism as a response to ethnic self-assertion. Moreover, he observes a curious ethnic complicity in cultural reification in order to sustain a sense of national belonging. Drawing attention to the lack of substantial meanings behind descriptive terms such as "Asian American" or "Chinese American," Dirlik emphasizes the importance of contextualizing such terms, or other terms like "ethnicity," "diaspora," or "culture," in a historical perspective, and draws attention to the historicity of the concept of "nation" itself.

Natascha Gentz, in her study "How to Get Rid of China: Ethnicity, Memory and Trauma in Gao Xingjian's Novel *One Man's Bible*," presents a textual analysis of the autobiographical novel of the first Chinese nobel laureate Gao Xingjian, and discusses his presentation of a Chinese's life in the Cultural Revolution in the context of the reconstruction of a fractured identity, individual and collective memory, and trauma. Gao's self-reflective novel presents an unique attempt at escaping the dilemma of the ethnic writer, as described by Arif Dirlik, through narrative techniques and explicit theoretical reflections upon this dilemma, which are inserted into the story of the novel. Analyzing the underlying narrative structure of the novel, as well as contextualizing his description as part of a transcultural discourse on the Cultural Revolution, Gentz shows how Gao's presentation is no longer restricted by narrowly defined narrative strategies chosen by most of the exile writers dealing with this period in the history of the People's Republic of China. Gao's construction of a multilayered, partly seemingly authentic, partly fictional identity for his main protagonist is an attempt to overcome essentialist categories, while at the same time revealing the sheer impossibility of such an approach—when oscillating between the attempt to escape orientalism and ethnic ascription and the simultaneous establishment of occidentalist stereotypes.

How strongly nationalist sentiments dominate the creation of film music is demonstrated by Roger Hillman in his essay "Film and Music, or Instabilities of National Identity." Hillman explores the cultural mediation of classical music in the cinema. Juxtaposing the usage of classical music in Australian, European, and American films, he differentiates specific modes and levels of referentiality to nationalist sentiments and their underlying cultural identity constructions. Hillman argues that the mix of national identity, cultural memory, and classical music is a potent, yet largely neglected, combination in film which forms an integral part of the narrative.

Irmbert Schenk's essay "The Cinematic Support to National(istic) Mythology: The Italian Peplum 1910–1930" shows, in a historical perspective, how a specific film genre fosters the construction of a national image of superiority in times of actual political and social crisis. Reconstructing the success story of the Italian monumental-historical films, the "collossal" or the "peplum," which occurred in the 1910s and became a very powerful genre in Hollywood decades later, Schenk ponders the question of how this popular genre could fall into oblivion in its home country and yet have such a successful career in different regions, gaining the strong attention of audiences all over the world for decades. Analyzing the aesthetic contribution that these Italian films have made to cinematography worldwide and to the language of cinema in this period of important changes in cinema history after 1911, he argues that the new visual aspect of the cinema in these films gained its own autonomous status for the first time, whereas their reference to a mythical past catered to the specific psychological needs of the audience of the time. Stressing the importance of a contextual reading of the viewing habits and the integration of cinema into the daily lives of the spectators, Schenk makes a strong case for new methodological approaches for analyzing the relationship between media and identity construction.

The specific political context of media presentation and reception in the construction of national identities is the focus of Tamar Liebes's essay "Their Master's Voice? The Coverage of Intifada II on Israeli Television," in which she offers an analysis of different modes of news coverage on Palestinean and Israeli TV and the U.S. presentation of war news in these areas. Whereas the Western news media coverage of this war has been the topic of many discussions, her approach to the modes and methods of coverage of "the other side" is a unique exploration into the complex psychological and political factors in the media negotiations between the Israeli and Palaestenian television. Moreover, in her historically comparative discussion of the dramatic changes undergone by global media between the Intifada I and II periods, she links her observations to the global context of simultaneous war reports on the Gulf War and the Anti-Terror War by the U.S. TV channels. This global horizon of war news coverage enables her to identify a current contradiction between the abandonment of the idea of a committed national media and the presence of war patriotism in contemporary U.S. news coverage.

Ratiba Hadj-Moussa's contribution "Drifted Liberties and Diffracted Identities? Algerian Audiences and the 'Parabola,'" on the function and uses of new media in a specific cultural environment, takes a media anthropological approach to the interplay of media and politics in the formulation of cultural identities. Separating three principle contenders in the Algerian public sphere, the state TV monopoly, the semiofficial Islamic Video and print publications and the new formation of satellite TV users, "le parabole," Hadj-Moussa discusses the transformation of social configurations through the usage of different media. These transformations, engendered by the incorporation the Algerian local communities into a global media, had a profound impact on the self-perception of the dish users, their cultural habits, and gender relations, even if it did not lead to the emergence of a politicized action-oriented public sphere. In her view, these findings challenge the common knowledge about dichotomies between the public and the private in respect to the political context of emerging civil societies.

The last contribution, by Peter Braun, is entitled "The Right to Be Different: Photographic Discourse and Cultural Identity in Hungary." It deals with the effects of visual material on scientific anthropological research. Braun illuminates how political change and innovative methodological usage of new media converge in the establishment of a new discipline of cultural anthropology in postsocialist Hungary. Identifying the major new features of this discipline established by Ernö Kunt and highlighting his special focus on cultural research through representations via film and photography, Braun shows how this technological device created novel representations and visions of local traditions.

The new technologically oriented media dealt with in this volume, from film to television up to the computer and the internet, seem to be eventually displacing the communication systems predating the widespread use of technical apparatuses, as both media critics and fetishists have depicted in apocalyptic or enthusiastic scenarios. But, on the other hand, they have also provoked a boom in the print market, which, at the same time, also strongly influences the aesthetics and the reception of these new electronic communications. In the digital age, this inherent intermedia character of postmodern media apparatuses might soon lead to a fundamental multimedia technology on the basis of a metama-chine combining all of the traditional media apparatuses. Such developments would bring up totally new questions concerning the formation of local and global identity between still extant political nation-states, on the one hand and, on the other, a globalization long since attained by the media. The authors in this book present new explorations into the field of these increasingly impor-tant complex interplays.

REFERENCES

Anderson, Benedict. *Imagined Communities. Reflections on the Origin and Spread of Nationalism,* Rev. ed. London, Verso 1991.

Baecker, Dirk. *Wozu Kultur?* Berlin, Kulturverl. Kadmos, 2000.

Bhabha, Homi K. *The Location of Culture.* London, New York, Routledge 1994.

Clifford, James. *Routes. Travel and Translation in the Late Twentieth Century.* Cam-bridge, Mass., London, Harvard Univ. Pr. 1997.

Kellner, Douglas. *Media Culture. Cultural Studies, Identity and Politics Between the Mod-ern and the Postmodern.* London, New York, Routledge 1995.

The Printing Press and the Internet:

From a Culture of Memory to

a Culture of Attention

ALEIDA ASSMANN

I.

Media thresholds are always accompanied by reflections about the possibilities of each new medium.[1] With every change in the technology of cultural communication, utopian visions and fantasies arise concerning the potential that is released with the advent of a new medium. These visions reveal much about the values, desires, obsessions, and fantasies of the respective era. In this chapter, I will compare the utopian visions of the print age to those of the internet age in order to better understand how these media supplement, contradict, or replace each other.

I begin with the utopian visions of the digital media which, surprisingly, not only point ahead and emphasize completely new configurations of word, image, and sound, but also hark back and promise the restoration of something past and lost. At the core of this backward-looking vision is the enthusiastic description of the digital era as a return to an oral culture. The conditions in McLuhan's "Global Village," of course, are not exactly those of an archaic tribal society. It is stressed, however, that the multisensuous and multimedia quality of an oral society is, in a new way, restituted in the electronic culture. The utopian claim is that something which had been marginalized, restrained, and even completely lost in literate and print culture is being restored by means of the new media. While the sharp contrast was emphasized separating digital culture from the preceding print culture, a new affinity was discovered that linked digital culture to primordial orality. Generalizing, we may say that the introduction of each new medium is accompanied by a discourse which dramatizes the contrast to the preceding media culture. The achievements of the electronic media are therefore praised as an overcoming of the Gutenberg era and as a restitution of that which print culture had in its turn conquered and displaced. Let me quote one of many references which emphasizes this new link to a lost oral culture:

> There's a lot you can do with text, as several thousand years of human culture can attest, but it seemed to me that what the computer enabled us to do was to reach back to the days before printing and recreate the old art of interactive storytelling. . . . It was the coming of print that took away the interactive element, and locked stories into rigid forms. It seemed to me that interactive computer-mediated storytelling might be able to combine some of the best of both forms (Adams 1997).[2]

These are Douglas Adams's words of introduction to his computer game *Starship Titanic* (1997). The new genre of interactive computer games is here presented as a mode of communication that combines aspects of both oral and literate culture. The interactive potential of electronic writing is, however, not only displayed by the computer game of pop culture, but also by the artistically ambitioned nonlinear hypertext. This is also presented in terms of a "second orality" which relieves the reader from the passive role to which he or she had been confined in print culture, turning the reader into the co-author of the plastic material of the text.[3]

Whether and how a reconciliation of oral and written cultures can so easily be achieved remains, however, an open question. It was in the 60s of the last century, when the technology of electronic organization of data was developed in its early steps, that studies started to focus on media history and on the important differences between oral and literate cultures.[4] These investigations made us aware of the fact that the new possibility of writing, namely the arresting of the flow of linguistic sounds in written signs on a material carrier, produced a serious and consequential imbalance in the former symmetry of face-to-face oral communication. To put this in the words of Walter Ong: writing separated the knower from the known. It separated language from voice and symbolic signs from the bodies of those who communicated. For this new form of communication mediated by writing, the German linguist Konrad Ehlich has offered the term 'extended communication' (*zerdehnte Kommunikation*), referring to a situation characterized by the mutual absence of sender and receiver (Ehlich 1983). In written communication, either one or the other of the communicative dyad is replaced and represented by the written text. Writing creates a form of communication that bypasses interaction. It produces a form of mutual absences. First it is the sender who is alone with the message, then it is the receiver. Writing introduced a series of divisions: between knowledge and initiate, language and voice, sign and body. In this respect, the printing press has not created anything entirely new, but has only increased a potential inherent in writing itself. Compared to manuscript culture where texts circulated among close circles of friends and confidants, the printing press further separated the writer, text, and reader from one another.

This development has been commented upon both positively and negatively. Since both evaluations are well known, I can be brief in summarizing the respective positions. The negative view of writing was emphasized by Plato. He saw the symmetrical interaction of oral communication threatened by the invention of writing. In this transformation of communication, he feared an assault on truth and unbridled possibilities for fraud, deception, and profanation. His plea for interactive orality, however, was not combined with a criticism of the authoritative gesture of writing or an argument in favor of the critical voice. He was concerned, rather, with the uncontrollable dissemination of written knowledge and looked for ways and means to protect truth within small circles of initiates who conversed in face-to-face communication. Plato's own highly literary use of writing seemingly contradicts these convictions; it can be understood, however, as a strategy to protect his texts against profane access.

Their positive view concerns the solution to the problem of writing as a technique of arresting utterances in arbitrary signs and fixating them on material carriers such as papyrus, vellum, or paper. This solution is hermeneutics. It is the answer to the threat of a distortion or vanishing of meaning, which is the inevitable fate that written texts incur over time. Hermeneutics, however, is not just a form of repair, it is the establishing of a second order communication which only presupposes the abolition of face-to-face communication. The suspension of reciprocity and the creation of a situation of stretched communication are among the positive potentials of writing that have led to our familiar institutions of textual interpretation in the domains of religion, law, and literature. These institutions are all based upon the fixation of signs and the asymmetrical form of communication that follows from it. The written message is further stabilized by turning it into a canonical text which must not be changed in its material substance, but which is required to be constantly reread and reinterpreted in ever new historical contexts.

Both the negative and positive perspectives on writing converged on one point: writing and face-to-face interaction, let alone printing and face-to-face-interaction, exclude one another.[5] This, however, was seen differently at the threshold of the Gutenberg era. At that time, a new vision arose that emphasized—of all things—the immediate and interactive, in other words: the semi-oral character of the new print medium. In the contemporary discourse on this new medium we hear much of new possibilities of direct communication via written and printed letters and precious little of the dire fixation of signs or the continuous estrangement of meaning. These latter themes become prominent only in the eighteenth century when, facing the new historical development of a mass culture, a new cultural distinction was constructed between the original and the copy. The humanists of the Renaissance did not yet share the anxieties about writing and printing which became such a prominent concern among eighteenth-century writers. On the contrary, they praised the medium as an extension of oral communication, which created the possibility of carrying on a dialogue across the gap of centuries. These humanists, who recovered ancient manuscripts and published them for the first time in philological editions, regarded the extended communication of writing as a kind of dialogue: a dialogue which took place across the abyss of time in a new dimension that we may refer to as 'virtual time.'

I want to refer to this form of interaction, which is based on writing and takes place in virtual time, as "diachronic dialogue." A hundred years before the introduction of the printing press, the diachronic dialogue was invented by the Italian poet Petrarch. He carried on a correspondence with the revered authors of antiquity with whom he felt he was sharing a common space—despite the great historical difference between their ages. "I wished you had been born in my time or I in yours," he wrote to the historian Livy. In the virtual space opened by writing in the language of classical Latin, Petrarch was able to converse with the great Livy as though they were meeting face to face. On the chronological axis, they were divided by what Petrarch called the 'dark ages,' the culture of medieval Christianity that had cut itself off from the world of pagan antiquity. Yet, this buried and forgotten world could once more be revived with the medium of written letters in which the spirit and wisdom of that age were stored. The Renaissance was possible via the magic of writing, which preserved ancient messages for a perpetual dialogue with the future. Petrarch found the kindred spirits that he could not find among his contemporaries in a distant age that became much more familiar to him than the period he lived in.

The diachronic dialogue that Petrarch had established with the authors of the past became a new mode of communication after the invention of printing and the establishment of secular libraries. Nietzsche later referred to the diachronic dialogue as 'a dialogue of spirits' (*Geistergespräch*). This became a goal and topos among Renaissance humanists who withdrew from the anguish of their time into the timeless niches of their libraries where they could join in an ongoing perpetual communication. Montaigne sold his public office to retire into his library; Cardano and Scaliger cherished their studies more than their worldly careers. The entrée billet into this transtemporal world was the command of classical Latin and a memory charged with the works of classical authors. The librarian from Leyden, Daniel Heinsius, wrote about his retreat into his library:

> I no sooner come into the library, but I bolt the door behind me, excluding lust, ambition, avarice, and all such vices, . . . and in the very lap of eternity, amongst so many divine souls, I take my seat.[6]

The German baroque poet Martin Opitz spoke of "a secret conversation and community of great and lofty souls who speak to us across so many hundreds, and even thousands of years" (Opitz 1954, 51). An amazing transformation takes place at the door to the library: the reader is divested of his mortal body and steps across the threshold as purely spiritual being.

This space of virtual time is inhabited by lofty spirits, resonating with the immortal voices of great authors. It is a space of memory as constructed by Renaissance humanists with newly printed scholarly editions of classical authors. When Nietzsche took up the topos of the *Geistergespräch* in the nineteenth century, he highlighted its exclusive and elitist quality:

> one giant calls to another across vast spaces of time, and the high dialogue of great spirits continues undisturbed by the under-current of the base noise of crawling dwarfs. (Nietzsche 1960, 317).

In referring to this memory space of virtual time, Nietzsche stressed the heroic monumentality that he praised as an exclusively male privilege. He defined his own claim to greatness against the background of the dwarfs that emerge and disappear with the changing tide of historical time. For Nietzsche, participation in this circle of the elect is gained by the creation of a great work, deed, or idea that carries an individual signature and transcends its historical limits. Participation in this circle of the elect is but another name for fame, which Nietzsche defined as "a belief in the community and continuity of the great achievements of all times, as a protest against the change of generations and against oblivion" (Nietzsche 1960, 260).

II.

The Gutenberg age produced cultural concepts such as greatness, immortality, and monumental heroism. These concepts are all anchored in the very medium of writing itself, which starts by stabilizing the letters of the alphabet on a material carrier and ends by elevating texts into canonized form. The electronic age has moved far away from these values. Its aim is rather the opposite: the speeding up the flow of information. To savor the contrast between the immanent drives of print culture and electronic culture, let us consider for a moment the institution of the chat room. The contrast cannot be greater between the highly stylized and elitist diachronic dialogue and the chatting on the internet that is carried out with the aid of a key pad. The demand for duration and eternity gives way to ephemeral brevity. Instead of highly formalized modes of initiation, the chat room provides ready access. Anybody can enter this space and create his or her personal profile. The utopian vision of elite exclusiveness as enforced in the *Geistergespräch* arose of course as a reaction against the increasing democratization of knowledge inherent in print culture. This democratization, which began with the publication, multiplication, and dissemination of printed books, has come to full flower in the internet age. Its utopian vision is the universal and unlimited access to information. This vision, of course, remains rather utopian, for it is already becoming apparent that the new technology's demanding and complex infrastructure also creates new social inequalities and new cultural hierarchies. In a world in which half of the population has never made a telephone call, the fulfillment of this promise remains erstwhile in the far distance.

In new ways, inequality and hierarchy are quickly reestablished in the internet. The new giants are created by a concentration of media attention. Attention has recently been introduced as a key term for the digital age. In 1998, two studies appeared, a book by Georg Franck and an internet publication by Michael Goldhaber, which presented and explored this term as a new category for internet communication (Frank 1998; Goldhaber 1998). The authors of these publications define attention as the new economy that has superceded the economy of money in the virtual space of the new media. Both authors argue that we no longer live in the age of an economy based on mass production and consumption, but in one that is dominated by the economy of attention. The main concern in this new age, they claim, is the search for and the maintenance of attention. The art of capturing attention via advertising, which had been a major force in capitalist consumer culture, has become, they claim, a ruling principle of the internet culture. The central protagonists in this economy of information are the stars, the prominent figures focused on by the public media. Stars are described in these new terms as 'capitalists of attention' that have managed to accumulate and maximize the precious resource of attention. The art of gaining and paying attention is presented as the new economy of the age of information. In a world that is more and more transformed into and inscribed with information, attention, as the capacity of selecting information and endowing it with value, has become the most important and scarcest of resources. The technology of information is seen to be dependent on a technology of attention as its necessary complement.

In the internet, attention perpetuates itself according to the simple law that "what has received attention engenders further attention."[7] Even a kind of stock market of attention capital is being established in the internet, which is constantly monitoring itself and becoming more and more aware of this new economy. There is a growing use of new statistical information about websites, listings of the top ten sites of the day, hour, and so on. These lists have gained a potent market value and acquired a logic of their own.[8] What the process of canonization was to the print culture, the intensification of attention is to the internet culture. The clusters of attention, however, are short-lived. They are whirls in the rapid flow of information, media effects that may implode at any moment. They are generated on a surface, disconnected from the material support and institutional infrastructure of a cultural memory.

III.

In the title of this chapter I have opposed the terms memory and attention. I will now try and probe their potential as cultural frames in describing the change of media technology and the concomitant (utopian) visions. Strategies of memory and attention are the respective answers that have been created to deal with the challenges of a continuous increase in the production of information. Nietzsche described this increase through a catastrophic water metaphor; he spoke of a broken dam of knowledge, of a rising flood sweeping away all vital markers of orientation. He feared that "historical knowledge streams (. . .) from sources that are inexhaustible, strange incoherences come together, memory opens all its gates and yet is never open wide enough." (Nietzsche 1957, 23). Water metaphors are also popular when it comes to describing the delimiting effects of the digital age. Digital books have no covers; digital libraries have no walls. The storehouses of knowledge have lost their material density and spatial anchoring. The catastrophic quality of water, however,—floods and bursting dams—has given way to more positive aspects of sport and leisure: one sails the high seas or enjoys surfing in shallower coastal waters.

The reason for the positive or negative thrust of the metaphor is grounded in the different cultural frames and utopian visions of both media. In the print age, the challenge of an inundation of information was answered with the limiting constructions of memory. The operation of arresting the sign and canonizing the text laid the foundation for hermeneutics and immortalization. Nietzsche's countervision of the catastrophic scenario was the educated man of *Bildung* who did not let himself be overwhelmed by the mass of stored knowledge, but was able to create boundaries which helped to limit his knowledge and made it serviceable to the demands of living. Nietzsche considered the ability to stem the flood of information and to select and limit the individual horizon of knowledge the most important task of *Bildung*, a term that, for him, is closely connected with memory.

In the electronic age, the flow of information has gained a speed and dynamic that can no longer be contained by the constructions of *Bildung* and memory. The new strategy designed to command the ever increasing and accelerated flow of information is the swift and targeted access to information as well as an equally swift and alert response to attention stimuli in the process of clicking through data configurations. For the flow of information in the internet is not only structurally organized in such a way as to make it accessible to search machines, it is also designed and displayed according to the economy of attention. Thus, the 'information technology' interacts with a 'technology of attention' which ensures that attention 'flows' against the current of the stream of information. These strategies of attention are much better adjusted to the new media than those of memory. Attention is repeatedly described as a capacity that is ideally adapted to the continuously changing and transient world of the new media. Florian Rötzer has called it "a primarily volatile capacity, functionally adapted to what is new and striking, reacting only to surfaces" (Rötzer 1999/2000). There is no sustained and continuous form of attention in the culture of the new media.

It should not be forgotten, however, that attention is not the opposite of memory but its prerequisite and necessary counterpart. There is no memorizing without previous attention; at-tention is the first step to re-tention. (This pun, by the way, also works in German: *mit dem "Auf-merken" fängt das (Sich) Merken an.*) Rötzer himself concedes that attention may be disciplined in cultures to "higher levels of concentration," thereby changing it into "a more intentional and continuous orientation." In this context, I would like to refer to another book on attention that appeared in 1985. This brilliant study by the English literary critic Frank Kermode has, in spite of its title, *Forms of Attention,* attracted little attention. It deals with attention as a resource not of the electronic age, but of the print age (Kermode 1985). In the print age, Kermode claims, attention was established as an intentional and continuous cultural orientation. He is interested in cultural attention as a process of selecting and valorizing cultural artifacts such as works of literature or paintings. In his book, Kermode analyzes the institution of canonization as a framework for selecting those creative works that merit continuous attention. According to Kermode, the attention due a canonized work is maintained in a process of ongoing acts of reading and interpretation. He writes:

> As we know of no venerable text that has an immanent capacity to survive, we may safely assume that the medium of such survival is the commentary (Kermode 1985, 36, 67).

Kermode described a form of attention that we can now retrospectively consider to be typical of the book age. It is related to selection, canonization, and continuous interpretation, described by him as social institutions that fixate a text or a work of art in the cultural memory. He showed how attention and memory tightly interact in the print age, one implementing the other. Kermode, then, described attention as a central resource of cultural appreciation and valorization, in other words, of cultural memory.

In the age of the new media, however, the operations that transform momentary attention into sustained attention and memory, meet with ever more averse circumstances. Through discipline it can be raised to a higher level of concentration and can assume the form of a deliberate long-term arrangement. The tie between attention and retention, between *Aufmerken* und *Merken,* becomes more and more precarious and is cut altogether. In the culture of the new media, memory is more likely to be destroyed than constructed. The internet, as we all know, is a medium that provides an unlimited plethora of information without actually storing it.[9] There seems to be an inverse relation between the capacity for drawing in information and making it accessible, on the one hand, and that of storing it for further use, on the other hand. The larger the supply of information, the shorter the period of its duration. The appropriate metaphor for the internet is no longer the library with its shelves, stacks, and archives, considered as shrines of knowledge, but the supermarket with its merchandise on display and ready for use. With regard to this new system of managing information, the traditional logic fails us. In the economy of a library, old items were valued just as much and sometimes even more than new ones. In a supermarket, however, what is new and fresh is considered most valuable. Whatever sits too long on the shelves loses its value and is sold at half price.

The internet, then, is a medium of an unlimited capacity for accommodating, presenting, and manipulating information without actually storing it. It may be compared to our short-term or working memory with its enormous capacity for altering and linking information, but it lacks the quality of a long-term memory. This change deeply impinges on the general cultural frame. The internet provides an unthinkable heterogeneity of information, but it contingently changes its supplies from wholesale availability to wholesale loss. The ways of the web as those of the hypertext may be intricate and labyrinthine, but they have no depth. The web is flat and all surface; but the term surface is already inappropriate because it implies depth as its dialectical other.

This structure differs considerably from that of the age of material writing and printing. What was abandoned and discarded in the era of material writing and printing did not necessarily disappear altogether. There is no equivalent to the easy delete function regulating the economy of remembering and forgetting in a culture of material writings.[10] The material remains of what is discarded may persist in niches or be dug up again by historians and archaeologists of a later period. We all know the question that has been raised frequently: What will remain of an internet culture for future cultural memory and historical scrutiny? The remains of print culture persisted in the structure of a palimpsest in which each layer of writing erases and covers up the former while, at the same time, occultly preserving its traces for a possible future restoration. Such a structure, which has characterized the cultural memory of the print age, is unthinkable in the age of the internet. We have left, I want to contend, a culture of memory and entered a culture of attention.

IV.

Let me summarize once more the steps of my argument. I started with the concept of face-to-face interaction, which is destroyed by writing and print culture and restored and reinstated as a value by electronic culture. In a second step the situation turned out to be much more complex, however, because, as I have tried to show, unmediated interaction became a utopian vision and *topos* of early print culture. The visions of direct interaction in the early print age and that of the internet culture obviously aim at different things. The one is developed in the frame of a memory culture, the other in the frame of a culture of attention. This new vision can be better understood if seen against the background of the old one. I want to contend that both exist in an inverse relation to each other. In my concluding paragraph I will try to make this enigmatic statement a bit more plausible.

The utopian vision of the early print age was aimed at transcending time. Francis Bacon praised the written letters which, like the ships of the great explorers, sail from one century to another, carrying the treasures of knowledge from one age to the next. The utopian vision of the electronic age, in contrast, aims at transcending space. The goal of transcending space has a long history, starting with the vehicles employing sledges, the wheel and the sail, and culminating in the ever more powerful engines propelling the vehicles of modern transport, such as trains, cars, planes, or rockets. With unimagined speed, our messages are transported by satellites, sent through a network of undersea cables, and are connected in a worldwide web of servers. The pace with which computers process information is measured in nannoseconds. The acceleration of time, movement, and experience, which has been identified and accepted widely as the formative experience of modernism, has been transferred from external vehicles unto the computing machines. The immanent goal of this technical development is towards an ever faster flow of information. What has been achieved in this process is the closing of the hiatus of distance and the realization of spatially extended communication in near real time. This means that distance has given way to global proximity and extended time has shrunken to an eternal now of a synchronic present.

While the utopian vision of the new electronic age is wholly focused on transcending *space,* that of the early print age stressed transcending *time* by connecting the present to a distant past and by extending the present indefinitely into the future. The Renaissance humanists, who were the first to acknowledge historical distance, saw the possibility of transcending this distance with the help of the new medium of printing, fusing different temporal horizons within the new synchronous horizon of virtual time. We may say that the utopian vision of the early print era constructed a *virtual time* in which a diachronic dialogue was possible; the utopian vision of the electronic age constructs a *virtual space* in which interaction is possible across vast geographic distances. Both the construction of virtual time in the print age and the construction of virtual space in the electronic age are staged as a return to orality and face-to-face interaction. Both make a claim to unmediated and corporeal interaction while both in fact exclude the body from the domain of communication. We have seen that, at the threshold of his library, the reader underwent a transformation as he was about to engage in the diachronic dialogue. He left behind his natural body and put on his spiritual body, with which he participated in the perennial *Geistergespräch.* Something similar happens to the user of the new electronic media. He or she leaves behind his or her natural body and puts on an electronic body in the shape of changing avatars. Before the realm either of virtual time or of virtual space can be entered, the physical body has to be left behind.

What underlies both utopian visions, be they spatial, or temporal, is an urge to transcend the given. I believe that an effort toward 'transcendence' lies at the heart of both print and digital media. Before both media, it was the exclusive task of religions to create a virtual space and make possible an experience of transcendence. Religious transcendence creates a divide between this world and another world, guiding us to the latter. The same holds true for the virtual time created by the humanists: they drew a borderline between historical time and transhistorical time, guiding us to the latter. This also applies to the virtual space of electronic media, which draw a borderline between physical locality and virtual ubiquity, guiding us to the latter. Every form of transcendence, and herein lies the utopian moment, involves a specific form of transformation, decorporation, excarnation, spiritualization. In religious transcendence, this decorporation is connected with the idea of holiness; in temporal transcendence, it is connected with the idea of immortality; in spatial transcendence, it is connected with the idea of disembodied ubiquity.

The concept of transcendence, then, used to be a religious concept that involved the possibility of communicating beyond this world. When it was readopted as a humanist notion, it meant communicating beyond the present, reaching into the past or the future. Readapted once by the new media, it means communicating beyond spatial limitations. While religious spiritual transcendence aimed at overcoming the limitations and trials of this world, and secular intellectual transcendence aimed at overcoming the limitations of time, cybernetic transcendence is aimed at overcoming the limitations of space. What was once conceived of in terms of religion and memory is now conceived of in terms of a new technology that liberates the human body from being physically tied to one place only. This utopian vision is elaborated in postmodern Gnostic myths that speak of a self-transcendence in avatars, thus liberating the self from the restrictions and constraints of the organic.[11]

In the various transcendences, which I have here presented in analogy to one another, there is an inbuilt tendency toward mutual displacement. Just as the temporal transcendence of the printing age asserted itself against religious transcendence in the early modern age, the spatial transcendence of the electronic age is now displacing the temporal transcendence of the print age. This, however, would be a simplified and even falsifying account of the complexity of the historical process. We know that in the history of technology, consecutive media do not easily replace and substitute each other. With my investigation into the cultural frames of media change and the utopian visions that are involved in it, I wanted to highlight and assert the specific logic of each of the respective visions. In a historical process, these cultural visions have become part and parcel of the technical and social structure of each medium, and we are sharing them consciously or unconsciously when we engage in the various media. My argument is, therefore, that as we live with different media, we also partake of different cultural visions which do not necessarily efface or exclude each other.

NOTES

1. When the situation of the new media is discussed historically, it is often presented as part of a technical history that goes back to Allan Turing, cybernetics, and the development of war technology in the twentieth century. If it is discussed at all in a

longer historical perspective, which goes back to include the print age, such a comparison is often invoked within a discourse of cultural critique that disparages the specificity and possibilities of the new media. I want to distance my presentation from both of these approaches. What I am interested in is a long view into the history of media that compares discourses of the present with those of a distant past. Such a comparative analysis will not automatically lead to pessimistic statements about contemporary culture if we withstand the pressure toward defining one side of the opposition as a standard and model for the other. Such an approach would be a normative one. My aim is rather an approach of mutual mirroring, describing the experience of the new media in the perspective of the old as well as discovering certain aspects of the old media in the light of our knowledge of the new.

2. I owe the hint to Frank Furtwängler.

3. On intertextuality and the discrepancy between promise and fulfillment of this promise see Matussek, "Die Gedächtniskunst und das Gedächtnis der Kunst."

4. Goody, *Literacy in Traditional Societies*; Ong, *Orality and Literacy*; Havelock, *The Muse Learns to Write*; Zumthor, *La lettre et la voix*; Assmann, *Schrift und Gedächtnis.*

5. In this respect, the printing press has not created anything entirely new, but has only increased the potentials hidden in writing. As long as texts were circulated as the manuscript culture in close circles of friends and confidants or recited at court, the bond of communication was not yet seriously stretched. It was the press that really separated writer, text, and reader from one another. The more stable and autonomous the text grew in the course of letter-press printing, the more definite became the mutual absence of writer and reader.

6. Cited by Robert Burton, *An Anatomy of Melancholy* (1621), ed. H. Jackson (London Dutton 1972) II, 2, 4: 91.

7. Kunstforum, 58.

8. I am indebted to Michael Taylor for this example, who has read this chapter and provided important criticism and associations.

9. There is a considerable change in the systems of ordering information from the title pages and catalogues of alphabetically arranged names of authors to the electronic search machines that can address every atom of the information directly and individually.

10. In spite of the delete key, which destroys only the reference to finding the stored information, there is still the trace of physical magnetic impression, allowing for much information to be recovered, for example, by law enforcement. As for Freud, who claimed a recovery of the repressed, there is now a technical recovery of what was (purposeful or inadvertently) deleted.

11. This rhetoric is inspected by Matussek, "Computer als Gedächtnistheater," 2000, 81–100; here: 85, 86.

REFERENCES

Adams, Douglas. Introduction to *Douglas Adams's Starship Titanic*. Edited by Terry Jones. London, Harmony Books 1997, 1–11.

Assmann, Aleida, Jan Assmann and Christof Hardmeier. *Schrift und Gedächtnis*. München, Fink 1983.

Brogsitter, Karl Otto. *Das hohe Geistergespräch. Studien zur Geschichte der humanistischen Vorstellungen von einer zeitlosen Gemeinschaft der großen Geister*. Bonn, Bouvier 1958.

Burton, Robert. *An Anatomy of Melancholy*. Edited by H. Jackson. London, Dutton 1972.

Ehlich, Konrad. "Text und sprachliches Handeln. Die Entstehung von Texten aus dem Bedürfnis nach Überlieferung." In *Schrift und Gedächtnis*. Edited by Aleida Assmann, Jan Assmann, and Christof Hardmeier. München, Fink 1983.

Franck, Georg. *Ökonomie der Aufmerksamkeit*. München, Hanser 1998.

Goldhaber, Michael H. "Die Aufmerksamkeitsökonomie und das Netz," Parts I and II. Translated by Florian Rötzer and reprinted in *Ressource Aufmerksamkeit. Ästhetik in der Informationsgesellschaft*. Kunstforum International 148 (1999/2000).

Goody, Jack. *Literacy in Traditional Societies*. Cambridge, New York, Cambridge Univ. Pr. 1968.

Havelock, Eric A. *The Muse Learns to Write: Reflections on Orality and Literacy from Antiquity to the Present*. New Haven, Yale Univ. Pr. 1986.

Kermode, Frank. *Forms of Attention*. Chicago, London, Univ. of Chicago Pr. 1985.

Matussek, Peter. "Computer als Gedächtnistheater." In *Metamorphosen. Gedächtnismedien im Computerzeitalter*. Edited by Götz Lothar Darsow. Stuttgart, Frommann-Holzboog 2000, 81–100.

———. "Die Gedächtniskunst und das Gedächtnis der Kunst. Erinnerungstechniken im Medienwechsel." In *Inszenierungen des Erinnerns*. Edited by Erika Fischer-Lichte and Gertrud Lehnert. Berlin, Akad-Verl. 2000.

Nietzsche, Friedrich. *Werke in drei Bänden*. Volume I. Edited by Karl Schlechta, München, Hanser 1960.

Nietzsche, Friedrich. *The Use and Abuse of History*. Translated by Adrian Collins. New York, London: Macmillan Publ. 1957.

Ong, Walter J. *Orality and Literacy: The Technologizing of the Word*. London, New York, Methuen 1982.

Opitz, Martin. *Buch von der deutschen Poeterey*. Tübingen, Niemeyer 1954.

Rötzer, Florian. "Inszenierung von Aufmerksamkeitsfallen." Kunstforum International 148 (1999/2000).

Zumthor, Paul. *La lettre et la voix de la "littérature" médiévale*. Paris, Seuil 1987.

Globalization and the Experience of Culture: The Resilience of Nationhood

WIMAL DISSANAYAKE

One of the defining features of the twenty-first century is the increasingly convoluted and complex interplay between localism and globalism, and its implications for the idea of nationhood. Clearly, this process has been in operation for centuries, but the velocity of it has risen sharply during the past fifty years. This interaction has produced remarkable transformations in the spaces of politics, economics, and culture, as newer forms of capital, originating largely in the west, began to imprint their local visibilities and inflect in unanticipated ways historically sedimented practices. How the symbolic forms and modalities of association of western capitalism are transformed, localized, and legitimized in most countries throughout the world in relation to their historical narratives and changing life worlds is at the heart of the discourse of localism. In the latter part of this chapter, I hope to show how this discourse is vitally imbricated with the experience of culture in the present world.

A productive way to understand the dialectic between the global and the local is through an examination of the production of newer and more complex localities. When we seek to interrogate the intersecting narratives of the global and the local, what we are aiming to do is to focus on the production of the local and its ever changing contours in response to the imperatives of the global. The local is never static; its boundaries, both temporal and spatial, are subject to ceaseless change. It is characterized by a web of power plays, agonistic interests, pluralized histories, and struggles over polysemous and asymmetrical exchanges. The local is constantly transforming and reinventing itself as it seeks to reach beyond itself and engage the translocal. What is interesting about the experience of culture in the contemporary world is that it foregrounds and gives figurality to these complicated processes in compelling and interesting ways within the national space. Indian and Hong Kong cinema, which I discuss in this chapter, furnish us with cogent examples illustrative of these trends. The well known anthropologist Clifford Geertz is surely right when he calls attention to the need in social understanding and cultural redescription for a continual tacking between the most local of local details and the most global of global structures in such a way as to bring them into simultaneous view (Geertz 1973). This simultaneous view will uncover many hitherto unmapped processes at work in the domain of culture. Deleuze and Guattari focus on this phenomenon when they allude to the notion of de-territorialization, in which the production of the local is inflected by the nexus of activities occurring elsewhere (Deleuze and Guattari 1986). What is interesting about the domain of culture, particularly cinema, is that it makes available the semiotized space for the articulation of the global imaginary and its formation within the phenomenology of the local and the space of the national. A study of Indian and Hong Kong cinema will make this complex symbiosis between globalism and nationalism apparent.

We are living at a moment in history when the local and the global are coimplicated in complex and unprecedented ways. As a result of the phenomenal growth of science and technology and the stupendous proliferation of media of communication, the world is shrinking as never before. This very shrinkage, paradoxically enough, has had the effect of generating local narratives and indigenous projects with undiminished vigor. A new world space of cultural products and national representation, which is simultaneously becoming more globalized and more localized as capitalism moves across borders, is also producing coalitions and resistances in everyday life. The interface of global forces, images, codes, sites, and technologies of transnationalization with those of local communities, tactics, and symbolic strategies confronts and challenges them in the production of locality (Wilson and Dissanayake 1996). These, along with the making of new everydaynesses, constitute some of the distinctive features of the contemporary world. Cinema presents us with a compelling cultural space in which we can observe how these phenomena are played out. The popular cinema of India and Hong Kong provides us with narratives, repertoires of images, frames of intelligibilities, and enfolding discourses that enable us to make greater sense of this interanimation of the local and the global.

Globalization, as I suggested earlier, has become a defining marker of the twenty-first century. It can be examined at different levels of analytical apprehension. At the level of economics, the worldwide spread of free market capitalism and the complex ways in which it inflects the local, the weightless economy that has come into being, the dominant knowledge economy that obeys different axioms from the industrial economy that antedated it, and the growing influence of multinational corporations are all important. At the political and social level, the challenges to the nation-state, the proliferation of nongovernmental organizations, and the new social order that has come into existence following the fall of soviet communism are all important. At the technological level, the increasing impact of new communications, technologies ranging from satellite communication to the internet and websites, are highly significant. At the level of culture, the impact of consumerism, commodification, the transnationalized forms of pleasures and desires and their concomitant impact on indigenous traditions becomes extremely important. David Harvey's characterization of globalization "time-space compression" has great implications for the experience of culture within a national space (Harvey 1989).

One useful way of understanding the experience of culture in the present globalized society is through the interplay of the two concepts culture and civilization. According to Raymond Williams, culture is among the two or three most complex words in the English language. This is so partly because of the way this word has developed in several European languages and partly because it has now come to be deployed for important concepts in a number of distinct disciplines and incompatible systems of thought. The word civilization, which has much in common with the word culture, is at times used interchangeably and at times antagonistically. For example, F. R. Leavis, following a line of thought opened up by Mathew Arnold, saw culture in an adversarial relationship with civilization. As the title of his book *Mass Civilization and Minority Culture* indicates, culture has to do the salvaged work consequent upon the leveling down impact of civilization (Leavis 1930). However, at other times and in the view of other critics, culture and civilization overlap very closely. In the present world what we are seeing is such a convergence of ideas of culture and civilization. In our globalized world culture and social life are related to each other in newer ways as is reflected in the growing power of the aesthetics of commodification, the cultural interests in consumerism, the emergence of the society of the spectacle and the crucial role played by image, and the collapse of the distinction between high culture and popular culture. Hence, one productive way of grasping the deeper currents associated with the experience of culture in our globalized world is through the convergence of culture and civilization.

The complex relationship between globality, locality, culture, and the experience of culture has to be understood in terms of the dynamics of cultural modernization. Contrary to what the theorists of the 1950s maintained, modernity is multifaceted and the process of modernization is never linear. It is evident that modernization is a global condition that reshapes our understanding of the self and society, time and space in culturally specific ways. Despite the overwhelming influence of modes of production on modernity, modernity is not reducible solely to the imperatives of the economic. Its relationship to cultural formation is vital and demands the closest attention. Its interaction with tradition is not one of simple opposition; it engages tradition at different levels, promoting revaluations and reinventions of tradition. Of course cultures are not timeless entities, but products of history, politics, and geography. They are terrains in which meanings related to everyday life are constantly made, unmade, and remade. As a consequence of the efforts by diverse groups in society to make sense of the vastly new conditions they encounter, newer understandings of the world and our place within it take shape. It is against this backdrop of thinking that we have to explore the relationship between globality and the experience of culture and its complex intersections with the discursive constructions of nationhood.

Globalization needs to be understood as a new structure of feeling in the sense that Raymond Williams uses the phrase (Williams 1979). Such phenomena as the movement of global capitalism, the transnational corporation and the new division of labour, the power of information technologies, the end of the cold war, the undermining of the nation-states, the resilience of nation-states, decolonization, feminist and ecological movements, global entertainment, and the rise of newer forms of imagination are central to this new structure of feeling. The experience of culture provides us with a useful terrain on which to examine the ontology of this structure of feeling. Walter Benjamin pointed out how, in the nineteenth century, a new sensibility based on new sensual perceptions emerged inflecting cultural textuality (Benjamin 1983). Similarly, from the late twentieth century onwards, a newer sensibility based on newer sensual perceptions is making its presence felt. In order to understand the current structure of feeling associated with globalization we need to explore this newer sensibility. The current experience of culture, especially as it relates to cinema, should enable us to undertake this task profitably.

As I stated earlier, globalism cannot be understood in isolation from localism and nationhood. This is not, of course, a simple opposition as some cultural critics seem to suggest. A more useful way of understanding this relationship between globalism and localism is through the trope of the chiasmus, in which one crosses with the other. Localism should not be seen as parochial or mythical; the natural tendency to romanticize it should be avoided. The local is both a site of hope and crisis, of accommodation and resistance, of acceptance and contradiction. What is interesting about the interplay between the global and the local is that both are in a constant process of interaction and evolution, one feeding into the other. The hybrid spaces, which we have begun to discuss in recent times, are a direct outcome of this chiasmic process. The interaction between the local and the global informs the experience of culture in modern societies. What we need to do, in order to understand the shape and movement of this experience of culture, is to undertake a more situated analysis, paying closer attention to issues of class, caste, and gender within the discursive domains of nationhood. We need new analytical vocabularies that go beyond simple binarisms to capture the essence of the experience of culture in the modern world.

The word experience has generated much discussion in recent times. The post-phenomenological trend in recent times has sought to devalue the concept of experience as being ideologically suspect, a product of discourse and irrelevant to contemporary theoretical discussions. The work of such scholars as Lyotard, Derrida, and Althusser tends to reinforce this point. The writings of Foucault and Bataille tend to take a position in between while Barthes and de Certeau underline the importance of experience. It is Lyotard's belief that experience is in terminal crisis and that it is being constantly undermined by the forces of techno-science, the mass life of the metropolis, and the absence of a sense of temporal direction, resulting in retrospective memory (Lyotard 1984). Critics like Raymond Williams see the value of the concept of experience while being sensitive to its fraught nature. Williams expresses the view that experience involves an appeal to the whole consciousness, the whole being, as against dependence on more specialized or more restricted faculties. Therefore, it is a part of that general movement which underlies the growth of culture. According to Williams, the strength of this appeal to wholeness, against forms of thought which would exclude certain forms of consciousness as being merely personal or emotional, is evident. However, within the form of appeal, in the domains of art and culture, the emphasis on wholeness can become a form of exclusion of other nominated partialities. Raymond Williams is fully aware of the problems with the concept of experience as it relates to his structure of feeling. It is my conviction that, despite all its drawbacks and ambivalences, the concept of experience can be used productively in the understanding of the role and function of culture in a rapidly globalizing world. Hence, my decision to discuss globalization in terms of the experience of culture.

The concept of experience seems to move between two extremes. Thinkers such as Althusser argue that experience is the medium of ideological illusion and that it is only through the production and utilization of concepts that we can apprehend reality. On the other hand, there are those thinkers like Leavis and, to a lesser extent, Raymond Williams who regard experience as the deepest space of truth. It is evident that both these extreme viewpoints are misleading. One should be able to anchor one's analysis of social reality while recognizing the crucial ways in which it is ideologically inflected and discursively constructed. It is my belief that there is a need to recuperate the concept of experience as a way of gaining access to reality.

In recent times, the trope for understanding globalization has changed from penetration to circulation. The idea of penetration of capitalism was widely used by those who embraced Marxist world system theory. This theory pointed to the complex ways in which various institutions and ideas travel across the globe and begin to influence life in various locations. The notion of penetration, with its suggestions of coercion and force and the wilful imposition of the interests of the powerful onto the less powerful, has been supplanted by the trope of circulation with its suggestions of the flow of blood in bodies. In a word, the focus is now on supposedly free and equal exchange. This trope seems to signal the collapsing of hegemonic divisions of nations, races, cultures, and languages and the ascendancy of freedom, mobility, and cultures in dialogue and hybridity. However, these global circulations conceal many hegemonic features associated with global capitalism. When one examines the work of a writer like Saskia Sassen, one begins to realize that global circulation conceals many problems and inequities related to social living. Hence, while it needs to be recognized that the dynamics of circulations are driving globalization and promoting challenges to traditional ideas of nationhood, race, culture, and language, it is also important to bear in mind that this circulation takes place in a decidedly asymmetrical space. While circulation-based capitalism and associated technologies and social formations signify a new phase in which the national capitalisms that existed from the seventeenth to the twentieth century are being made and remade at the same time globally, they nonetheless represent a constitutive aspect of capitalism with all its inequities. Consequently, in seeking to understand the newer thinking of globalization and the experience of culture, one has to increasingly direct one's attention to the notion of circulation; one should do so in full awareness of the potential concealments that it effectuates. How cultural experience and nations define and shape each other has to be accorded very close attention.

It is against this backdrop of thinking that I wish to focus attention on two important cinemas of the world—those of India and Hong Kong. India is the largest film producing country in the world while, until very recent times, Hong Kong was the third largest. The interplay of localism and globalism marked the growth of Indian cinema from the very beginning. Cinema is not an indigenous form of artistic communication in India; it was an importation from the west. However, it very quickly put down roots in the Indian soil and the consciousness of the people and succeeded in assuming the status of a local art form. When one examines the genealogy of Indian cinema, one realizes how central the interaction between the global and the local has been to Indian filmmakers (Gokulsing and Dissanayake 1998). Simultaneously, the reimagining of the national space has been a crucial preoccupation. In this regard, five formative influences present themselves as being significant and far-reaching in their power of inflection. Firstly, the two highly esteemed epics, *Ramayana* and *Mahabharata*, played a very significant role. From the very beginning of Indian cinema, these two epics, which were an animating force in classical poetry, drama, art, and sculpture, also exercised a profound influence on the growth of cinema. This influence can be explored at four levels: thematics, narrativity, ideology, and communication. From its inception up until today, the two epics have continued to furnish Indian filmmakers with themes and story lines. The very first Indian talkie, *Raja Harischandra*, was based on the *Ramayana*, and, interestingly, the filmmaker was deeply involved in the Indian freedom movement. Since then, hundreds of films have drawn on the *Ramayana* for their plots. In addition, thematics related to motherhood, femininity, patrimony, and revenge, enunciated in themes like Mother India, Awaara, and Zanzeer, repeatedly find an emphatic articulation in popular cinema; here we perceive the direct influence of the two epics. What is interesting is that the attempt to make use of the two epics was informed by a modern sensibility. Hence, we see the coming together of the local and the global from the very beginning.

It is only by paying close attention to the structure of narrativity in popular cinema that we can begin to understand its uniqueness as a cinematic discourse. Although, as I shall indicate later, Indian cinema was manifestly influenced by

Hollywood, the art of narration, with its endless circularities, digressions, detours, and plots within plots remained characteristically Indian. Once again, the influence of the two epics is readily apparent. Instead of the linear, logical, and psychologized narratives, which we find in Hollywood cinema, the mainstream Indian cinema offers us different orders of diegesis which can be understood most productively in terms of the narrative discourse enunciated in the *Ramayana* and *Mahabharata*. What we find then, even at the very inception of Indian cinema, is the interplay of the local and the global and the preoccupation with the idea of nationhood

Next, I would like to focus attention on the classical Sanskrit theatre as a formative influence on popular films. Sanskrit theatre constitutes one of the richest legacies of classical Indian culture. It was highly stylized and its preferred mode of presentation was episodic, placing great emphasis on the spectacle. In it, music and dance and mime came together in an exquisite union to create a complex artistic unity. We can identify several features of classical Indian theatre, which have had an important bearing on the construction of popular cinema in India. Classical Indian plays were spectacular dance dramas, in contrast to the tightly organized placed on the characteristic of the west. They were non-naturalistic, stylized. One can see in the general tenor of popular Indian cinema some of the features of Sanskrit theatre. However, Indian filmmakers sought to draw on this tradition from a sensibility inspired by the modern. In other words, as with the epics, we see the coming together of the local and the global.

After about the tenth century, Sanskrit theatre began its downward trajectory. There were a number of factors that precipitated this situation. Concurrently, several dramatic forms emerged or matured in the various provinces of India, which, albeit of an unrefined and inelegant nature, preserved and embodied some of the central features of the classical Indian theatrical tradition. The Yathra of Bengal, Ram Lila and Krishna Lila of Uttar Pradesh, Bhavai of Gujerat, Terukkuttu of Tamilnadu, and Vithinatakam of Andhra are the most prominent among them. These various regional folk dramas, which are basically the work of untutored folk artists, contain one common feature: namely, that in varying degrees of reliability, they incarnate in living form some of the outstanding inscriptions of classical Indian drama. An examination of the central features of these folk plays makes it evident that they have been influenced by and carry over the style and techniques of Sanskrit theatre. In the deployment of humor, music, dance, the structure of the narrative, and the informing melodramatic imagination, the folk dramas of India have clearly had a deep impact on the makers of popular commercial cinema. It is interesting to note that these folk dramas, which are given to improvisation, very often incorporate contemporary experiences related to modernization. Once again we see the interface of the global and the local.

In our inquiry into the genealogy of popular cinema, the next important cultural force that we need to explore is the Parsi theatre, which came into existence after the nineteenth century. The Parsis, who were rich and gifted partly because of the unavailability of a deep-rooted cultural tradition of their own in the Indian soil, took up drama both in Gujerati and in Hindustani. During the nineteenth century, the Parsis succeeded in gaining a wide reputation as resourceful playwrights and versatile technicians who influenced the theatres of North and South. Many Parsi theatrical companies toured the country, performing before packed audiences. Some of the more notable among them, like the "Elphinstone Dramatic Company" of Bombay, visited neighboring countries like Sri Lanka, then Ceylon, and played to enthralled audiences. Stylistically, these plays, displayed an odd mixture of Western realism and Indian fantasy, narrative and spectacle, music and dancing, all amalgamated within the narrative discursivities of melodrama. These Parsi plays, with their lilting songs, crude humour, *bon mots*, sensationalism, and dazzling stage craft, were aimed at appealing to the vast mass of theatregoers. The Parsi theatre, which drew on both Western and Indian forms of entertainment, represented an attempt to pander to the lowest common denominator in taste. These plays also exercised a profound influence on the imagination of the Indian filmmakers. Indeed, the Parsi plays bear an uncanny resemblance to the generality of commercial films made in India. The conjunction of the local and the global is there for everyone to see. If the folk theatre is based in rural areas and seeks to present the lexicon of inherited theatrical articulations, the Parsi plays indexed an urban theatre exposed to Western styles, sensibilities, and semiotics of commodified desire and entertainment. In terms of thematics, textuality, visuality, cultural inscription, narrative discourse, and modes of presentation, the Parsi theatre and commercial cinema in India share much in common. Once again the intersections of the discourses of localism and globalism and the concern with nationhood are evident.

In discussing the genealogy of Indian poplar cinema, the next important cultural force that invites close attention is Hollywood cinema. Indeed, in the Asian context, the absorption of Hollywood by indigenous film industries represents a telling example of globalization, with all its myriad problems. The influence of Hollywood on the makers of commercial cinema in India is both deep and pervasive. Indian filmmakers were greatly impressed by Hollywood and sought to adopt the codes and conventions of Hollywood cinema to suit local tastes, sensibilities, and conventions. Indian film directors found the technical resources that their Hollywood counterparts had at their disposal most attractive and sought to imitate them and create an Indian world of magic and make-believe. Makers of commercial cinema in India, very often, took directly from Hollywood film story lines, character types, and memorable sequences, and reshaped them to suit local sensibilities. For example, Raj Kapoor was an admirer of Charlie Chaplin, Harold Lloyd, Laurel and Hardy, and Buster Keaton.

Indian film directors were greatly fascinated by the enticements and possibilities of the Hollywood musicals. Hollywood musicals stood in a very interesting relation to performance in the classical and folk theatre as well as the Parsi theatre. The heyday of Hollywood musicals was from about the 1930s to the 1950s. It is evident that a large number of musicals had as their privileged subject the world of entertainment itself. The narratives of these films were largely conventional, even predictable, while the songs and spectacle cleared a representational space in which both characters and the audiences could indulge in flights of fantasy. It was through the instrumentalities of the plot that the apparent disparities between the narrative and spectacle were reconciled. This is, of course, a trait discernible in the commercial films made in India.

Many of the popular films in India sought to adopt pathways that differed considerably from some of the conventions and preferred modalities of presentation valorized by Hollywood filmmakers. One of the fundamental tenets of Hollywood filmmaking, for example, is the desire to cover up the artifice, the constructedness of their efforts. All aspects of film production were perceived as ancillary to the projection of a realistic and convincing narrative. As a result, camera angles were largely at eye level; lighting was unobtrusive; framing was aimed at focusing attention on the central action of a given sequence; cuts were made at logical junctures in the unfolding of the narrative. These devices served to foster an illusion of reality and to promote ready identification with characters appearing on the screen. Popular Indian cinema, on the other hand, grew out of somewhat different roots: there was never a deeply felt desire to conform to the 'invisible style' pursued by Hollywood. Hence, while makers of commercial films in India were fascinated by Hollywood and sought to imitate its products in certain ways, they also chose to ignore some others in the pursuit of their own agendas. Questions of national cultural space figured prominently in these calculations. The interanimation of the local and the global is indeed a complex process of selective adaptation.

Musical Television of comparatively recent origin, has taken on the force of a global phenomenon. It is a force that has begun to inflect popular cinema in India in interesting ways. During the past two decades, with the growing exposure of Indian audiences to MTV, which is disseminated through national and international channels, Indian filmmakers have seen in MTV a rich resource for stylistic innovation. The pace of the films, the quick cutting, newer forms of presenting dance sequences, and the camera angles that now seen in Indian films are a direct result of MTV films. The work of Mani Ratnam or popular films like *Satya* or *Kuch Kuch Hota Hai* bear testimony to this fact. One reason for the mass appeal of cinema has always been the clever mixture of entertainment and technology. Hence it is hardly surprising that modern film directors in India associated with popular Indian cinema are seeking to establish newer connections between technology and entertainment and set in motion newer circuits of desire and pleasure.

The increasing influence of satellite television in India also has had a profound influence on the reshaping of Indian film culture. Rupert Murdoch's

"STAR" (Satellite Television Asian Region) network, Subhash Chandra's "Zee Television," "Sony," and "Doordarshan" have begun to inflect Indian cinema in interesting ways. These television channels have begun to use films and programmes related to films and film stars in interesting ways as a means of increasing their viewership. Telefilms have become an important segment of the programming of "Doordarshan" as well as satellite television networks. This has resulted in, among other things, the interanimation of film and contemporary televisual cultures in complex ways, thereby introducing newer elements to the experience of expressive culture and the self-understandings of nationhood.

The intensification of the process of globalization has begun to influence the audiences for Indian films as well. The markets for Indian films abroad have begun to make their presence felt on the calculations of Indian film producers in significant ways . In this regard, popular films made in Hindi and Tamil are most important. Like most diasporic communities, Indian audiences too, living in the United States, United Kingdom, Canada, and Australia, for a variety of reasons, are becoming more and more interested in films that deal with themes of Indianness, Indian history, and Indian nationhood, thereby underlining the emergence of deterritorialized nationalisms. Film producers are quite sensitive to this propensity. What this means is that in the new globalized world, Indian film culture is turning toward the Indian national imaginary in paradoxical ways.

There are a number of interesting points that need to be made regarding these formative influences on Indian cinema, which foreground the intersections of localism and globalism in interesting ways. First, it is clear that these forces never congealed into a neat unity reinforcing each other. Instead, they retained their identities and distinctiveness and followed their own path of giving popular cinema its characteristic amorphousness. This also resulted in the dominance of 'force' over 'form' in the Deleuzian sense. Second, these diverse influences are filtered through an evolving and modernizing consciousness and the interpretations put on the more ancient influences in particular take on an emphasis of contemporaneity. Third, the meaning and relevance of these forces change in accordance with newer social and cultural discourses that come into play, thereby investing Indian popular cinema with a timeliness that is vital to elicit popular participation. Hence, as we explore the genealogy of popular Indian cinema, what we find is not a smooth confluence of diverse forces leading to an elegant unity, but a problematic coexistence of different influences within the evolving matrix of cultural modernity and the space of national imaginary. This underlines the complex nature of the chiasmic relationship between the local and the global.

The complex and multivalent relationship between the global and the local is most powerfully articulated in modern world cinema. Indian cinema furnishes us with a convincing example of this interplay. It foregrounds, in interesting ways, issues of cultural modernity, nationhood, secularism, capitalism, consumerism, ethnicity, citizenship, cosmopolitanism, and collective agency. Cinema originated in India, as indeed in all other countries, as a result of the complicated dynamics of globalization and localization, hence the need to situate cinema at the intersection between the global and the local in order to grasp its true importance. One of the defining features of the contemporary world is the increasingly complex representation of urban experience in films. Cinema made its appearance as a work of visual spectacle and commodification associated with the city. As a consequence of the interaction between the local and the global, cities like Bombay and Calcutta not only represent themselves but also clear a space in other global cities to make their presence felt. It is almost as if Foucauldian heterotopias are in operation here. To represent Bombay is also to partially represent Los Angeles. And these transformations have deep implications for the production of newer libidinal economies and spectatorial subjectivities in Indian cinema. It is evident then that the interplay of localism and globalism in cinema has great implications for the experience and understanding of culture and for ways of reimagining the nation.

If we pause to examine some of the newer trends in the space of Indian cinema we begin to see how the coming together of the local and the global tends to add newer layers to the experience of culture and provoke reimaginings of the national space. For example, the critical, theoretical, and interpretive writings on popular cinema are increasingly drawing on current western formulations. Similarly, the newer audiences for Indian cinema and the way they tend to shape the nature and form of Indian cinema testifies to this fact. Moreover, as a consequence of the intensification of globalization, transnational television has begun to make its presence felt in the domain of popular Indian cinema. All these trends then serve to underline the fact that the increasing interplay of the global and the local has deep and far-reaching consequences for the experience of culture and the self-understanding of nationhood. In the contemporary discussions of popular cinema in India, despite all the globalizing imperatives, the nation remains an untranscendable horizon.

Let us now turn to Hong Kong cinema. Here, my focus is on martial arts films, which have come to assume the status of the signature of Hong Kong cinema and a badge of nationhood. When we examine the origins and the growth of this genre in Hong Kong we begin to see the complex ways in which the conjunction of the global and the local, and the paradoxical intersections of the affirmations and negations of the national space, have inflected it. In this chapter I am using the term martial arts film to denote a generic category that includes swordfights as well as hand-to-hand combat. There is a certain terminological confusion that should be clarified. Normally, the Mandarin term *"wuxia pian"* is used to refer to martial arts films with swordfights, such as King Hu's movies or Ang Lee's popular film *Crouching Tiger, Hidden Dragon.* The term "kung fu" is employed to denote martial arts films containing unarmed fistfights. This category really became internationally popular in the 1970s. The works of Bruce Lee and Jackie Chan belong to this category. However, outside Hong Kong and at times inside, the term kung fu is used to denote films with swordfights as well. This confusion itself is a symptom of the transnationalization of Hong Kong cinema and the tendency of western action films to draw on the codes and strategies of martial arts film. When most moviegoers outside of Hong Kong think of Hong Kong cinema, what immediately comes to mind is the heroics of the martial arts films. As with any film genre, there are different subcategories within the general rubric. In the case of martial arts movies, there are films devoted to sword fighting and horsemanship, hand-to-hand combat, comedies, technologized versions, and so on. And these movies have evolved during the past eight years or so, responding to newer challenges and reshaping them. They also have become interesting sites for foregrounding commerce and the imperatives of the national imaginary as well as the dynamics of transnational space in cinema, testifying to the power of the intersections of the local and the global to inflect the experience of culture.

The growth and expansion of the discursive boundaries of the martial arts films testifies to the ever increasing interplay between the local and the global. The martial arts are closely linked to the deepest well springs of Chinese culture. Originally, kung fu designated, not a form of martial arts, but the undertaking and successful completion of daunting tasks. It focused on a certain attitude of mind and a disciplining of the body. According to legend, Bodhidharma, who was involved in the propagation of Buddhism in China, came to the famous Shaolin monastery. It is here—a monastery well known for the translation of Buddhist scriptures—that kung fu took root. As with all legends, this one points toward an important historical fact, in this case the deep religious and cultural roots of this art form in the national imaginary.

As far as cinema is concerned, martial arts movies began to be produced on the mainland in the 1920s. They were designated by the compound phrase "*Wuxia shenguai pian*" which literally meant martial arts-magic spirit films. They combine modern technology with a traditional sensibility, a coming together of the global and the local. At first they generated a great measure of enthusiasm among audiences, bringing a new sense of cinematic excitement. For a short while this new form of filmic entertainment dominated cinema. At this early stage of martial arts filmmaking, martial arts movies were heavily influenced by the aesthetics, codes of representation, and rhetorical strategies of stage plays. These were combined with a desire to make use of the available technical resources for the enhancement of the visual effect. However, this newfound enthusiasm did not last long, and the enthusiasm for these films began to wane quickly. There was also a strong reaction from certain quarters of society, which saw them as promoting a retrogressive valorization of feudal values at the expense of social progress.

It was only in the 1950s, with the Huang Feihong film series, that kung fu movies sprang back to life, and this time it was in Hong Kong. Between 1949 and 1959, nearly seventy episodes of the Huang Feihung series were produced. This film series succeeded in giving a strong boost to the Hong Kong film industry, infusing it with a new vigour and the films with a broad-based appeal. Huang Feihung began to lose some of its attracting power in the 1970s, although the series continued to be made until the 1980s. Nearly one hundred episodes of the Huang Feihung series were made, marking them as constituting a significant stage in the growth of the Hong Kong visual enter-tainment and the self-understanding of national values. The interplay of the local and the global that was seen in the early martial arts films took on a more intense and complicated form in these films.

These films are important, not only on account of their promotion of the kung fu tradition in Hong Kong and an interest in it abroad, but also for creat-ing a distinct image of this form and displaying its cinematic possibilities. In particular, a certain kind of easily recognizable hero, who was strongly moti-vated and capable of enlisting the admiration of the generality of moviegoers emerged. He was idolized as he sought to live by and disseminate community-sanctioned values. He was a respecter of tradition, upholder of cultural norms, altruistic, generous, and quick to react to injustices and rectify them. In creat-ing such an idealized hero, the Hong Kong filmmakers drew, not only on the traditional repertoires, but also on western film culture. Once again, the inter-face between the local and global and the salience of the national imaginary become apparent.

The martial arts movies were invested with a new vibrancy in the late 1960s and 1970s with the work of King Hu and Zhang Che. They sought to revitalize the martial arts form. As King Hu is the better known of the two internationally, his work merits some consideration. King Hu attempted to draw on the representational strategies, visualities, and oralities of the Peking opera as well as traditional Chinese paintings to create a martial arts film tradi-tion that emphasized poetry of physical motion. A highly acclaimed film like *A Touch of Zen* illustrates this point. When one examines King Hu's films, one begins to perceive the way traditional sensibility and modern filmmaking inter-act at different levels of artistic expression, underlining the significance of the meeting of the forces of localism and globalism. In the 1970s, Bruce Lee gave an added impetus to the kung fu films by investing them with certain elements that had a transnational appeal. He succeeded in making kung fu movies rele-vant to contemporary times by infusing them with a sense of modernity, even as he focused on the importance of patriotism and the discursive constructions of Chinese greatness. He focused on the male body in novel ways by making clever use of the apparatus of the cinema. What is interesting to note here is that he focused on the male body as a way of drawing attention to the idea of nationhood and its significance in the national imaginary. Films such as *Fist of Fury* and *The Way of The Dragon* served to promote a discourse of nationhood on the basis of the power of the male body. It is also interesting to observe that a new note of hybridity—ark of globalization—entered the kung fu movies with the work of Bruce Lee. As critics like Kwai-chung Lo have pointed out, although he focused on issues of Chineseness, nationhood, and patriotism, he himself was an American citizen, born in California, and had a Eurasian mother (Lo 2001). And biographical factors have a way of intervening in the cultural products of entertainment in interesting ways.

The next stage in the development of Hong Kong martial arts movies is marked by the emergence of Jackie Chan. This emergence also marks the further intensification of the forces of globalization on Hong Kong cinema. Chan succeeded Bruce Lee, who died in 1973, as the leading figure associated with martial arts films. The image of the hero too underwent a change, signifying an important departure from the past. While focusing on elements of physicality and performance of stunts, Chan introduced an element of the slapstick which had a transformative effect on the genre. Instead of portraying patriots and men of indefatigable valour, he brought characters that were ordinary to the screen. In films like *Drunken Master* and *Snake in the Eagle Shadows,* one sees the trademark features of Jackie Chan's art. With the work of Bruce Lee and Jackie Chan, martial arts films began to exercise a greater influence on the imagination of western audiences, thereby calling attention to a newer aspect of the interplay between localism and globalism. In the 1990s, there was a revival of the swordplay films, notably with the launching of the swordsman film series. Today, martial arts films have become a worldwide phenomenon, generating interest among moviegoers in America, Europe, Asia, and Latin America and inflecting the global vocabulary of action films the world over. The recent spectacular success of Ang Lee's swordfight film *Crouching Tiger, Hidden Dragon* generated an unprecedented interest in martial arts films in the west, and Zhang Yimou's film *Hero* promises to intensify this appetite. Interestingly, the dynamics of martial arts movies have now been absorbed by Hollywood films such as *The Matrix, Tomb raider,* and *Charlie's Angels.* This reflects the power of globalization as well as the technologization and transnationalization of the martial arts film. This quick survey of the martial arts films of Hong Kong points to the fact that martial arts films represent the increasing intensification of the interplay between the local and the global at different levels and in diverse registers, raising significant issues related to the experience of culture.

What this discussion of the popular cinema of India and Hong Kong points to is the need to reunderstand and reexplore the experience of culture, which is subject to massive transformations. The concept of culture advanced by Raymond Williams, which I alluded to at the beginning of this chapter, sees it as a whole way of life that underlines integration, unity, and boundedness. However, the culture that is coming to being as a consequence of globalization gives pride of place to multiplicity, transgression of boundaries, and hybridity. It is evident that cultures cannot be contained within bounded spaces and that through the flow of people, ideas, and images across boundaries a new volatility has come to characterize the experience of culture. In addition, it needs to be noted that, as a result of globalization, forces of culture are no longer unidirectional, flowing from the west to the rest of the world, but rather are multidirectional and disconnected. They are instrumental in bringing about unpredictable and strange juxtapositions. However, the important point is that these phenomena do not announce the demise of the nation-state. To the contrary, they refocus on its importance. The global flows of capital, commodities, images, technologies, labour markets, and ideologies both challenge and reinforce the nation-state. Some critics of contemporary culture seek to understand globalization and culture in terms of cultural imperialism. To my mind, this captures only a part of the experience. By cultural imperialism is understood the imposition of western culture on the rest of the world with the mass media of communication playing a pivotal role. Critics argue that the economic and cultural processes unleashed by global capitalism result in this cultural imperialism. Hence, cultural imperialism refers to the coercive domination of the rest of the world by the west through culture and, along with it, the imposition of western values, life ways, commodities, and outlooks.

While there is much to be said for this notion of cultural imperialism, it tends, at times, to simplify matters and be reductive; the flow of culture, as we noted earlier, is not unidirectional and we need also to recognize the power of cultural spaces to put up resistance. What we see is not a sense of homogenization, as cultural imperialism theorists would have us believe, but a heterogenization and hybridization. Moreover, the concept of cultural imperialism is based on a center periphery model that many find unpersuasive; for example Arjun Appadurai, who wishes to emphasize the complex and intersecting and disjunctive orders, says that, for people of Irian Jaya, Indonesianization may be more worrisome than Americanization, as Japanization may be for the Koreans, Indianization for Sri Lankans, Vietnamization for Cambodians, and Russianization for the people of soviet Armenia and the Baltic Republics (Appadurai 1996). At a minimum, then, we need to pluralize the concept of cultural imperialism and talk in terms of cultural imperialisms. In order to convert the idea of cultural imperialism into a more productive tool of social analysis, we need to explore its inner dynamics in the light of contemporary cultural experiences, relate it to the forces of global capitalism in a more complex manner, and tie it to the discourse of nationhood.

The dynamic of globalization cannot be understood without paying adequate attention to the political economy that subtends it. Indeed, this is a point that has been repeatedly and emphatically pointed out by critics like Arif Dirlik. The way a select group of multinational corporations dominate global nexuses of production, promotion, and consumption is important in this regard. Hence, the ways of global capitalism and capitalist modernization offer us valuable information regarding the process of globalization and its impact. The interplay between political economy and cultural meaning in globalization deserves closer and sustained attention. As Dirlik points out, to fall victim to a kind of culturalism that serves to divorce culture and cultural textualities from the political economy will only result in a distorted vision of reality (Dirlik 1996).

A significant problem for contemporary cultural analysts is how to frame the discussion of the new globalized culture. The concept of hybridity has been pressed into service by some astute critics. In the hands of commentators such as Homi Bhabha, Stuart Hall, Paul Gilroy, and James Clifford it has attained a hermeneutic sophistication and analytical power. However, the concept of hybridity, as critics like Ella Shohat have argued, needs to be unpacked very carefully so as to bring out the different levels and valences embedded in it (Shohat 1992). One cannot ignore the fact that hybridities operate within power structures and political economies. Without adequate attention being paid to these vital aspects, it is impossible to map the full implications of hybridity, both positive and negative. Pheng Cheah is most cogent when he remarks that hybridity theorists seem to argue that if culture is perceived as a discursively constructed entity, then the subject of culture is transformed into a terrain of permanent contestation (Cheah 1998). The idea of subversion is apparently built into it. However, as Cheah observes, there is a tendency among hybridity theorists to glorify hybridity into motive force for the political interrogation of diverse forms of cultural symbolization and the articulation of marginalized political identities without providing any substantial arguments why this should be so. Hence, despite its undeniable heuristic value, the concept of hybridity should be examined and reformulated more carefully. In seeking to understand the nature of cultural experiences in the new globalized world, we need to think beyond the concept of hybridity. Paradoxically, one way to think beyond is to go back to the notion that it putatively surpassed, namely, that of the nation.

One consequence of the widespread acceptance of the concept of hybridity as an analytical tool has been the relative neglect of the power and resilience of the nation-state as a site of cultural assimilation and resistance. This propensity ties in nicely with the axiomatics of globalization, which proclaims the demise of the nation-state and the emergence of postnational societies. This is indeed a hasty move, the nation-state still exercises a great influence in the arbitration of cultural matters. When we examine the popular cinemas of India and Hong Kong, we see that the idea of the nation-state, however problematic it may be in both cases, still wields immense power. In the case of India, with its diverse ethnicities, languages, and religions, the idea of the nation-state is constantly subjected to diverse challenges. In the case of Hong Kong, which is now only a Special Administrative Region, where issues of postcoloniality, globality, citizenship, subjectivity, and cultural identity are discontinuous and contradictory and take on a special resonance, the idea of nation is indeed problematic. However, what is interesting in both these cases is that the experience of culture, with all its cosmopolitan and hybridizing inflections, is still understood largely in terms of the framework of nation, despite the ambivalences associated with that term.

In many of the writings on globalization, there is a tendency to brush off the nation-state all too hastily as if it did not have function in the contemporary world. One has only to examine the various conflicts taking place in the globe to realize the importance that the nation holds in the social imaginary of people. For example, Arjun Appadurai, an astute observer of globalization, believes that the global economy, with its disjunctive floes, serves to undermine the hegemony of the nation-state and move in the direction of a postnationalism (Appadurai 1996). Speaking of the globalization of culture, John Tomlinson writes,

> the idea of globalization suggests interconnections and interdependency of all global areas which happen in a far less purposeful way. It happens as the result of economic and cultural practices which do not, of themselves, aim at global integration, but which nonetheless produce it. More importantly, the effects of globalization are to weaken cultural coherences in all individual nation-states, including the economically powerful ones—the imperialist powers of a previous era (Tomlinson 1991, 175).

This is indeed an oversimplification. To think that hybridity and its associated practices have the effect of weakening the nation-state is to ignore the many-sidedness of capitalist globalization and to reduce its complex interactions to just one arena. Despite all the forces of cosmopolitanism and hybridization, the experience of culture in contemporary society is still largely determined by the imperatives and imaginations of the nation. Our inquiries into the popular cinemas of India and Hong Kong certainly reinforce this point. Discussions of and explorations into these cinemas still take place within the discursive boundaries of the nation. Hence in our reunderstanding of the experience of culture in the modern globalizing world, we need to keep in focus the hold that the nation, with all its political and economic implications, has on the social imaginary of the people. The image of the nation may be undergoing changes as a consequence of the influence of capitalist globalizing forces; however, the idea of the nation is still very much alive. It is well to remind ourselves that the experience of culture is vitally linked to economics, politics, and the play of the global and the local within the matrix of the nation.

As we discuss the importance of the idea of nation in understanding the experience of culture in the contemporary world, it is important to keep in mind the fact that global circulation of capital, commodities, pleasures, and desires has a way of inflecting nationhood and forcing us to rethink its ontology afresh. However, the important point is that we cannot afford to ignore it. The attributions of and investments in meaning and significance to the idea of nationhood, as well as questions of citizenship, collective identity, and national belonging, are subject to far-reaching changes. It is for this very reason that the experience of culture in our rapidly globalizing world has to be anchored in nationhood. The capitalist global economy, to be sure, with its emphasis on movements of capital, commodities, and information, has contributed significantly to the reimagining of nationhood. In the ultimate analysis, the processes of globalization, the interplay between globalism and localism, and the creation of new transnational mobilities have to be rethought against the backdrop of global capitalism and nation-states. These issues can best be understood as elements in the national allegories of modernity. The transformations taking place in the national space provide us with a significant point of departure as well as productive point of reference for the analysis of globalization and the experience of culture. An examination of the popular cinemas of India and Hong Kong testifies to this fact.

On the basis of this discussion, we can formulate some tentative ideas regarding globalization, the experience of culture and nationhood.

1. Despite the apparent emergence of a globalized monoculture, and the increasing deployment of hybridity as an analytical tool in the understanding of globalization, there is a deeply felt need to keep the idea of nation as a focus of interest.

2. A focus on the idea of nation enables us to pay closer attention to the interactions of global capitalism and nation-states. Benedict Anderson's seminal work on nations as "imagined communities" does not address the divisions and fault lines within nations. It is important that we pay attention to these aspects in terms of the experience of culture.

3. Etienne Balibar talks of the 'nation form' in his desire to focus on the nation-state as structure. In his view, the nation form constantly draws on various external forces as a way of refashioning itself (Balibar 1991). This is a part of the narrative construction of nationhood. As we explore the imbrications of globalization and the experience of culture, this phenomenon deserves careful attention.

4. As scholars like Arif Dirlik have persuasively argued, in our euphoria over globalization and transnational cultures, there is a tendency to ignore the significance of place (Prazniak and Dirlik 2000). Hence, place-based critiques assume great significance. Once again, this focuses our attention on the changing ontology of the nation.

5. As commentators like Fredric Jameson have argued, in our globalized world, culture itself has expanded, becoming coterminous with the market society in a way that inevitably calls attention to the everyday consumption of culture (Jameson 1998). This phenomenon cannot be understood by ignoring the salience of the nation. Ideas of collective identity and location, which are being revitalized as a consequence of the march of globalization, have to be understood in terms of the nation.

6. A point that has been foregrounded in the analyses of critics such as Arjun Appadurai is that, in our globalized world, the work of imagination

has assumed unprecedented and significant proportions, and that in order to comprehend the full force of globalization we need to map the diverse ways in which new imaginations operate. This cannot be usefully undertaken without investigations into the ways in which new imaginations redefine nationhood.

These observations are vitally connected with the central theme of this volume, namely, the relationship between media representations and cultural identity. Films, in the modern world, play a crucial role as a medium of entertainment and culture and in the dissemination of pleasure and desire. Filmic representations, in the context of globalization and the experience of culture, which I have discussed, create, challenge, and refashion identities in complex ways. It is often contended that identities are not essences but discursive constructions that cannot exist outside the space of representation, hence the importance of media representations. The globalizing of cultures has resulted in the creation of newer identities. These identities are many and diverse: ethnic, fundamentalist, hybrid, cosmopolitan, progressive, reactionary, fragmented, displaced, and rooted. Identities are linked to dislocations and relocations, attachments and detachments, fixities and volatilities. To map the full force and complexities associated with these diverse identities, we need to situate them within the discursive space of the nation-state and inquire into their nature and significance in relation to globalization and the experience of culture.

The production of identities in the present world is often discussed in terms of the axiomatics of postmodern theory, which valorize such phenomena as fragility, instability, and a multiplicity of identities. The very notion of identity has been characterized as illusory. It is argued that identities are constructed through role-playing and appropriation of images; identity is matter of leisure and playacting. People are able to pick and choose their identities at will. Against this approach to identity, one has to counterpose the very real need that people, say, in Asia feel for a sense of collective belonging and group agency. Instead of the disappearance of identity, what one perceives is an attempt to recognize its centrality and to redefine and resituate it in newer social contexts. The need for identity is very real, and for most people living in Asia today, one important aspect of their identity is that they are victims of neocolonialism and global capitalism.

REFERENCES

Appadurai, Arjun. *Modernity at Large: Cultural Dimensions of Globalization.* Minneapolis, Univ. of Minnesota Pr. 1996.

Balibar, Etienne. "The Nation Form: History and Ideology." In *Race, Nation and Class.* Edited by Etienne Balibar and Immanuel Wallerstein, London, Verso 1991.

Benjamin, Walter. *Charles Baudelaire.* London, NLB 1973.

Cheah, Pheng. "Rethinking Cosmopolitan Freedom in Transnationalism." In *Cosmopolitics: Thinking and Feeling Beyond the Nation*. Edited by Pheng Cheah and Bruce Robbins. Minneapolis, Univ. of Minnesota Pr. 1998.

Deleuze, Giles and Felix Guattari. *Kafka: Toward a Minor Literature*. Minneapolis, Univ. of Minnesota Pr. 1986.

Dirlik, Arif. "The Global in the Local." In *Global/Local*. Edited by Rob Wilson and Wimal Dissanayake. Durham, Duke Univ. Pr. 1996.

Geertz, Clifford. *The Interpretation of Cultures*. New York, Basic Books 1973.

Gokulsing, K. Moti and Wimal Dissanayake. *Indian Popular Cinema: A Narrative of Cultural Change*. London, Trentham 1998.

Harvey, David. *The Condition of Postmodernity: An Enquiry into the Origin of Cultural Change*. Oxford, Blackwell 1989.

Jameson, Fredric. *The Cultural Turn*. London, Verso 1998.

Leavis, Frank R. *Mass Civilization and Minority Culture*. Cambridge, Minority Press 1930.

Lo, Kwai-cheung. "Transnationalization of the Local in Hong Kong Cinema." In *At Full Speed*. Edited by Esther C. M. Yau. Minneapolis, Univ. of Minnesota Pr. 2001.

Lyotard, Jean-François. *The Postmodern Condition: A Report on Knowledge*. Manchester, Manchester Univ. Pr. 1984.

Prazniak, Roxann and Arif Dirlik. *Places and Politics in an Age of Globalization*. Lanham, Rowman & Littlefield 2001.

Shohat, Ella. "Notes on the 'Postcolonial,'" *Social Text* 1: 32 (Spring 1992), 99–113.

Tomlinson, John. *Cultural Imperialism*. London, Pinter Publisher 1991.

Williams, Raymond. *Politics and Letters*. London, NLB 1979.

Wilson, Rob and Wimal Dissanayake. *Global/Local: Transnational Imaginary and Cultural Production*. Durham, Duke Univ. Pr. 1996.

Transcultural Narrations of the Local:
Taiwanese Cinema Between
Utopia and Heterotopia

STEFAN KRAMER

From its very beginnings, Taiwan's cultural self-concept has been characterized by the many and diverse contacts between its societies and the other. This circumstance has repeatedly affected Taiwanese social and cultural self-reflection—both in peaceful and in violent ways. Hence, it has also had a decisive influence on Taiwanese communicative structures and systems of media representation. In this way, it has led to a continuous internal and external dialogue, which has manifested its own peculiar *dispositifs*. From this perspective, then, the confrontation with others who in some way or another constantly inscribed themselves into this self-concept began as early as 239 A.D., when the island in the South China Sea (called Formosa, 'beautiful,' by the Portuguese) was violently appropriated by the Chinese Wu state. This development continued under the Mongol reign of the Chinese Yuan dynasty and during the subsequent colonization by the Portuguese and Spanish, then by the Japanese, and finally by the Dutch (Gernet 1996). Terminating the Dutch occupation, Manchu Qing rulers reconquered the island in 1661 and remained in power there until the late-nineteenth century. Then, following the Chinese defeat in the Sino-Japanese War, Taiwan came under Japanese rule once again in 1895. As a result, the expanding Japanese empire transformed the island into one of its strategic outposts in the South China Sea and reigned over Taiwan until Japan's surrender in the Pacific War in 1945. At the same time, the Japanese were the first to confront primarily agricultural Taiwan with industrial modernity, that is, with the technical, economic, and ideological/cultural conditions of the European and North American other. Decades before, from the time of the Meiji restoration, Japan itself had successfully appropriated these conditions and used them as an instrument of its own imperialist ambitions in East and Southeast Asia (Tsang 1993).

Not least among the attendant circumstances of Taiwan's conquest by the Japanese colonial rulers were (in addition to the wartime technology) the unfamiliar media, the power to generate meaning with the industrial printing press imported from Europe, with photography since the middle of the nineteenth century, and with the cinema, brought to Taiwan by the Japanese as an instrument of warfare. But beyond the colonial period, the technical inscriptions of the other have persisted up to the current transnational cable and satellite television networks and to the internet. They have accompanied the process of modernization and the economic miracle on the island that came under Chiang Kai-shek's Chinese rule in 1945 and have been a decisive factor in the determination of the island's position between Chinese exile, Taiwanese tradition, and enthusiastic openness to the west. The media systems of representation of a cultural self-concept in Taiwan were exported under these conditions, complete with their ideology and specific perceptual *dispositifs*, to Taiwan from Japan, Europe, and the U.S. (which appeared on the scene as Taiwan's protective power against the 'communist threat' after the Korean War, 1950–51). In Taiwan, these media systems were appropriated by society in one way or another and integrated into its cultural system.

Binding the other's place into Taiwanese self-reflection already begins to emerge with the forms for appropriating foreign technology and economic structures. In addition, this aspect is covertly present, not only in the media-transfused meanings of the colonial Chinese, European, and Japanese channels or of the postcolonial ones of the transnational media industry. Rather, it is especially to be seen in the use of the originally alien apparatuses themselves. The intrusion of the other was able to attain a new quality through the accelerated developments during the twentieth century and the rapid modernization of the island, enmeshed as it still was, up to that point, in rural local structures—a modernization characterized by intensified economic contacts, developed consumer goods industries, and increased travel activities and stays abroad on the part of the population. Thus, Taiwan's postcolonial search for identity coincides precisely with the era of efforts at globalization, an era which, with its formation of dominance at deterritorialized, more or less neocolonialist and transnational levels, motivated a corresponding discourse of adaptation or resistance at the local level. Accordingly, this search is decisively influenced by the current definition of the cultural position as one between Taiwanese localism, China, and a new globalization and by the accompanying reappraisal of Taiwan's colonial past. The end of the Pacific War in 1945 was, indeed, also the end of this colonial past, yet, with the occupation of the island by the Han Chinese, it has practically persisted up to the present. Thus, the current position of Taiwan primarily becomes clarified within the struggle (additionally stimulated by political debates on Chinese reunification) between intrinsic Taiwanese tradition on the one hand, and the involvement in Chinese culture (with its cultural symbols and myths), and an industrial and technical modernism imported both from the Japanese and through the postcolonial economic openness on the other. In the form of a practically uninhibited industrialization and disbandment of formerly rural structures and in the materialization of culture and everyday life, this modernism has shaped at least the social and economic aspects of Taiwan's development and the *dispositifs* of her national self-constitution in the last fifty years.

Nevertheless, this struggle is not primarily a process of dialogue and conflict between Taiwan and China, Japan, or the West. It testifies to an internal hybridity that characterizes Taiwan's identity as an inherently open-ended and dynamic system. In the most inner processes of Taiwan's social and individual search for identity, its system of order is also characterized by the constant exchange between self and other at a number of levels and by the uninterrupted appropriation and cultural reproduction of foreign elements. For this reason, the constantly active circulation between other and self, which exposes every propagated fixed form of identity (e.g., national) as an illusion is inevitably reflected in painting and in the theater, and especially in literature and cinema. At the interface between its economic and ideological/political determination and its capacity for reconstructing and storing the traditional (thus accepted as part of the self), cinema, in particular, was able to establish itself as the decisive representation system of the Taiwanese self-concept during the past decades. In the course of this development, filmmakers have formed various strategies of resistant discourse for the aesthetic and narrative representation of their own identity between the constant shifts from self to other and back again. At the same time, this is a conflict carried out in the media and by artistic means, a conflict between the myths of the Greater Chinese or the Taiwanese nation, which, from the perspective of life in exile, articulates utopian constructs of ideal societal conditions presumed lost and to be striven for once again, and a pragmatic multiperspectivism on the hybrid present between local characteristics and a globalism having ever more influence on society as a whole. In the process, this last element is constantly forced to incorporate that other, which positions itself locally into its trains of thought and representation strategies.

The French historian Michel Foucault was the first to make productive use of the *topos* of heterotopia for scientific discourse—in a lecture 'Of Other Spaces' (Foucault 1993) and in the Preface to his pioneering work, *The Order of Thing* (Foucault 1994b, XV), both written in 1966. Foucault discovered the *other space* designated in this way in Jorge Luis Borges's description of the perceptual indifferences that ostensibly appeared while reading "an old Chinese encyclopedia" (Borges 1964)—indifferences, with which, incidentally, Taiwanese discourse also had to cope in the course of the violent introduction of ever more elements of Chinese culture. Foucault also used the term heterotopia, which again became a fundamental theme of his thought after his encounter with Japanese Zen monks (Foucault 1994a) twelve years later, to provide a critical reflection of the illusion of mimesis, of the conceptuality and reproduction of external reality, of utopian thought oriented to an imaginary future. Thus, Foucault was able to introduce into systematic debate an issue already suggested by Claude Lévi-Strauss (Lévi-Strauss 1966) decades before and already of a certain significance within philosophical hermeneutics (Gadamer 1975): the question of the not only imagined but material other in one's own discourse on the other and, not least, on oneself.

Foucault confronted thought on the self, which up to that point had only been possible within the dichotomous model between perceptible being and the unreal, virtual spaces of its utopian countermodels or schemes for perfection, with a different 'place' of thinking. Consequently, the discourses on post-colonialism and postmodernism, but also the debates on transnational media society between its global and universalist, geopolitical and economic structures and the local, discrete conditions of its production and perception, must deal with this possibility in one way or another. Moreover, this issue of another space has definitively inscribed itself in the relevant societies themselves. In Taiwan, the societies must define their own cultural positions, especially in relation to local traditionalism, Chinese hegemony, European and Japanese colonial traditions, the protectionism of the U.S., and, not least, the globalism that inevitably invaded the Southeast Chinese island republic in the midst of the 'economic miracle,' and the numerous relocalizations that followed in its wake.

The imaginary utopian thought at the basis of Foucault's concept of heterotopia, expressed in these parameters and the corresponding myths, determines its own position exclusively within its own epistemological space and under the conditions of its materiality, its *dispositifs*, and its media characteristics. For all of the various possible interpretations in historical discourse, in that of cultural or literary history, or even in sociological discourse, utopia, as characterized by the hegemonic discourses of Chinese and Taiwanese nationalism, always amounts to the formulation of the vision of a genuine and just order of life in a removed, imaginary era. This order constructs and communicates the image of its (spatially or temporally defined) other exclusively under the cultural, social, linguistic, ideological, and, not least, economic and high-tech, material conditions of the self here and now. Thus, by linking itself to the social utopias of its place and time and by always simultaneously helping to produce these, the alienation of such conditions, construed within the context of colonial or anticolonial discourse, also produces, with one stroke, difference, which is, not least, also an economic and power-politics strategy of the self. This is illustrated by numerous examples from the cultural history of Taiwan as the residence of Chinese exiles since 1949. Whether in literature, theater, or the new medium of film, these are media reconstructions of an imaginary Greater Chinese past and of a desirable future, which, at the same time, present the illusion of the (re-)production of an ideal world that does, in fact, only exist in the imagination.

For decades, the themes of the Chinese nationalist Taiwanese cinema were largely confined to the genres of swordsmen epics or of present-day melodramatic romances. There were also anti-Communist documentaries and propaganda films. All of these films constantly outdid the preceding ones in the presentation of traditional Confucian hierarchies and in the dissemination of moral values highly endorsed by the government—as a sort of opposite pole to the Communist state doctrine in the neighboring country. An antagonistic schema of good and evil, according to moral and ethical criteria, was at the base of the swordsmen epics. The villains, presented to the audience as robbers, traitors, and public enemies who threatened the peace of fictitious or authentic earlier Chinese societies, were also always personified metaphors for the neighboring Communist 'realm of evil.' One can easily imagine whom the audience was to project onto the heroes who, in the end (precisely following the tradition of storytelling still flourishing in the dime novel), reestablished peace, justice, and the harmony traditionally aspired to through self-sacrificing efforts and strict adherence to the Confucian moral code. By means of such heroic stories, with their elaborate offers of identification, and through the indoctrination of traditional (thus, anti-Communist) values, the nationalist rulers attempted to legitimize their claims to power over all of China. At the same time, they facilitated the indigenous public's escape from disillusioning social and political reality and from their own everyday life in exile on the island. Accordingly, the virtual images of society imparted to the audience via the screen were to help gradually restore the lost sense of national identity and to direct it toward new, future goals. In this respect, films such as Xu Xinfu's *Sweet Smelling Blossom Among the Troops* (*Junzhong Fangcao,* 1952), Hu Jie's *An Admirable Girl Amidst the Flames of War* (*Fenghuo Liren,* 1953), or Xiong Guang's *Escape* (*Ben,* 1955) fulfilled the national function of constructing a closed system of order (Foucault) which is assigned to them for the movie-going public.

On the other hand, the melodramatic romance films made a very direct attempt to provide a clear view of the future and to disrupt the collective national depression. Most of the films consisted of originally unhappily proceeding love stories mixed with success stories from professional life. Then, in an often repeated plot structure with only a few variations, the economic success of the usually young lover and the attendant social recognition finally also brought about the long-awaited success with the female beauty of his desires: an obvious appeal to actively participate in building the economy, which met with impressive success in the social reality of everyone's life. Examples of film productions in this genre are Chen Wenrong's *An Admirable Husband* (*Qianjin Zhangfu,* 1954), Xu Xinfu's *On the Wrong Path* (*Qilu,* 1955), and Zong You's *Brilliant Prospects* (*Jinxiu Qianchen,* 1956), whose titles already reveal much of their simple plot structure and the values imparted by the films.

In the final analysis, for all of these films, utopian representation, perception, and its semantics remain forever excluded from thinking of the other in terms of a real (media) space—if, for instance, they reproduce for the thousandth time the triumph of the Confucian hero over (Communist) evil, or if, on the other hand, they produce perfect success stories of the economic and social ascent of their citizens and of their society itself, situated as it is on the fringe area of world politics, and thus imagine a collective identity of Taiwan and let it become real in the media-materialized imagination. Hence, the utopia within the national, hegemonic myths of Taiwan is actually nothing other than a tool for the political, economic, and, not least, aesthetic project of defining one's own culture, and for the self-concept of identity. The utopia, then, was created to confront contemporary Taiwan as a place of exile with the optimum of an imagined, future vision based on a nostalgically tinged construction of the past and, finally, to directly refer back to the (adverse, but meliorable) present conditions. In this way, with its construction of a concept of order, the utopia remains exclusively within the framework of its own present way of thinking, less analytical and to a much greater extent simply concerned with naïve and vivid oppositions.

By contrast, Michel Foucault made a clear distinction between his heterotopias as—material—other places of thought and utopias. He approached the changing conditions of the postcolonial and globalized present era, which have decisively formed Taiwanese society (which, at any rate, is not preoccupied with fixed patterns of identity and the illusion of historical continuity) and have been forcing that society to unceasingly undergo transformational processes since the early-twentieth century. Despite the national Chinese or Taiwanese propaganda of fixed systems of identity, in reality the people of the southeastern Asian island experience identity primarily in the form of cultural heterogeneousness and of a multiperspectivism that is constantly in flux. Thus, despite certain cultural and social specifics that attribute uniqueness and a certain incomparability to Taiwan, the island can be presented as an example of that inherent interculturalism that equally characterizes postcolonial societies and others increasingly linked to the current process of globalization in East and West, in North and South. In the case of Taiwan, this interculturalism exposes every assertion of a hermetic national identity to be a myth. In Taiwanese societies, interculturalism presents itself both as a dialogue with and as a discourse on the other, which is represented in various direct and mediated forms, but, at the same time, as an inner hybridity of the people and of society itself, subject to a constant dynamics. The self-concept of the people and of society still depends primarily on their difference, that is, on the actual or imagined other from which they differentiate themselves, only to also make it an indispensable part of the self in the moment of its perception as other.

Foucault's heterotopias, which can be found as local or, just as often, as global counterdiscourses in ever more works of antihegemonic literature, painting, and film that have been produced since Taiwan's liberalization in 1987, serve as a distorting mirror of both the lost reality in the translation of the cultures under observation and of the utopias put in that reality's place. They urge the reflection on the self to change its place, so that by taking in nonvirtual, but real and effective, material places such as have long influenced the external reality of the *beautiful island* Formosa in any case, new ways of grasping and interpreting communicated meaning can enter into one's own thinking. This reverse effect calls the multifocused preconditions of one's own reasoning into question—reasoning that, in its dominant discourses, still strives to construe and communicate a fixed self as a system of identity.

In this sense, the heterotopias of the Taiwanese media's self-concept are results of both cultural translation and intermedia transmission. Since, in each case, they require, as Foucault puts it, a "system of openings and closures which they simultaneously isolate and make permeable" (Foucault 1993), the heterotopias allow the other room for its penetration into the self. A great number of artists has had to learn this by using the imported media apparatuses in order to analyze themselves and their culture in the entirety of its economic and political order and in its semantics—and in opposition to the full range of hegemonic discourses geared to the production of monosemic, Taiwanese national narratives and meanings. Within this context, the cultural construction of meaning and the perception of the world, for most Taiwanese, are also more strongly determined by the media today than ever before. They take less and less recourse to real domains of experience, as these were disrupted by the introduction of the industrial printing press and even more so by the audiovisual technical apparatuses of the mass media. On the contrary, they take place in light of a media culture that increasingly detaches itself from its geographical frames of reference (as described in Douglas Kellner's book *Media Culture*, 1995), especially under the conditions of a transmedia and increasingly transnational media and cultural industry engaged in reciprocal quotation and thus in increasing mutual dissolution. Along with the other, this industry has also appropriated the corresponding systems of communication and representation and merged them with the thought and representational structures of the self to constantly renew forms of that third space that Homi K. Bhabha has described as an "in-between" space (Bhabha 1994). Thus, the question of utopia and heterotopia is always a question of the order that constitutes the media construction of the self and of the other. But, to the same extent, it is also a question of the material and media conditions of representation and communication itself. In this way, the media of cultural representation are decisive in constituting those systems of order that they themselves communicate in order to define the self-concept of cultural communities and their concepts of the other as, in Benedict Anderson's term, "imagined communities" (Anderson 1991). These do not only constitute themselves through the content conveyed by the media in order to thus constitute imaginary worlds and worlds that become real in the imagination. Rather, they originate primarily through their material and media nature itself, through the *dispositifs* that are inscribed economically and ideologically, in aesthetic and apparatus-related ways and that, according to Jacques Lacan (Lacan 1988), always inscribe the apparatuses themselves as the other of one's own self-concept.

In the postcolonial, late modern, or postmodern present state of affairs in Taiwan, the culture that is thus discharged into self-reflective thought processes in view of the authentic other and of the mediated other that is perceived as a cultural text, appears under the conditions of a media culture that increasingly detaches itself from its traditional localities and thus from its (no longer fixed) geopolitical and linguistic-cultural identities, and simultaneously constitutes new, real and virtual, cultural and symbolic spaces. As a major constructor and communicative instrument of knowledge and meaning, this media culture has inscribed itself in the society and societies of Taiwan. Within the tension between the discourses of the global and the local, which arise in this way and comprise the "in-between" space that is constantly in motion, interculturalism is not simply defined as the attempt at communication between Taiwan's societies and systems of order and the other that represents itself in other societies. On the contrary, interculturalism expresses itself primarily as the confrontation of Taiwanese society and of every individual with itself, with one's own person, and with the multiple internal and external influences from which the self and the other are both imagined and constructed. This confrontation, in turn, takes place primarily through and in the media. In the process, the consciousness constituting culture always also includes dealing with the actual or imaginary other that only becomes real through its reproduction in the media. Thus, according to the model of German system theorist Dirk Baecker (2000), mediated Taiwanese culture that also mediates itself is, in its materialized form, also part of the order that it transports and conveys to its public, and is inevitably also intercultural and a product of comparative analysis and, in the most favourable case, also of heterotopia.

In this way, the experience of the other through and in the media of the transnational cultural industry, that is, through print media just as much as through the technical apparatus media of mass communication, but also through consumer goods industries and their symbolic language, determines the self-perception that results from the differentiation from its other. Thus, on the surface, it still requires a fixed identity-difference construction, including corresponding utopias or anxieties, in order to exist as imagination at all. Yet, in the moment of experiencing the other, this other has become, as Dirk Baecker puts it, an inherent part of the self and thus, in a certain sense, has already taken on characteristics of a heterotopia. It has changed the *dispositifs* of cultural and media perception and inscribed itself in the internal processes of the self. In the process, it has entered into an inherent intercultural dialogue with its other, which is a prerequisite for a heterotopia in the first place.

From the moment of its media perception under specific material conditions, the other (and thus the media of representation of culture) can no longer remain really alien. On the other hand, this also applies equally to the assertion of the self, since the other, by way of which the self defines itself, is no longer alien, but has become part of the self in the form of an 'other' that locates itself within its media representation. According to Baecker, the response to and the stimulus of cultural self-determination constantly intersect and indissolubly overlap in their mediated perception. Thus, processes of media culture become an inevitable part of the confrontation, not with the colonialist other, but primarily with the self, which thus, in the final consequence, resists any cultural colonization by, in turn, realizing its own discourses through the same media. Accordingly, regardless of their specific themes, the literary, performative, and cinematic expressions of Taiwan's current cultural and societal state are primarily a discourse on Taiwanese identity and culture, which takes place under the conditions of the media *dispositifs*. But they do not always present themselves in the form of a rigid arrangement of a dichotomous categorization of self and other in the ways demanded by hegemonic discourses (and the debates on "otherness"), as in alternatives such as "Confucian" or "Christian" (or "Communist"); "Asian" or "Western;" "traditional" or "modern;" "national" or "transnational;" "global" or "local;" "good" or "evil;" or, not least, "Taiwanese" or "mainland Chinese." On the contrary, they first define themselves at a level of indeterminacy that comprises all of these categories and develops into something new, which, however, is constantly changing. The main characteristic of this phenomenon is, above all, that indeterminacy and changeability, its nature as a process, the ability to appropriate and monopolize on something, which characterizes the actual identity of Taiwan as a dynamic and open-ended system.

Under such preconditions, *Taiwanese New Cinema* catapulted cinema in the Republic of China on Taiwan to the status of national art cinema after decades of propaganda and simplistic commercial cinema. In this way, the history of Taiwanese cinema has become independent, liberated from the restrictions of politics and artistic tradition. It is unmistakable that in the aesthetics and narrativity of most of the films of this genre, the imagination of the self and that of the other collide. Thus, it is no accident that the urban world of modern Taipei is the favoured background of the works of many filmmakers, and that elements of Western aesthetics are also manifest in their films. Such films have long since discovered the gradually disappearing back-country (on the small island, scarce at any rate) as a paradise worthy of protection and they projected their obsessive visions of harmony onto it at a time when, on the Chinese mainland, urban life and modernization were only starting to become considered.

But with the themes of the films of the *New Taiwanese Cinema*, many of the omnipresent problems of modern society have been reflected on in impressive ways and have been captured on the screen in subtle images. Filmmakers have begun to demonstrate personal signatures in their films. For example, many of the discourses of contemporary Taiwanese culture are succinctly presented in the film *The Peach Blossom Land* (*Anlian Taohuayuan*) by the film and play director Stan Lai (Lai Sheng-chuan, 1954)—a film made in 1991, under conditions of a gradual liberalization and democratization. The film contains numerous referential levels. On the one hand, it is based on a traditional tale of the Jin era by the Chinese poet Tao Qian (Tao Yuanming, 365–427) (Hightower 1970; Bauer 1971). Tao Qian's story of the *peach blossom land* (Taohuayuan), adapted for the film plot, tells of a fisher who, during a westward boat trip on a river, chances on a paradisiacal land where the secular world and the hereafter mingle so as to be indistinguishable. Already at this level of the dissolving dichotomies between the reality of the life-world and the (un)reality of the afterlife, to be found in numerous novellas of the Tang dynasty (618–907) (Edwards 1937–38) with their themes of the 'extraordinary' and 'supernatural' events, the contemporary cinematic reconstructions reflect the conflicts of Taiwanese culture between good (paradise) and evil (life-world), or between the self and the other. But these originally so clearly distinct categories of the dominant social discourses soon begin to dissolve in Stan Lai's film text and under the conditions of the "hot" cinema *dispositif.* The audience no longer knows what in the cinematic presentation can be thought of as good and desirable and what as detestable, and, ultimately, what as the self and what as the other. Here, an open discourse on those of dichotomizations displaces the reproduction of dominant discourses or of discourses of direct resistance.

This deconstructive intention of dissolving and questioning not only fixed positions, but also traditional discursive structures also applies to formal elements of Lai's staging of the presentation. He combines various stylistic elements of traditional drama with modern forms of theater imported from the West and confronts both of these theatrical realities with that of film and with the focus of his own production. In the course of this surreal exchange, cinematic and theatrical reality constantly offset each other and put each other into question. Thus, the audience is faced with a formal potpourri that is difficult to decode and for exactly this reason, in the "in-between" space of the cinematic reception, reveals a large number of possible connotations from mythological codes, traditional theatrical practices, more typically Western elements oriented to realism, and, not least, scenic elements from Chinese trivial literature. Throughout the entire plot, the presentation maintains the dialogue between these elements, wandering along the borderline between tragedy and comedy, even to the point of provocative ludicrousness. This dialogue is the only central theme of the entire film in which the viewers, influenced as they are both by their own myths and by the viewing habits and the *dispositifs* and reception standards of the Western mass media, and desiring confirmation of their illusions and searching for clarity, can find a secure position.

Especially those categories connected to the dichotomizing of self and other, the categories of time (nostalgic backward-looking or future-oriented utopias) and space (the land beyond the mountains, the sea, etc.), which cinema can manipulate better than any other art form, by focussing the represented events in the here and now of the screening room, produce a distinction to contemporary Taiwanese society in Stan Lai's film. On the other hand, they also provide, more than any other media of cultural representation, the freedom to construct and to deconstruct national utopias and individual fantasies—freedom that is necessary for allowing heterotopias to enter into one's thinking. Only here does a differentiated analysis of one's own identity and its differences become possible. At any rate, with its perceptional *dispositifs* the illusory medium of film counteracts the distinction between its underpinnings in the here and now and in the hereafter, and between the reality of the media and that outside the media. Thus, with the aid of its illusory and, at the same time, deconstructive effects, the film promotes the internalization of these paradises and facilitates a unique convergence between them and self-awareness, self-concept and mediated self-representation. In this way, it also causes new processes of intermediality and changes in literature and in the theatrical arts themselves. In Taiwan, in any case, the hegemonic as well as the resisting discourses now find their audience primarily at the cinema and in television series. This has decisive effects on the design and dramaturgy of these arts (now adapted to film and to television) and especially on their perception and on the circumstances of their consumption. The auditorium in the cinema and, ultimately, the living room at home have long since replaced the tea houses, just as the two-dimensional screen or the two-dimensional television monitor have replaced the three-dimensional stages open to the theater auditorium.

In his film *Anlian Taohuayuan,* Stan Lai constructed his discourse on precisely these—cinematic—forms of literary narrative, Western theatrical production and traditional Chinese drama and shadow play—in order to transform them, film itself, and their position in the *dispositifs* of Taiwan's contemporary society and identity into matters of a higher-level discourse. Consciously disrupting conventional schemata and viewing habits and provoking the cultural self-reflection of the audience, the formal elements of the production correspond to the content and message of this film to a great extent. Three distinct strands outline this message. First, there are the mythical visions of reality and the idea of paradise as they correspond to that analytic reconstruction of the legend about the fisher between this world and the hereafter in the play *The Peach Blossom Land* (*Taohuayuan*). In addition, there is a nostalgic look at the Chinese past. In the film, this appears in a second play rehearsed and performed simultaneously on the same stage after a mistake has occurred in renting the theater: in the play *Secret Love* (*Anlian*) about the tragic love story of a couple separated by the historical events surrounding the division of China. Finally, there is the cinematic reality of the frame story (providing yet another addition to the original theatrical performance of Stan Lai's play), which represents contemporary Taiwan. Through their disillusioning effects, which at the level inherent in the film with its falling set pieces, interruptions by the director, or conversations among the actors approximately correspond to a blackout and thus call critical attention to the media aspects of the presentation itself, the two plays, the film, and, not least, every cultural construction, are constantly relegated, as if at a metalevel, to the realm of fantasy and imagination. In Stan Lai's film, all of the temporal and spatial categories intersect one another and overlap; this also applies to the levels of vision and reality, of stage, film, and the reality represented, and, not least, of media representation and nonmediated reality. Such overlap occurs, for example, when the two plays cross over into each other's stage space or into the reality taking place beyond the stage, and the borderlines between present and past, between experienced reality and imagined dream world, and, not least, between film and audience, dissolve. Just as all of the levels of perception enter into a dialogue with one another and thus, ultimately, all ostensible and constructed boundaries dissolve, all moral-ethical antagonisms of the world and the hereafter, of order and chaos, of Taiwan and China, of China and the West, of tradition and modernity, of familiarity and alienation, of family and individuality, of innocence and guilt, of good and evil, of vision and disillusionment, and between self and other finally counteract one another in this dialogue. These conflicts shift from the societal level to the individuality of each person, who is constantly forced to construct his or her own identity and the other among all of the decisive influences and mediations; this almost naturally allows the space of the other to enter one's own thinking and its representations.

REFERENCES

Anderson, Benedict. *Imagined Communities. Reflections on the Origin and Spread of Nationalism.* Revised edition. London, New York, Verso 1991.

Baecker, Dirk. *Wozu Kultur?* Berlin, Kulturverl. Kadmos 2000

Bauer, Wolfgang. *China und die Hoffnung auf Glück.* München, Hanser 1971.

Bhabha, Homi K. *The Location of Culture.* New York, Routledge 1994.

Borges, Jorge Luis. "Die analytische Sprache John Wilkins'." In *Other Inquisitions (1937–1952),* Austin, Univ. of Texas Pr. 1964.

Dirlik, Arif. "The Global in the Local," In *Global/Local. Cultural Production and the Transnational Imagery.* Edited by Rob Wilson and Wimal Dissanayake. Durham, London, Duke Univ. Pr. 1996, 21–45.

Edwards, Evangeline Dora, *Chinese Prose Literature of the T'ang-Period A.D. 618–906,* 2 Vols. London, A. Probsthain 1937–1938.

Foucault, Michel. "Andere Räume." In *Aisthesis. Wahrnehmung Heute oder Perspektiven einer anderen Ästhetik.* Edited by Karlheinz Barck et al. Leipzig, Reclam 1993, 34–46.

Foucault, Michel. *Dits et Écrits,* Vol. 3 (1976–1979), Paris, Gallimard 1994a, 618–624.

———. *The Order of Things. An Archaeology of the Human Sciences.* New York, Vintage 1994b.

Gadamer, Hans-Georg. *Truth and Method.* London, Sheed and Ward 1975.

Gernet, Jacques. *A History of Chinese Civilization*, 2nd Ed. Cambridge, Cambridge Univ. Pr. 1996.

Hightower, James R., *The Poetry of T'ao Ch'ien*. Oxford, Clarendon 1970.

Kellner, Douglas. *Media Culture. Cultural Studies, Identity and Politics Between the Modern and the Postmodern*. London, New York, Routledge 1995.

Lacan, Jacques. *Radiophonie/Television*. Berlin, Quadriga 1988.

Lévi-Strauss, Claude. *The Savage Mind*. Chicago, Univ. of Chicago Pr. 1966.

Tsang, Steve Yui-Sang, ed. *In the Shadow of China: Political Developments in Taiwan Since 1949*. Honolulu, Univ. of Hawaii Pr. 1993.

Garifuna Song, Groove Locale and "World-Music" Mediation

MICHAEL C. STONE

INTRODUCTION

Many observers celebrate the transculturation of local traditional musics as a mutually edifying synthesis of dissimilar cultural influences, conducive to a more generalized democratizing of the planetary sonicsphere, and as a welcome interaction of world musics seen as indexing a more egalitarian "multicultural" future. But this optimistic assessment of affirmative diversity and progressive politics stands opposite a view of "world music" as the penetrating mediation of transnational commodity forms and practices connecting various local and international audiences, in a separation of sound ("schizophonia") from local sources, traditions, artists, and communities, and its multiple recursive recombinations ("schismogenesis") under the rubric of "world beat" (Feld 1994a, 1994b).

A creative dialectical tension conditions a new world of musical diversity governed by forces of investment, copyright ownership, licensing, promotion, distribution, and overall corporate control. In this context, creative local energies constitute the raw materials of world-music-as-commodity, a selective extraction of sonic otherness under terms of global capital accumulation, presented to western consumers who seek to distinguish themselves as patrons and connoisseurs of the culturally unfamiliar.

The international production, circulation and consumption of world music entails a concerted mediation of local expressive traditions, faulted by critics as the global music industry's commercial exploitation of exoticized musical forms. In this view, the phenomenon undermines musicians' vital connections with their artistic heritage and home communities, the foundations that make their musics and societies unique. The argument has the familiar ring of the Frankfurt School mass culture critique. A "cultural imperialist" reading of world music detects an appropriation of local style as a curio for exhibition and a vehicle of unapologetic accumulation, in a process that corrupts its object, extracts value on inequitable terms, reinforces unexamined assumptions of western cultural distinctiveness and superiority, and threatens the cultural viability of its nonwestern authors.

Absent in the preceding is an informed historical perspective. Unlike most popular genres, world music's diversity and hybrid character make it an umbrella category rather than a singular, identifiable style, even if the most popular genres reflect influences of the percussive, eminently danceable musics of West Africa and the African diaspora. Unlike the more diffuse history of other popular music genres, the genesis of the world-music tag is recent and well-documented, making it easier to evaluate the cultural-imperialist indictment.

World music emerged as a marketing category developed by independent English record labels seeking to distinguish their eclectic inventory of "international-roots" music from mainstream popular tastes. In mid-1987, label owners, disc jockeys, promoters, musicians and writers met to discuss "ways of achieving a greater awareness of their music in the retail trade, in the press, and among the public." As the transcripts relate, "The main aim [was] to broaden the appeal of our repertoire," and to establish a "short-term marketing plan that resulted in World Music becoming a 'genre'" identifiable by consumers, the press, and industry types (Anderson 2000).

Ian Anderson, editor of Folk Roots, the London world-music monthly, says that collaborators sought a coherent, coordinated strategy to promote "music from 'outside' Western pop culture" to a nascent western audience. A community of knowledgeable and engaged promoters and aficionados invited listeners to explore unfamiliar sounds and thus differentiate their tastes from pop sensibilities. Anderson and fellow tastemakers sought

> . . . an established, unified generic name [to] give retailers a place where they could confidently rack otherwise unstockable releases, and where customers might both search out items they'd heard on the radio . . . and browse through a wider catalogue. Various titles were discussed . . ."World Music" seemed to include the most and omit the least . . . Nobody thought of defining it or pretending there was such a beast: it was just to be a box, like jazz, classical or rock (Anderson 2000).

Given a plain-spoken emphasis on promoting and marketing commodified forms of cultural distinction to savvy western patrons, a populist egalitarianism, and an emphasis on cultural authenticity, what is world music? As the terms "international-roots" and "music from 'outside' Western pop culture" suggest, the world in question is one of traditional communities and their artistic purveyors, struggling to express their cultural identity and make a living somewhere on the western periphery (Guilbault, 2001).

But this grassroots emphasis stands in contrast with "world beat": ethnic-pop hybrids, international dance-oriented musics and mixed genres of exotic pedigree whose audiences celebrate "a new, postmodern species of 'authenticity,' one . . . precisely guaranteed by its obvious blendings, its synthesis and syncretism" (Feld 1994a, 266). This is the music of (often, oppressed) cultural others, produced and distributed for the vicarious enjoyment of western consumers—whether by independent specialty labels who scout and develop most artists, or by the major labels who seize upon and elevate those acts they perceive as the most globally marketable.

But world music's bifocal formulation, its deliberate juxtaposition of multiple cultural realities, and its dialogical, intertextual, interreferential character also reflect latent political potential. In bringing local traditions to sympathetic western audiences, these projects of global musical fusion proffer a progressive vision of "a common culture based on families of resemblance and similarities of emotion and experience" that is "capable of challenging the ideological hegemony of Anglo cultural domination" (Lipsitz 1986, 164, 165).[1] The dialogic, intertextual musical groove of this prophetic stance, while clearly versed in local idioms, is no longer strictly local. Mixing the new and the familiar, it advances, indeed, celebrates an affirmative aesthetics of human agency in everyday life. It represents a strategic emotional, kinaesthetic, intellectual, and political response to present global conditions, in praise of human sociability, and an effort to perpetuate the spirit of styles and practices rooted in local practice, custom, and history (DeNora 2000; Keil and Feld 1994).

Anderson wrote in response to attacks on world music's inventors as exploiters romantically enamored of the "rudimentary, exotic and inaccessible qualities" of nonwestern musics and musicians. There is no denying the conditioning commercial relationship, Anderson readily admits, but he adds that if inventing world music "was good for business, . . . it was automatically good for the incomes of the artists too." He continues,

> It's not all positive, but World Music . . . sells large quantities of records that you couldn't find for love or money two decades ago. It has let many musicians in quite poor countries get new respect (and houses, cars and food for their families), and it turns out massive audiences for festivals and concerts. It has greatly helped international understanding and provoked cultural exchanges—people who've found themselves neighbours in the same box have listened to each other and ended up making amazing music together . . . I call it a Good Thing (Anderson 2000).

In an optimistic, progressive perspective showing genuine enthusiasm for the music, Anderson implicitly rejects the Frankfurt School pessimism of the cultural-imperialist critique, its spectral view of late modernity as an inexorable, cold-blooded hijacking of democratic human history, a moral horror chargeable to the brutal structural adjustments of late global capitalism (Jowers 1993). Here, world music becomes an opportunistic, depthless pastiche, an eclectic, seductive Babel of accidental sound whose power to appropriate, distort and deracinate leaves source societies in ruins. Human displacement, the creation of new transnational populations, the emergence of novel cultural hybrids, these are products of the "creative destruction" of global financial restructuring, the relentless commodification of cultural forms, and the opportunistic interventions of global mass communications media (Harvey 1989).

By contrast, Anderson perceives a considerate, generally beneficial project ("musicians in quite poor countries get new respect . . . houses, cars and food for their families"). World music becomes a celebration of local human agency, a mutually fortuitous encounter between traditional and modern (i.e., "western") sounds ("international understanding . . . cultural exchanges . . . making amazing music together"). The optimistic view endorses egalitarian values that guide a politically progressive, engaged, humanitarian transnational community of artists, activists, culture workers, intellectuals, and their audiences.

This framing highlights the contingent, socially constructed nature of the world-music project, whose oppositional temperament anticipates alternative approaches rich with emancipatory potential. Indeed, numerous efforts have musically championed the cultural survival of threatened peoples around the world. Consider Amnesty International's collaboration with World Music Network; the work of Music for Change (M4C, the English charity "promoting cultural respect through music"); the Bosavi People's Fund (Feld 1994a, 2001a, 2001b) for highland New Guinea communities, founded by ethnomusicologist Steven Feld and ex-Grateful Dead drummer Mickey Hart; Hart's Endangered Music Project (Hart 1993); Peter Gabriel's recording and promotion of Third World musicians (Cheyney 1990); Putumayo Records' aid and public education efforts; Refugee Voices, the recording, concert, and video initiative of the United Nations High Commissioner for Refugees; or the musical activism of Afropop Worldwide, the syndicated radio show (N'Dour 2001; UNESCO 2001). Precursors include the folk-singing activists who lent their voices to the U.S. Civil Rights Movement (Cantwell 1996), and the Ravi Shankar-George Harrison concert to aid Bangladesh.[2]

These more optimistic manifestations are consonant with a reading of late modernity cast in the heroic mode (Jowers 1993). World music becomes a valiantly creative, positive popular response to global capital's indiscriminate, far-reaching wealth accumulation strategy. But to foreground world music's egalitarian, emancipatory potential is not to annihilate contradiction: inequities remain, naturalized in the structured inequities and bottom-line rationale of global capital accumulation and consumption. Anderson concedes,

> Small wonder that virtually all world music producers and promoters have at least one sad tale to tell of an unfortunate misunderstanding or relationship breakdown over money with a musician they'd worked so hard to help (Anderson 2000).

Althusser's remarks on the character of ideology pertain: as a self-interested gloss on everyday practice, ideology only sets for itself the kinds of questions it is prepared to answer, working thus to dispel the real contradictions of lived experience. Put another way, there are concrete conditions, and there are the ways we represent those conditions to ourselves and others. The problematic inscribed in much of the staging discourse of world music calls for a symptomatic reading of what Barthes would call the falsely obvious—an interrogation not so much of what is said, but more importantly, of the absent, collusive silences in discursive convention. Such lacunae mask popular music's actual operative forms and practices, and how its unexamined propositions play out, presently and historically, in the quotidian experience of artists and their home communities.

Consider the work of Paul Simon, David Byrne, Peter Gabriel, and Sting, high-profile pop artists whose global-fusion experiments have drawn criticism for a naive disavowal of political intent, eliding past and present conditions of oppression, ignoring the power relations that condition differential financial reward, finessing creative credit, and keeping traditional artists at the circle's edge of global stardom. In actual practice, world music cannot avoid a basic tension: its artistic and commercial success depends on traditional artists whose creative energies are essential to a marketing category that "sells large quantities of records" and "turns out massive audiences for festivals and concerts" (Anderson 2000).

Are there principled, nonexploitative ways to render traditions comprehensible to western audiences without effacing the meanings its originators and local audiences inscribe through their own artistry and reception? Efforts like those already noted offer some models to sustain an ethical relationship with local artists and cultures. But it is another issue to inform and engage receptive audiences in the broader cultural, socioeconomic and political realities that confront people in societies which, among many other things, happen to produce "world music" that, whatever else it may do, assumes commodity form. Indifference on this point will mark the separation of traditions from the music's source of expressive vitality and culturally transcendent potential. Yet western audiences' receptiveness to the bifocal, intertextual, interreferential character of transnational musics and their political potential to promote a cross-cultural aesthetics of human agency, means that the issue is far from settled.

WORLD MUSIC, LOCAL HISTORY

Beyond the music's obvious aesthetic pleasures, media representations convey little concern with how tradition bearers and their home audiences create cultural meaning or cultivate an insider's sense of cultural history. What perspectives do musicians and audiences cultivate in the transnational communities where they reside, socialize, make music, and seek a living? These are questions to which ethnography and ethno-history are well suited. Consider the expressive heritage of the Afro-Amerindian Garifuna people of Caribbean Central America.

Any appraisal of Garifuna musical tradition confronts the complicated history of colonial Belize,[3] where the Garifuna first arrived as wage laborers in 1802, bearing a proud, militant history of resisting enslavement.[4] I propose to explore the relationship between early accounts of Garifuna music and dance and contemporary media portrayals, situating analysis in the broader context of the historical insertion of Garifuna culture into the regional political economy, and, more recently, into transnational circuits of labor, capital, and commodity forms.

Garifuna music's historical unfolding reveals an expressive repertoire uniquely responsive to a people's changing fortunes, expanding geographic and cultural range, and consequent shifting of identities. Only recently logged in the world-music registry, the music powerfully articulates the historical tensions and displacements of Garifuna experience as a population long conditioned to transnational forms of existence as a means of cultural survival.

Garifuna music performance accordingly manifests a kind of "strategic antiessentialism": in any moment it sustains

> the appearance of celebrating the fluidity of identities, but in reality seeks a particular disguise on the basis of its ability to highlight, underscore, and augment [aspects] of one's identity that one cannot express directly (Lipsitz 1994, 62).

Garifuna expressive traditions thus enact a dynamic performance strategy long versed in the cultural artistry of subaltern endurance. Their chronicle illustrates that Caribbean peoples, as the first truly modern human precipitate of global capitalism, have long grappled with the material, aesthetic, and ethical predicaments that now, as a generalized condition of postmodernity, confront humanity at large (Yelvington 2001).

An analysis of music's place in Garifuna everyday life, past and present, speaks to the intersubjective workings of culture, identity, geography, commerce, and power, and to the resilient agency of human history in the making. Strategically, such an approach underscores the privileges and contradictions of relative social location, and the responsibilities that such positioning confers. Any analysis, however informed and sympathetic, cannot evade its own complicity in the dominant (or leading, as Gramsci would say) institutions and practices that underpin efforts to sustain a self-interested ideological consensus while aestheticizing and commodifying sonic otherness.

With reference to Althusser, I argue that the mediation of traditional expressive traditions produces answers to only those questions that leading ideology is prepared, in practice, to entertain. Music among Garifuna themselves, in local and overseas communities alike, takes varied forms, which an ethnographic approach may help to elucidate, forms distinct from their commercially mediated representations. By contrast, the narrow utilitarian focus of world-music-as-commodity—generally indifferent to local cultural histories and the prevailing asymmetries of power traditional peoples have endured—fails to register the signification of local meaning in everyday performance.

The global convergence of music, culture, politics, and commerce produces novel artistic, social, and material meanings that are anything but self-evident, and where local culture and international capital intersect, both danger and opportunity reside. But a fascination with the new, the hybrid, and the exotic can mask how today's paradoxes are embedded in the unresolved contradictions and inequities of the past. Missing from most analyses of world music is an account of the asymmetrical legacies of colonialism and local people's sustained, articulate struggles for historical recognition, respect, and cultural equity. This chapter offers a preliminary reflection upon such questions, as inscribed in Garifuna musical dynamics.

TRACING THE PRESENT IN GARIFUNA MUSIC

In the racialized polity of Belize, colonial commentators reduced the actual diversity of African-inspired performance traditions to a racially essentialized unity. To wit, Garifuna music was only one among many local cultural tradition with African roots, and it was first specifically noted only in the mid-nineteenth century. Prior to emancipation (1838), enslaved and free laborers (Garifuna and free Jamaicans among the latter) worked side-by-side in the timber camps of Central America's Caribbean coast. Garifuna players thus interacted with enslaved Africans, sharing musical skills, traditional lore, and aesthetic pleasures. Yet no slave-era account of music-making in the mahogany camps has surfaced. Hence, we know little of Garifuna music's colonial performance contexts, musical conceptions, genres, rhythms, melodies, lyrical texts, dance forms, vocal and playing styles, instruments, or modes of learning and cultural transmission, let alone (as Raymond Williams might have put it) the structure of Garifuna musical feeling.

The earliest textual evidence is an 1847 sketch of a Carib (i.e. Garifuna) "John Canoe" (Jonkonnu or Wanaragua) masquerade dance, which, along with palpable African and Amerindian features, showed the carnivalesque influence of English mummery and fife-and-drum traditions. Enacted between Christmas and New Year's, and linked to forms described in nearby Jamaica and New Orleans, Jonkonnu is still performed today in Belize and other parts of the English-speaking Caribbean, and was once found as far afield as the Carolinas.[5] Young described one such ethnically mixed workers' bacchanal in nearby coastal Honduras:

> Whilst the natives were enjoying themselves, handing the mushla [cassava beer] from one to another, the sound of the drums were [sic] heard rapidly advancing, and in a short time there arrived several mahogany cutters, who had just come down from some mahogany works on the Wanks River, consisting of Creoles, from Balize [sic], and the Caribs, from Little Rock, to the

westward of Black River; who, after greeting their Mosquito [Indian] friends, and making very low bows to the English, commenced dancing with might and main, the drums being played very well with their open hands. The scene to us was so perfectly strange, so much like a burlesque on Old Drury, and yet so real, and in such vivid colours, as to be striking and picturesque; the Caribs with their red trowsers, caps, white shirts, and dark complexions, the Creoles, in snow-white clothes, and their shiny black and merry faces, the copper coloured Indians, and the pale faced Englishmen (Young 1847, 32).

For Young, the most striking Garifuna expressive practice was the sacred dugú, an extended trance-possession ceremony to conciliate the gúbida, the ancestral spirits of the dead.[6] He reported that "the Caribs have various feast days," including "Christmas, and those termed Devil feasts" (Young 1847, 132). Jesuit priests called the latter the "Mafia-devil" feast or dance, whose sacred dimensions, cultural syncretism, and intense sociability they were too busy condemning to actually detail; their accounts of the dugú overlooked the aesthetics and social orientation of the associated singing, drumming, and dancing, casting a disapproving eye on its alleged "blasphemy" and "African degeneracy." Compare Young's description, which despite its high-romantic style and failure to perceive the dugú's social and spiritual orientation, sustains a nonjudgmental tone quite distinct from pejorative Jesuit portrayals:

> Some time previous to a Devil feast, the inhabitants . . . send messengers to summon their friends and relatives, however distant, and they surmount every obstacle to attend; coming from Balize [sic], Stann Creek [Dangriga, coastal southern Belize], Truxillo [coastal Honduras], &c. in their creers [sailing craft] (Young 1847, 132).

Notably, the dugú drew people from throughout the Caribbean coast, and plainly, the Garifuna freely incorporated English customs and goods into its intensely sociable ritual performance. The ceremonial synthesis of traditional Garifuna forms with emblematic borrowed elements offers striking early evidence of a guiding strategic antiessentialism among a subordinate people versed in the uncertain politics of cultural diplomacy. The ritual abundance and conviviality catered to a diverse human commons, demarcating an arena of mutual cultural esteem and exchange in a figurative expenditure of material abundance that Europeans read as a deferral to their ideological authority and material dominance. The performance expressed a considerable political aesthetic, articulating a distinctive cultural identity, strategically enacted as a striking communal expression of convergent humanity.

> This feast lasts from three days to a week, and they all contribute, by bringing their offerings of liquor. Strangers are welcomed with evident pleasure, but the white man, with all the courtesy and delight they can possibly testify. The feast commences at sunset, when the drums as well as the liquor are put into

requisition, and the play and singing commence, and are kept up with all the vigour and enjoyment so characteristic of the Caribs. Glass decanters, glass tumblers, white table cloths, and English earthenware, raise a familiar sensation in an Englishman's mind. The liquor handed round in glass tumblers, English fashion, in one part, and the bottle in another. Numerous large and beautifully clean cotton hammocks are slung around . . . It is a maxim, on these events, that good drinking ought to be accompanied by good eating. They therefore take care to have a number of little tables well, and even sumptuously furnished, at which all enjoy themselves without ceremony or limitation. In one place several tables may be seen, about three feet high and two or three feet square, covered with clean white cloths, and ornamented with red or yellow fringe. On some of the cloths are placed large pieces of cassada [cassava] bread, which serve as dishes and plates; others for the captains, have decanters, and every sort of crockery ware required. On one dish is either fresh or salt pork, on others fresh or salt fish or fowl. Here you may feast yourself on game of the choicest kind, such as venison, warrie [wild boar], qualm [wild turkey]; there you may satiate yourself on turtle, or tashajo; pepper-soup, in various large basins, being placed in all directions to dip the cassada bread into, thereby to soften and improve it. This being one of the St. Vincent customs, it is held in great esteem. As family meets family they greet each other with much warmth and cordiality, and even in the midst of all their hilarity, no such thing as quarreling takes place. Towards the morning the tables begin to look remarkably empty, nearly everything being consumed, dishes and all, shortly however to be replenished by the provident masters of the feast, who, as soon as daylight appears, begin to put down fresh dishes and meats (Young 1847, 132–33).

The performance may well have served to "raise a familiar sensation in an Englishman's mind," but in doing so it reproduced a locally-based performance style, a participatory mode of ritual recreation enacted in a pleasurable dialectic entailing concurrent expressions of cultural convergence and distinction. Young's account offers evidence of Garifuna renegotiation of the cultural stereotypes and expectations of that privileged outside observer,

the white man [who enjoys] all the courtesy and delight [his Garifuna hosts] can possibly testify . . . with much warmth and cordiality, and even in the midst of all their hilarity, no such thing as quarrelling takes place. (ibid.)

Young's tone resonates with the delight a savvy, supportive, politically progressive audience might express at a contemporary world-music concert, and the upbeat reportage on Garifuna musical style in the world-music press. Historical and present-day accounts share the advantaged perspective of outsiders describing a palpable yet simultaneously imaginary space wherein, as Young related, "It is a maxim, on these events, . . . [that] all enjoy themselves without ceremony or limitation." This is, of course, a matter of perception and privilege, as anonymous cultural others bear the burden of producing a suspended moment of enjoyment mediated from without by cultural perceptions not necessarily attuned to Garifuna cultural cues and norms. This is not to suggest that Young or modern audiences entirely deceive themselves. A good time may be had by all, but only insofar as dominant discourse ideologically conceals and erases extant cultural, socioeconomic, and political inequities.

GARIFUNA MUSIC:
GROOVE LOCALE, TRANSNATIONAL CIRCUIT

World music today enjoys bona fide status as a vibrant industry genre, trading upon a putative authenticity perceived in the rough-edged, elusive, exotic quality assigned to "discoveries" that are anything but new to local artists and audiences. As one anthropologist wryly remarked upon meeting a popular traditional lambada musician on his home turf in northeastern Brazil, "We were in search of authentically obscure game, someone who embodied a regional style which could still be encountered in pre-culture-industry form" (Nugent 1994). Stephen Nugent points to a key aspect of world-music popularity, a danceable, rhythmic vitality characteristic of African diaspora musics in all their naturalized Dionysian glory, seen as produced by racialized subjects specializing in a bodily abandon whose performance invites western audiences to cast off their inhibitions in a seizure of vicarious sensual gratification (Radano and Bohlman 2001). Nugent also notes how local traditions gain global hearing precisely through an assay of their commodity potential:

> I don't get it. The World Music I'm presented with in London is either stuff I've listened to all my life ... or ... late colonial retread. What "World" means in London is "Lost Empire," music from the continent they never cracked, Africa. [Other music] doesn't qualify as World Music because it too successfully resists appropriation . . . It falls just the wrong side of the folk art divide—uncoverable by First World artists, yet still not up for a museum display (Nugent 1994, 168).

Nugent's irony signals the operation of what I call the groove locale, the interactive field of commodified popular reception that creates the intangible cultural allure (and thus the commercial viability) of sonic otherness. The groove locale entails a dialectical process wherein dominant and subordinate subjects, influences, forms, and forces converge and act upon one another to create a covariable (and accordingly unstable) field of musical dialogue. Encompassing a production, circulation, and reception circuit that juxtaposes local and global-popular aesthetic values, the groove locale entertains a provisional estimation of musical authenticity to validate certain world-music forms, while disallowing others. In a shifting consensus regarding a given traditionally-based style's popularity, actors coproduce a mutable domain of musical "tradition" and "truth" in a discourse that rewards particular mediations of local roots traditions at the expense of their commodity-resistant counterparts. Paradoxically, the groove locale masks concrete local musical foundations while derivative styles take commodified transnational form.

In the Garifuna case, ethnomusicologists began documenting the music in the early 1950s (Stone 1953; Jenkins and Jenkins 1982a and 1982c; Sandahl 2000), but industry cachet came much later, after independent recording efforts and revival groups like the Ballet Folklorico Garifuna of Honduras drew international attention. By the early 1990s, Garifuna musicians were long rooted in expatriate communities in New York, Miami, Chicago, New Orleans, Houston, and Los Angeles, and were performing widely in Europe and Japan.

Early press accounts of Garifuna music bear out Nugent's wry reflection on the colonial character of appropriation, the music's association with illicit sensuality and, paradoxically, its imputed accessibility. As the Associated Press reported in 1991, "An addictive dance music called punta rock has become the beat of Belize and a symbol of pride to one of the world's most dispossessed people." C. C. Smith, publisher of The Beat, a world-music monthly, is quoted: "It's good-time party music. It's very accessible. Most of it's in English, for heavens sake . . . soca with a twitch."[7] Compare a National Geographic report whose title informs that Garifuna villages "pulse with . . . joyous rhythms" (Rust 2001). Such would seem to be the safely habit-forming, ever so slightly racy, danceable musical product of the culturally exotic. (But as argued in the final section, the music's "accessibility" may also contain a political potential antithetical to the pessimism of the Frankfurt School mass culture critique.)

Writing in 1991 for The Beat in one of the earliest media reports, Amy Miller made a pilgrimage to Central America after hearing Garifuna punta rock tapes in an independent, Belizean-owned Los Angeles recording studio, missing the fact that she had encountered the transnational product of a cosmopolitan cultural hybridity. A romantic, hackneyed style says more of the writer than the subject:

> In search of the roots of this music, I travelled to Belize . . . then took an old
> rickety bus on rough dirt 'highways' and a dugout canoe over aqua waters until
> I reached white sands by clear waters in a world without electricity . . . among
> miles of thatched-roof huts [on] the Caribbean shoreline, [to] the home of
> the well-known drummer, Dionicio 'Thin Skin' Flores (Miller 1991,40).

Making her way to his "hut" as darkness falls, Miller sketches a scene signifying cultural authenticity, ageless wisdom, earthy character and noble poverty, set against a whimsical "American-style" bricolage of Third-World postmodernity:

> A kerosene lamp illuminated the dirt floor, bamboo walls and a palm-leaf ceiling, and shone on a large black disco box. His dress combined American pop
> fashion with the style of a timeless seaman, the way tropical and Hollywood

mingled throughout Belize, a country that survived TV-less until the 1980s. Two strands of large seashells around his neck rested on a bright blue body-building T-shirt. His gray, lower-chin beard clashed with his dark hair. A blue bandanna was tucked behind glasses that framed intense, knowing eyes (Miller 1991, 40).

Later, in Belize City, Miller meets an English sound engineer whose authority rests on claims to have worked with Elton John and the Psychedelic Furs. Reportedly "in Belize to promote the nation's culture," he asserts that "even if it is well-produced—unlikely, given the lack of equipment and capital in Belize—punta rock could easily be 'ghettoized into coffee-table music' like much ethnic music." He offers Miller the unwitting paradox of eccentric local "professional musicians" who dare seek recognition and compensation commensurate with their artistry. He declares—in a classic expression of imperialist nostalgia—that professional musicians should stick it out at home. Looking out the window of the Belize City Cultural Center at an overgrown and undernourished seaside shanty town, he says,

> It's difficult to make people realize that they should stay and make music here, but the best, truly great music has been [made] when people are in their own environment (Blanca 1999).

To paraphrase the sound engineer, Belizeans have neither the money nor the technology to make high-quality productions, and their 'ethnic music' would just become a middle-class decorative accessory, so they should stay put, because picturesque poverty, racism and human suffering have created 'the best, truly great music.'

The "cultural promoter" conveys a telling indifference to the material conditions that have led both Garifuna musicians and their audiences to emigrate in hopes of making themselves heard and improving their life chances.

To paraphrase Marx, history unfolds the first time as tragedy, the second as farce. The engineer seems unaware that Garifuna recordings had been made in Belize by the mid-1980s, and were readily available when he was there (indeed, surviving cassettes are collector's items). Meanwhile, a Honduran (but non-Garifuna) group topped the U.S. Latin dance charts in 1991 with "Sopa de Caracol," a disco reworking of the Garifuna punta rhythm that Sony quickly licensed for international distribution (Blanca 1999). So even before Garifuna musicians played at the Festival of Caribbean Culture in Mexico (1992), their music was making international waves (Duran 1998).

Also in 1992, the independent Arhoolie label issued the first recording of U.S. Garifuna music (by Chatuye, a Belizean group formed in 1983 in Los Angeles), and a Mexican label released a compilation of African diaspora music that included Garifuna songs. In 1993, Mickey Hart's Endangered Music Project issued a survey of indigenous music from Latin America's rainforests, including ten tracks of Garifuna sacred music from the Library of Congress vaults. In 1994, Lita Arian, a Honduran Garifuna group, toured Japan and recorded there (Pillich and Mejia 1992; Llerenas 1992; Hart 1993; Lita 1994).

In 1995, Ivan Duran founded Stonetree Records, a Belizean company dedicated to regional traditional music, and in 1998 Warner Music's European division licensed Stonetree's Garifuna paranda recording, which quickly climbed the European world-music charts. After a tour by the Garifuna All-Stars, the album was excerpted in a best-selling African diaspora compilation in 2000, the same year the definitive Rough Guide world-music reference took note of Garifuna music for the first time. In 2001, UNESCO declared Garifuna language, dance, and music to be "Masterpieces of the Oral and Intangible Heritage of Humanity" (Duran and Abarbanel 1998; Rosenberg 1998; Scholze 2000; Graham 2000; UNESCO 2001). In 2002, Stonetree began recording a Garifuna women's group, and Belize was set to host its first world-music tourism junket, organized by Afropop Worldwide, the syndicated music program broadcast on National Public Radio. Characteristic of industry workings, in a relatively short time a handful of independent recording efforts fueled a "world-music" phenomenon that quickly gained exposure via global mass media.

Extending the "discovery" process, New Yorker David Whitmer, a conga drummer seeking an exotic sonic upgrade, travelled to Honduras for "a quick and efficient introduction to the hand-drumming styles of Garifuna punta music" (Whitmer 2000, 33). The Fordist language of speed and efficiency betrays an underlying cultural conceit. In a portrait of picturesque tropical decay, Whitmer describes strolling a poor Garifuna neighborhood in search of a drum and someone to teach him to play. His teacher (whom he identifies only as "David") assumes a heroic subaltern folk dignity, the authentic intuitive genius and intense physicality of the racialized musical other,

> a rough, unkempt looking fellow, with bushy and uncut hair receding on the temples and fat, lamb chop sideburns framing his cheekbones. An unlit cigarette dangled from his lip. He was not tall but he held himself very straight . . . He took the drum away from me, sat down . . . and played. His fingers were like thick, blackened slabs of meat, with dried, cracking skin peeling from around the nails and callused palm. They seemed barely to move at all over the drumhead, but the snare sang and danced at his light touch, and the steady double tone finishing each measure was deep and resonant and packed a punch (Whitmer 2000, 35).

The author also met a younger player who spoke "very good" English and who had lived in New York for a time. Whitmer observes, "He was not half the player David was," but his style "worked better with contemporary music." Whitmer relates,

> I suspect that in these days of electronic instrumentation and cassette record-
> ings there have been drastic changes in the sound and rhythms of punta
> music and that the young man on the beach had been much influenced by
> these changes (Whitmer 2000, 87).

The process has been underway longer than he thinks. Garifuna music and
dance began to be widely reported in U.S. cities in the early 1980s, and the
Ballet Folklorico Garifuna of Honduras performed in New York and Houston.[8] Whitmer could well have stayed in Manhattan and studied with Garifuna drummers in nearby Brooklyn and the Bronx, but for a world-music
readership, the U.S. inner-city groove locale of immigrant Garifuna, starkly
emblematic of the transnational postmodern condition, would not have
offered the same cachet as a quixotic, imperially nostalgic musical safari to
Caribbean Central America in search of "authentically obscure game" that was
already fully in international circulation.

WHICH WORLD, WHOSE MUSIC?

Prevailing media accounts of traditional Garifuna music render a superficial
reading of cultural history that mutes Garifuna voices, restricting them to the
musical performance itself. But in the early-twentieth century, Garifuna
men—working as stevedores and deckhands on cargo steamers connecting
Caribbean Central America with Galveston, New Orleans, Mobile and U.S.
east coast ports—inaugurated a migration process that continues to connect
expatriate and home communities (Gonzalez 1988; Taylor 1951). The music
entails far more than the "pulsing joyous rhythms" reported by National Geographic. It speaks to Garifuna experience at home and abroad, expressing profound sentiments of longing and loss, but also a celebratory sense of identity
rooted in a conflictual history of encounters with dominant cultural forms and
institutions under conditioning forces of global capitalism, wage-labor experience, and metropolitan racism.

The cultural impact of return migration was already manifest in Central
America early in the twentieth century. Colonial reports bemoaned Belizean
appetites for U.S. popular culture. Migrant Garifuna brought home acquired
foreign tastes, and, like other Belizeans, incorporated them into local cultural
practice. As early as 1927, from a remote Garifuna coastal village, a Jesuit
priest noted,

> The young folks show an aptitude for playing the organ that is remarkable,
> and nearly all the Carib teachers are organists as well, purchasing their
> 'portable Estey' with their savings and practicing faithfully and patiently in
> their every spare hour (Anonymous 1927).

They seem to have pursued a strategy of adopting and refashioning dominant
forms as a means of expressive assertion and cultural survival, a process evident

even in Young's account of the ethnically plural musical encounter in a coastal settlement in Caribbean Central America, circa 1847.

Young's is a magical, fetishized account of Garifuna performance. If ideology works to dispel the actual contradictions of lived experience, what symptomatic erasures does Young's account perform? Where are the human actors in Young's radiant tale of Garifuna ritual celebration and abundance? There are no palpable Garifuna voices or personalities, no individual actors, women or men, no sense of the human planning, organization, and labor required to bring off the feast—and only passing acknowledgment of the power inequities embedded in the performance. Enchanted music issues from the booming drums, nameless dancers astonish with their acrobatics, and immaculate tables miraculously replenish themselves with food and drink throughout a night of unmitigated communal pleasure—all in an animated romantic style echoed in much contemporary world-music journalism.

For western fans, the music represents a vicarious transcultural pleasure whose mediated accessibility renders invisible the actual human histories embedded in it. This perspective misses how traditional artists and audiences inscribe musical performance and appreciation with meanings both convergent with and distinctive from those it elicits in commodified mediation and reception. Media representations at best make only superficial note of what is primary in original context—the music's intense sociability, embedded in a participatory ideal, its fiercely historical character, its potent expression of local identity, social agency and cultural survival, all values carefully transmitted to the younger generation.

By contrast, world music offers a set of consumer choices through which to imagine (and thus concretely produce) a seemingly benign relationship with a world of sonic otherness, whose subordination to western material practice, essential to the encounter, is ideologically veiled in the exchange. But a Frankfurt School-like condemnation of this engagement as a vulgar commodifying process that denatures traditional musics in rendering them accessible to global audiences overlooks another dynamic worthy of consideration.

World music's calibration of local traditions with western tastes under the structural logic of global capitalism cannot silence a strange but oddly familiar articulation of culturally convergent counternormative sentiments and values. In actual practice, world music encompasses multiple subject positions, aesthetic perspectives, and political dispositions with far richer political potential than a crude mass culture critique is capable of rendering. If the opportunistic mediation of traditional expressive forms and cultural identities constitutes a self-concealing act of simultaneous exploitation and erasure, paradoxically, it also enables a groove locale with utopian potential, one in which novel, more inclusive cultural and political possibilities are latent, if not fully articulated.

In a mediation process conditioned by market-value calculation, global-popular reception may well entail an exercise in ideological misrecognition, one less concerned with traditional artist and audience than with trading in a commodified "lifestyle" identity. But if local traditions gain global cachet, insofar as they resonate with the popular cultural and aesthetic expectations of world audiences, the encounter presents not only risk but also opportunity. Artists may gain an opening by coproducing, with nontraditional audiences, an inviting new groove locale, pursuing a process of strategic antiessentialism that opens ground for common understanding, even as it masks aspects of cultural identity and political history too volatile to bear direct expression.

Preliminary consideration of Garifuna musical traditions in a transnational context indicates a potential to repudiate popular cultural stereotypes in a subtle fashioning of irony, exaggeration, and ebullient stylistic display. The music appeals to a systemic sense of alienation widely perceived under late capitalism, but in variable terms conditioned by an audience's particular subject position. Music compellingly articulates and sets into motion those ultimately political sentiments of human estrangement that resist customary logical and verbal expression, and that question the ideological contours of hegemonic consensus-seeking.

This preliminary impression of Garifuna music dynamics in a global sonic domain offers lessons generalizable to the analysis of other world musics, and anticipates ethnographic work to explore trends whose cultural contours are only outlined here. Without discounting the potentially debilitating effects of roots music's separation from local performance contexts, as these sounds gain planetary audition, the music need not surrender its wellspring of artistic dynamism, its participatory vitality, or its animating vigor as a countermedium of simultaneous social affirmation and critique. Traditional artists working in a mediated global arena inspire new audiences by initiating a conscious dialogue with dominant musical idioms, refusing reductive stereotypes while sustaining the locally-honed sensibilities of their own cultural particularity. A dialectical remediation of dominant forms through the grassroots agency of a unique aesthetic and social-historical consciousness calls to life, celebrates a more globally resonant groove locale, conditioning novel expressions of identity that surmount cultural and political challenges and sustain a creative tension between local and transnational experience, sentiment, and signification.

NOTES

The Wenner-Gren Foundation for Anthropological Research, Fulbright-CIES, and Fulbright-IIE supported this work. I thank Dr. Joseph Palacio and staff, University of the West Indies, Belize; staff at the Belize Archives, Belmopan; the Benson Latin American Collection, University of Texas at Austin; Bancroft Library, University of California, Berkeley; Vatican Microfilm Collection, St. Louis University; Midwest Province Jesuit Archives, St. Louis; and Dawn Baker, Stevens-German Library, Hartwick College. David Bruno, Shanna Castillo and Kristyn Wilcox provided unstinting student research assistance. Particular thanks to the Universität Konstanz

FB Literaturwissenschaft and the SFB Literatur und Anthropologie for the chance to develop this work. Kudos to unindicted co-conspirator Cliff Furnald, who provided an early venue to air the project; Gina Melendez and Armando Crisanto Melendez of the Ballet Folklorico Garifuna, Honduras; Nestor Rodriguez-University of Houston, Pat Jasper-Texas Folklife Resources, and Cathy Ragland for aiding preliminary research in the Houston Garifuna community; Ivan Duran and Mark Langan, Stonetree Records, Belize; and Sten Sandahl, Caprice Records, Stockholm. Personal thanks to Rick and Betty Adams for opening the door; to Milton Jamail and Brad Barham, whose interest, encouragement and principled self-fashioning offer continued inspiration; to Silvia Mergenthal and Robert Calder for general indulgence, provocative conversation and generous hospitality; and to Gabrielle Winkler and Solana Winkler Stone, who better than anyone know why and wherefore.

1. A similar argument applies to the global resonance of "conscious reggae's" cultural politics of liberation.

2. Another illustration of music's ability to undermine ideological barriers, the *Buena Vista Social Club*, features the music of Cuba, a nation long isolated and stigmatized by a hostile U.S. government. Enthusiastic international reception has enabled Cuban musicians to skirt the U.S. economic embargo, bring their music to appreciative world audiences, and without having set out to do so, undercut the outmoded cold-war rationale of U.S. Cuban policy (Fairley, "The 'Local' and the 'Global' in Popular Music").

3. Belize (formerly British Honduras) stands on Central America's Caribbean coast, bounded to the north by Mexico's Yucatán region, and by Guatemala to the west and south.

4. The first Garifuna arrived in Belize in 1802, only five years after British forces defeated them in their aboriginal territory, the island of St. Vincent, and deported them en masse to the Caribbean coast of Honduras, where they hoped the Garifuna would become a thorn in the side of England's colonial rival, Spain (Burdon, *Archives of British Honduras*, 57). Ethnohistorical sources include Anderson, "The Significance of Blackness;" Conzemius, "Ethnographic Notes;" Gonzalez, *Sojourners of the Caribbean;* and Taylor, *The Black Carib.*

5. See Bettelheim, "Jamaican Jonkonnu" and "Jonkonnu and Other Christmas Masquerades;" Dirks, "The Evolution of a Playful Ritual;" Greene, "Belize;" Gullick, "Piaye and Pia Manadi;" Hadel, "Carib Dance Music;" Kerns and Dirks, "John Canoe;" Rommen, "Home Sweet Home;" Sands, "Carnival Celebrations;" Stone, "Jonkonnu;" Whipple, "Pia Manadi."

6. Foster, *Heart Drum;* Greene, "The Dugú Ritual;" Jenkins, "Ritual and Resource Flow;" Jenkins and Jenkins, *Dabuyabarugu* and "Garifuna Musical Style;" Kerns, *Women and the Ancestors;* Wells, "Spirits See Red."

7. Rice, "Punta Rock;" for a Garifuna view, see Palacio, "Punta Rock."

8. See Anderson, "Dance;" Barnes, "Neighborhood Report;" Gershanik, "Music Sheds Light;" Hutchinson et al., "Community Life;" Kugel, "Neighborhood Report;" McCallister, "African Arts Festival;" Miller, *Bridges;* Otis, "Music Heralds Cultural Revival;" Perry, *Garifuna Youth in New York City;* Pillich and Mejia, *Chatuye;* Renwick, "Home Away from Home;" Rice, "Punta Rock;" Shepard, "Going Out Guide;" Wildman, "Expecting Salsa."

REFERENCES

Anderson, Ian. "World Music History." *Folk Roots* 201 (2000): 36–39.

Anderson, Jack. "Dance: Honduras's Folklorico Garifuna Company." *The New York Times,* 7 December 1986.

Anderson, Mark. "The Significance of Blackness: Representations of Garifuna in St. Vincent and Central America, 1700–1900." *Transforming Anthropology* 6, no.1/2 (1997): 22–35.

Anonymous. "In the Toledo District 1927, Monkey River." *The Clarion* [Belize], 26 May 1927.

Barnes, Julian E. "Neighborhood Report: South Bronx; Feeling the Spirit: Preserving a Culture in an Alien City." *The New York Times,* 31 January 1999.

Bettelheim, Judith. "Jamaican Jonkonnu and Related Caribbean Festivals." In *Africa and the Caribbean: The Legacies of a Link.* Edited by Margaret E. Crahan and Franklin W. Knight. Baltimore, Johns Hopkins Univ. Pr. 1979, 80–100.

Bettelheim, Judith. "Jonkonnu and Other Christmas Masquerades." In *Caribbean Festival Arts.* Editied by John W. Nunley and Judith Bettelheim. Seattle, Univ. of Washington Pr. 1988, 39–83.

Blanca, Banda. *Sopa de Caracol.* Miami, Sonotone 1999.

Bolland, O. Nigel. *Colonialism and Resistance in Belize: Essays in Historical Sociology.* Benque Viejo, Belize, Cubola Productions 1988.

Burdon, John. *Archives of British Honduras,* vol. 2. London, Sifton, Praed & Co. 1934.

Cantwell, Robert S. *When We Were Good: The Folk Revival.* Cambridge, MA, Harvard Univ. Pr. 1996.

Cheyney, Tom. "The Real World of Peter Gabriel." *The Beat* 9, no. 2 (1990): 22–25.

Conzemius, Eduard. "Ethnographic Notes on the Black Carib (Garif)." *American Anthropologist.* 30 (1928): 183–205.

DeNora, Tia. *Music in Everyday Life.* Cambridge, Cambridge Univ. Pr. 2000.

Dirks, Robert. "The Evolution of a Playful Ritual: The Garifuna John Canoe in Comparative Perspective." In *Forms of Play of Native North Americans: Proceedings of the American Ethnological Society 1977.* Edited by Edward Norbeck and Claire R. Farrer. St. Paul, MN, West Pub. Co. 1979, 89–109.

Duran, Ivan and Gil Abarbanel. *Paranda: Africa in Central America.* Benque Viejo, Belize, Stonetree Records STR CD 018, 1998.

Duran, Lucy. "More Itself Than Ever." *Folk Roots.* 35 (1992): 35–37.

English, Merle. "Into the Spotlight: Focus on Little-Known Peoples." *Newsday,* Brooklyn Edition, 29 June 1993.

Fairley, Jan, "The 'Local' and the 'Global' in Popular Music." In *The Cambridge Companion to Rock and Pop.* Edited by Simon Frith, Will Straw, and John Street. Cambridge, Cambridge Univ. Pr. 2001, 272–89.

Feld, Steven. "From Schizophonia to Schismogenesis: On the Discourses and Commodification Practices in 'World Music' and 'World Beat.'" In *Music Grooves:*

Essays and Dialogues. Edited by Charles Keil and Steven Feld. Chicago, Univ. of Chicago Pr. 1994a, 257–89.

———. "Notes on 'World Beat.'" In *Music Grooves: Essays and Dialogues*. Edited by Charles Keil and Steven Feld. Chicago, Univ. of Chicago Pr. 1994b, 238–46.

———. "A Sweet Lullaby for World Music." *Public Culture* 12, no. 1 (2000): 145–71.

———. *Bosavi: Rainforest Music from Papua New Guinea*. Washington, DC, Smithsonian Folkways Recordings 2001a.

———. *Rainforest Soundwalks: Ambiences of Bosavi, Papua New Guinea*. Taos, NM, Earth Ear-Bosavi People's Fund 2001b.

Foster, Byron. *Heart Drum: Spirit Possession in the Garifuna Communities of Belize*. Belize, Cuban Productions 1986.

Frith, Simon. "The Discourse of World Music." In *Western Music and Its Others: Difference, Representation and Appropriation in Music*. Editied by Georgina Born and David Hesmondhalgh. Berkeley, Univ. of California Pr. 2000, 305–22.

Gershanik, Ana. "Music Sheds Light on Garifuna Roots." *New Orleans Times-Picayune*, 10 September 2000.

Gonzalez, Nancie L. *Sojourners of the Caribbean: Ethnogenesis and Ethnohistory of the Garifuna*. Urbana: Univ. of Illinois Pr. 1988.

Goodwin, Andrew and Joe Gore. "World Beat and the Cultural Imperialism Debate." *Socialist Review* 20, no. 3 (1990): 63–80.

Graham, Ronnie. "Belize: Drum 'n' Flute Legacies." In *World Music: The Rough Guide*, vol. 2. Edited by Simon Broughton and Mark Ellingham. London, Rough Guide 2000, 325–31.

Greene, Oliver N. "Belize." In *Garland Encyclopedia of World Music*, vol. 2: South America, Mexico, Central America and the Caribbean. Edited by Dale A. Olsen and Daniel E. Sheehy. New York, Garland Publ. 1998, 666–79.

———. "The Dugú Ritual of the Garinagu of Belize: Reinforcing Values of Society through Music and Spirit Possession." *Black Music Research Journal* 18, no. 2 (1998): 167–81.

Guilbault, Jocelyne. "World Music." In *The Cambridge Companion to Rock and Pop*. Edited by Simon Frith, Will Straw, and John Street. Cambridge, Cambridge Univ. Pr. 2001, 176–92.

Gullick, C. J. M. R. "Piaye and Pia Manadi." *Belizean Studies* 4, no. 6 (1976): 7–12.

Hadel, Richard E. "Carib Dance Music and Dance." *National Studies* 1, no. 6 (1973): 4–10.

Hart, Mickey. *The Spirit Cries: Music from the Rainforests of South America and the Caribbean*. Salem, MA, Rykodisc 1993.

Harvey, David. *The Condition of Postmodernity: An Enquiry into the Origins of Cultural Change*. Cambridge, MA and Oxford, UK, Blackwell, 1989.

Hutchinson, Janis Faye, Nestor Rodriguez, and Jacqueline Hagan. "Community Life: African Americans in Multiethnic Residential Areas." *Journal of Black Studies* 27, no. 2 (1996): 201–23.

Jenkins, Carol L. "Ritual and Resource Flow: The Garifuna Dugú." In *Blackness in Latin America and the Caribbean: Social Dynamics and Cultural Transformations*,

Vol. 1: Central America and Northern and Western South America. Edited by Norman E. Whitten, Jr. and Arlene Torres. Bloomington and Indianapolis, Indiana Univ. Pr. 1998, 149–67.

Jenkins, Carol and Travis Jenkins. *Dabuyabarugu: Inside the Temple, Sacred Music of the Garifuna of Belize.* New York, Folkway Records 1982a.

———. "Garifuna Musical Style and Culture History." *Belizean Studies* 10, no. 3/4 (1982b): 17–24.

———. *Traditional Music of the Garifuna (Black Carib) of Belize.* New York, Folkway Records 1982c.

Jowers, Peter. "Beating New Tracks: WOMAD and the British World Music Movement." In *The Last Post: Music after Modernism.* Edited by Simon Miller. Manchester, Manchester Univ. Pr. 1993, 52–87.

Keil, Charles, and Steven Feld. "Getting into the Dialogic Groove." In *Music Grooves: Essays and Dialogues.* Chicago, Univ. of Chicago Pr. 1994, 1–50.

Kerns, Virginia. *Women and the Ancestors: Black Carib Kinship and Ritual.* Urbana, Univ. of Illinois Pr. 1983.

Kerns, Virginia, and Robert Dirks. "John Canoe." *Belizean Studies* 3, no. 6 (1975): 1–15.

Kugel, Seth. "Neighborhood Report: Bronx Up Close: A Quest to Count the Descendants of Islanders and Castaway Slaves." *The New York Times,* 5 August 2001.

Lipsitz, George. "Cruising around the Historical Bloc: Postmodernism and Popular Music in East Los Angeles." *Cultural Critique.* 5 (1986): 157–77.

Lipsitz, George. *Dangerous Crossroads. Popular Music, Postmodernism and the Poetics of Place.* London, Verso 1994.

Lita, Arian. *Honduras: Songs of the Garifuna.* Tokyo, JVC 1994.

Llerenas, Eduardo. *Africa en América.* México, DF, Corason 1992.

McCallister, Jared. "African Arts Festival at Boys and Girls High." *New York Daily News,* 25 June 2000.

Miller, Amy. "Punta: Dispatches from the Diaspora." *The Beat* 10, no. 4 (1991): 38–41, 54.

Miller, Linda Ruth. *Bridges: Garifuna Migration to Los Angeles.* Ph.D. dissertation, University of California, Irvine, 1993.

N'Dour, Youssou. *Refugee Voices—Building Bridges.* Geneva, United Nations High Commissioner for Refugees 2001.

Nugent, Stephen. *Big Mouth: The Amazon Speaks.* San Francisco, Brown Trout Publishers 1994.

Otis, John. "Music Heralds Cultural Revival of Belize's Garifuna Indians." *Miami Herald,* 13 August 1993.

Palacio, Andy. "Punta Rock: The Sound of Belize." *Belize Today* 3, no. 11/12 (1989): 12.

Perry, Marc David. *Garifuna Youth in New York City: Race, Ethnicity, and the Performance of Diasporic Identities.* M.A. Thesis, University of Texas at Austin, 1999.

Pillich, G. Simeon and Sidney Mejia. *Chatuye: Heartbeat in the Music.* San Pablo, CA, Arhoclie Records 1992.

Radano, Ronald M. and Philip V. Bohlman, eds. *Music and the Racial Imagination.* Chicago, Univ. of Chicago Pr. 2001.

Renwick, Lucille. "Home Away from Home: Belizeans Bring Sights, Sounds, Smells of Their Native Country to South-Central." *Los Angeles Times,* 3 July 1994.

Rice, John. "Punta Rock Becomes the Beat of Belize." *Los Angeles Times,* 30 December 1991.

Rommen, Timothy. "Home Sweet Home: Junkanoo as National Discourse in the Bahamas." *Black Music Research Journal* 19, no. 1 (1999) pp. 88–89, 92.

Rosaldo, Renato. "Imperialist Nostalgia." In *Culture and Truth: The Remaking of Social Analysis.* Boston, Beacon Pr. 1993, 68–87.

Rosenberg, Dan. "Parrandalised." *Folk Roots.* 182–183 (1998): 47–51.

Rust, Susie Post. "Fishing Villages along Central America's Coast Pulse with the Joyous Rhythms of This Afro-Caribbean People." *National Geographic* 200.3 (2001): 102–13.

Sandahl, Sten. *Music from Guatemala 2: Garifuna Music.* Stockholm, Caprice 1999.

———. *Music from Honduras 2: Garifuna Music.* Stockholm, Caprice 2000.

Sands, Rosita. "Carnival Celebrations in Africa and the New World: Junkanoo and the Black Indians of Mardi Gras," *Black Music Research Journal* 11, no. 1 (1991) pp. 217–28.

Scholze, Christian. *Musica Negra in the Americas.* Frankfurt am Main, Network Medien 2000.

Shepard, Richard F. "Going Out Guide." *The New York Times,* 21 April 1983.

Stone, Doris. *The Black Caribs of Honduras.* New York, Folkway Records 1953.

Stone, Michael C. "Jonkonnu (John Canoe)." In *Historical Encyclopedia of World Slavery.* Edited by Junius P. Rodriguez. Santa Barbara, CA: ABC-CLIO, 1997, 383–84.

Taylor, Douglas MacRae. *The Black Carib of British Honduras.* New York: Wenner-Gren Foundation, Viking Fund Publications in Anthropology no. 17, 1951.

UNESCO. "The Garifuna Language, Dance and Music." UNESCO Proclamation of Masterpieces of the Oral and Intangible Heritage of Humanity, 2001. http://www.unesco.org/opi/intangible_heritage/belize.htm

Wells, Marilyn McKillip. "Spirits See Red: The Symbolic Use of Gusueue among the Garif (Black Caribs) of Central America." *Belizean Studies* 10, no. 3/4 (1982): 10–16.

Whipple, Emory. "Pia Manadi." *Belizean Studies* 4, no. 4 (1976): 1–18.

Whitmer, David. "Garifuna Beat." *Folk Roots.* 202 (2000): 33–35, 87.

Wildman, David. "Expecting Salsa, You Get Punta Rock." *Boston Globe,* 9 September 2001.

Yelvington, Kevin A. "The Anthropology of Afro-Latin America and the Caribbean: Diasporic Dimensions." *Annual Review of Anthropology.* 30 (2001): 227–60.

Young, Thomas. *Narrative of a Residence on the Mosquito Shore; with an Account of Truxillo, and the Adjacent Islands of Bonacca and Roatan.* London, Smith, Eldes & Co. 1847.

The Thousand Faces of Xena:
Transculturality through Multi-Identity

MIRIAM BUTT, KYLE WOHLMUT

This chapter examines the television action series *Xena: Warrior Princess* (XWP) in the context of expanding use of new media, increasing globalization, and the phenomenon of identity detached from place, concluding that XWP is a response to the need for an action hero(ine) capable of responding to the current crisis of cultural identity as described by Appadurai and others (Appadurai 1996). Success in the world of rising globalization and new media depends on versatility and adaptability, characteristics not typical to the traditional action hero. This new situation calls for a mass media heroic figure that can be admired by the onlooker for the ability to adapt and succeed in a dynamic world.

MULTIDIMENSIONALITY

In the pre-Electronic Present[1] the archetypal action hero was a predictable, stock character. The action hero could be seen as a descendant of the heroes of the ancient heroic epic (a source drawn on heavily by XWP) and the romance of chivalry of the Middle Ages. An action hero was typically a flat character, a character who only ever faced one type of situation and could only respond to any situation in the same, predictable way: through (usually violent) action. Examples from pop culture are too numerous to mention here,[2] but the heroic 'one way' approach is succinctly described in the 1991 film *City Slickers*, in an exchange between the weathered cowboy Curly and Mitch, the urban denizen thrust into Curly's wild and uncontrollable world:

CURLY: You want to know what the secret of life is?

MITCH: Sure.

CURLY: It's this. [holds up one finger]

MITCH: Your finger?

CURLY: One thing. You've got to find your one thing, and be that.

MITCH: What's the one thing?

CURLY: That's what you've got to figure out.

Here, the cowboy action hero Curly is explaining the one approach that works for him in all situations ('I am a cowboy. How would a cowboy respond to this situation?') to Mitch, the hapless city dweller who is unable to cope in Curly's environment because in his own complex urban world (which the filmmakers would have us believe is more complicated than Curly's 'simple' rural existence), he must face a wide variety of situations in different ways, and thus has no real mastery of any one 'way.' It is interesting to note that the film *City Slickers* dates from 1991, just before the rise of the 'new media,' while XWP began its run in 1995, when that development had already become a widely recognized phenomenon.

The character of Xena continually demonstrates her ability to approach problems from different angles. While excelling in methods involving brute force and violence, she is equally adept at subterfuge, often resorting to disguise and stealth. She has superhuman abilities (strength and speed), but is also a renowned strategist with a remarkably analytical mind. At the same time, she is a shrewd negotiator and exhibits an innate understanding of any opponent's motivations, often using this to her great advantage. Indeed, unlike her predecessor action heroes, she appears to be the consummate master of many 'ways' and is in fact confused when confronted with the idea that any person can only excel in one 'way' (in the season four episode entitled 'The Way'):

XENA: Hanuman, you've been walking the Earth for centuries. How
       do you know what is the right code, or, lifestyle, or . . .

HANUMAN: . . . way?

XENA: Yes—how do you know what's the right way for you?

HANUMAN: My way is the way of obedience and loyalty. I can see it's not
          your way. You are too proud.

XENA: What happens when a person gets caught between two ways?

HANUMAN: That is not good. For each person, there can be only one way.

XENA: [pensive look]

Questions of one way versus many ways and the concept of identity are explicitly thematized in XWP, and the exploration of these themes sets the character of Xena apart from the traditional action hero.

In the Electronic Present, success requires the ability to respond to vastly divergent demands and the concept of identity is an increasingly blurred one. Until the end of the twentieth century, an essentialist concept of identity (Woodward 1997) was the ideal, and versatility was, to some extent, viewed with suspicion and mistrust. As recently as the 1960s, multilingualism was believed to be linked to brain deficiency and lower IQ. This belief was based on studies like Goddard's (1917) who invented the Binet (IQ) test and administered it to fresh Jewish immigrants, concluding that they were mentally deficient, or Smith (1949), who examined Hawaiian children of Japanese descent and concluded that their exposure to multiple languages impaired their ability to speak English properly. Smith did not take into account that the children she examined were actually speaking an undocumented and unfamiliar (to her) Pidgin. These and other studies mirrored the basic belief system of the time (as also expressed in the older writings of the famed Danish linguist Otto Jespersen (1922), for example), which has since been proven to be baseless by a host of linguistic studies.[3] Today, in the context of international commerce, multilingualism is a quality highly sought after on the employment market.

This is partly because success in the Electronic Present requires the ability to adapt instantly and to be multifaceted. One has only to look at today's job market to see that any chance of gainful employment requires excellence and experience in various areas. In addition to competence in an employable skill, applicants for any position must at a minimum have the computer skills requisite to any position (mastery of the 'new media') as well as organizational skills, and, of course, the ubiquitous 'ability to juggle multiple complex tasks simultaneously.' Clearly, Curly's concept of 'one way' or 'one thing' is outdated. It is the transition from an essentialist to a nonessentialist vision of identity that lies at the root of the crisis of identity in the Electronic Present.

To put this change in context, another useful comparison is found in *Star Trek,* arguably the most monumental action series of all time, and one that predates XWP by nearly thirty years. *Star Trek* is set on a space vessel in a pseudo-militaristic context, and, as a result, each character's role is clearly defined by his or her position on the ship, so much so that one of the show's many catchphrases was Dr. McCoy's recurring line, 'I'm a doctor, not a . . . ' Whenever Dr. McCoy is called upon to do anything not falling directly within his purvies as the ship's medical officer, he uses this line to peremptorily point out that, in effect, what he is being asked to do does not fall within his job description. By contrast, the most frequently recurring catchphrase used on XWP is: 'I have many skills.' This line occurs in at least thirteen episodes (and counting); in the vast majority of cases it is uttered by Xena after demonstrating some uncharacteristic and surprising skill, astonishing the other characters (even her constant companion Gabrielle). Xena is able to draw on a huge body of skills in her background, never refusing a task she is faced with, overcoming obstacles through her multidimensionality. Thus, she is a role model to those in the Electronic Present having to cope with ever-changing job requirements, in contrast to the former (static) 'action hero.'

Both the character Xena and the program XWP itself are fundamentally multidimensional. The on-screen visual elements present a striking, at first glance almost incoherent, mixture of styles. The show's creator and executive producer, Sam Raimi and Rob Tapert respectively, are American veterans of the 'Hong Kong' style of action film. As a result, the action sequences stand out from the standard American fare, even to the untrained eye. Yet, at the same time, the show makes constant reference to mainstream Hollywood filmmaking and American pop culture. Furthermore, the show, set in ancient Greece, is actually filmed in the temperate rainforests of New Zealand with predominantly American actors and actresses (speaking in completely modern, colloquial American English). Where possible, Polynesian influences found in the New Zealand setting, such as huts, monolithic statues, and fishing equipment, are used in the shots. The multifaceted nature of the show's look parallels the heroine's inherent multidimensionality.

Similarly, Xena's character allows for a broad spectrum of interpretation. She is, first and last, an exciting action hero, and, if interpreted solely on this level, the character succeeds. The action sequences are engaging, and the character can be seen to be following 'the way of the warrior.' The fact that she is female, however, and acting in the traditionally male role of warrior (and vanquishing males at every turn by dishing out varying amounts of abuse) begs for a feminist interpretation of the character, and the show provides no shortage of evidence to support that interpretation as well. Beneath that, there is perhaps the show's most talked-about element, the suggestion of a lesbian relationship between the two main characters, Xena and Gabrielle. The show's writers, producers, and actors all have a hand in the deliberate creation of this angle, known among the show's fans as 'subtext,' and there is always enough evidence to support this interpretation for those looking to find it, while remaining subdued enough to be ignored by those who don't.[4]

Thus, the construction of Xena's identity is never based on a static set of characteristics but transcends notions of gender, sexuality, and 'one thing.' She uses her 'many skills' to successfully respond to challenging situations and to extract useful information, which she can then use to construct a more coherent worldview. This is an interesting point to note within the context of this chapter because Xena does manage to project a coherent identity, despite her multifaceted nature ('many skills') and the many levels on which her character can be interpreted. Thus, Xena does manage to follow 'one way' without necessarily being committed to doing this in a one-dimensional manner, that is, she is not confined to 'one thing' in order to hold on to a coherent personality. She is thus the archetypal cosmopolitan and ideal hero figure for the crisis of identity in the Electronic Present: she can travel and survive in many different adverse environments by using diverse survival skills, while still projecting a coherent identity. In the Electronic Present, when a shrinking, increasingly globalized and dynamic world demands that we cope with a ceaseless tide of new situations and technologies and thereby uproots us from an essentialist identity tied to locality and culture, Xena is a role model for the construction of identity.

Appadurai (1996) speculates that the present crisis of identity is caused by the introduction of new media in conjunction with global migration. Mass migrations and the resulting diaspora are not new, but the ability to maintain a cohesive cultural identity detached from place (as fostered by the new media) is. In Appadurai's view, agency is provoked by (among other things) the consumption of mass media. As the nation-state loses its power and relevance, agency is sought in virtual communities such as those fostered by internet communication and computer-mediated multiuser discourse (Wellman 2001), where the most important communal basis between community members is a common pursuit or the consumption of a particular product of interest (Cherny 1999). Clearly, XWP fits into the latter context. Some writers have speculated that the success of XWP is linked to the concurrent success of the internet as a medium for communication.[5]

Additionally, the increasing rate of disappearance of real world cultures[6] appears to leave room for the formation of imagined cultures. As increasing globalization puts the pressure of a certain degree of conformity on all cultures, questions of the construction of identity arise. As the average Indonesian becomes more Americanized, the average American may begin to question what exactly separates him or her from the average Indonesian. The ensuing cultural vacuum leaves participants in the Electronic Present searching for means of differentiation in new ways, which are found in the Agency of the Imagination. Where a retreating sense of community in the Electronic Present leaves a void in the lives of the participants in the obsolete nation-state, some seek to fill that void with the imagined community of 'fandom,' detached from place, and that community is fostered by the new media's potential for communication independent of location. XWP has been a beneficiary of this new form of community for several reasons: (1) the development of the show has coincided with the rise of the new media; (2) its multidimensional construction, as outlined above, is ideally suited to generate interest among the members of a community detached from place; (3) it offers impulses for identity construction (e.g., the perceived need to construct a personal and coherent multidimensional identity to meet the demands of the Electronic Present) in a mass media context.

Identity construction is explicitly thematized in XWP on a number of levels. One of the most overriding and recurring identity issues of the series revolves around the relationship between Xena and her sidekick, Gabrielle. Before the series begins, Xena is a ruthless and brutal warlord bent upon killing and conquest.[7] She spends the duration of the series trying to do well and rectify her evil past. Along the way she meets Gabrielle, a peaceful villager with a flair for poetry. As they travel together each begins to have an effect on the other; Gabrielle, while remaining true to her character, does begin to develop a warrior aspect and often wrestles with the question of whether she is coming under the sway of Xena's darker side. In one exchange (from 'The Dirty Half-Dozen'), the characters address this question:

GABRIELLE: Can I ask you something? These people—all of them—were they murderers before you met them? I mean, it seems like, maybe they . . .

XENA: Gabrielle, it was me. I changed them. Before they met me, they were . . .

GABRIELLE: They were like me. Real people. Maybe even good people. Walsim, I . . . I could see him as a farmer at one time.

XENA: He was a carpenter.

GABRIELLE: I wonder, what would have happened if I had met you before . . . before . . . you know.

XENA: Gabrielle, I could never see you as being evil. There is a difference between them and you.

GABRIELLE: What difference? Xena, I have changed so much since I met you. I wonder how much of that is timing.

XENA: Does it really matter?

GABRIELLE: Am I really who I am? Or am I what you made me?

XENA: [pensive look] We better get going. If I'm going to stay up all night, I want to get an early start.

It would be a mistake to equate this question (whether identity is inherent or whether it is the sum of experiences) with the question of whether identity is ultimately essentialist or non-essentialist, as a subsequent exchange from the same episode shows:

XENA: I've got that answer to your question—are you who you are, or are you who I made you?

GABRIELLE: And?

XENA: You're Gabrielle: bard, Amazon Princess, best friend. Nobody made you who you are—it was already there. The question is, who would I be without you?

GABRIELLE: Hmm . . . I can answer that. You'd still be heroic Xena. You were on that path when we met.

XENA: Are you crazy? Without you to keep me on the straight and narrow?

GABRIELLE: You'd have managed . . .

The question is not one of whether essentialist identity exists or not. The question is one of maintaining a coherent identity despite inner conflicts and despite experiences and skills acquired along the way—following your 'way' with confidence, responding dynamically to a dynamic world while maintaining your identity.

XWP also explores the theme of identity construction and reconstruction. In the episode 'Forgiven,' Xena gives advice to Tara, an unruly teenager striving to be what Xena is: a good character with an evil past, as if that in itself is an identity that can be constructed, with no regard to the epiphany that Xena experienced, which shaped her identity.

> TARA: This doing good thing—how do you know what's really good and what's not? I mean, those boys from the gang, they think they're good. How do you really know?
>
> XENA: It's not always that simple. I usually go with my gut. And when in doubt, I ask her. [gestures to Gabrielle]
>
> TARA: No—She would know?
>
> XENA: Not always. But I know that her first instinct is usually an unselfish one, and that's a really good place to start.
>
> TARA: Do you think she was born good? I mean, my father always told me that I was bad from day one.
>
> XENA: That is not true. You are what you do. You can recreate yourself every second of your life.

Here, in a nutshell, is the essence of Xena's ability to interact in a dynamic manner with a dynamic world, the reason she is a role model for the Electronic Present. Xena is able to reinvent herself within the context of her 'way.'[8] The key to understanding why Xena represents a coherent but multidimensional character, instead of simply an unfocused character, lies in understanding 'the way.' This is examined in the next section.

TRANSCENDING IDENTITY

From its onset, XWP has been an extremely successful show, its success far outstripping that of the show that spawned it, *Hercules: The Legendary Journeys*.[9] This success is largely due to the fact that the character Xena is able to appeal to a wide range of audiences through her multidimensionality. Unlike the archetypal action hero Hercules, she is able to offer many different segments of the viewing audience what they want to see. In this way she transcends the notion of identity itself, able to consistently draw on an array of character traits that appeal to a wide audience. It was apparent even to the initial viewers of the show that the character appealed to a broad spectrum of subcultures, some of which might normally be considered to be mutually exclusive. As one writer on XWP put it,

> It is impossible to receive a monolithic message from Xena because different people bring different cultural backgrounds to their viewing of the show and carry away many different messages, ranging from the conservative to the radical (Innes 1999).[10]

For example, one would not expect a typically flat action hero to be able to have a fan base among both heterosexual males and lesbians, but as we will see below, Xena does just that. It is clear that "Xena's appeal cuts across all age, gender and sexual preference lines" (Dickinson 1996).

TRANSCENDING HEROISM

First and foremost, Xena can hold her own as an action hero. As alluded to above, each episode is full of 'Hong Kong' style action[11] and the action sequences in and of themselves are sufficient to keep the most ardent action film fan engaged. Furthermore, the viewer looking just a little deeper will see an abundance of allusions to the action genre, both ancient and modern. Xena finds herself involved in many of the most seminal historical events of her time[12] and the astute viewer will recognize both subtle and not-so-subtle references to the canon of ancient heroic epics (from the *Iliad* to *Beowulf*) and the modern action genre (*Indiana Jones, Buffy the Vampire Slayer*, and others). Xena parades around in bronze and leather; she gallops on a stalwart steed and vanquishes evil wherever she finds it, equally adept with her trusty sword as with all manner of improvised weapons such as frying pans and fish. In short, a viewer simply looking for an action series will not be disappointed by XWP.

With that in mind, it is interesting to note that, in contrast to other action heroes (both male and female), a large part of Xena's adventures consist of facing the more mundane obstacles that the audience is much more familiar with, such as being sick, domestic squabbles, bodily functions, and the proverbial 'bad hair day.' As one example, in the episode 'In Sickness and in Hell,' Xena is plagued by an epic case of head lice, Gabrielle is afflicted by a painful skin irritation, and both have to deal with intestinal distress brought on by the cooking of their erstwhile companion Joxer, all the while countering the plans of the episode's nominal villain, an evil warlord.

> JOXER: Meet Xena, the Warrior Princess, and her sidekick, Gabrielle!

[enter XENA and GABRIELLE; Xena is disheveled and scratching lice from her unkempt hair; Gabrielle's skin is covered in outbreaks of unsightly fungus which she scratches on every available protuberance; both are in a sorry state and clearly smell bad.]

> VILLAGER: They're going to defend our village?
>
> XENA: Yeah. But we're gonna need a little help. Uh, go to your houses and collect together all your—your tools and—your weapons . . .
>
> JOXER: [giggles idiotically]
>
> XENA: Give Joxer a list of every able-bodied villager . . . and secure the outhouse.

VILLAGER: The outhouse? Is that important?

XENA: [in some distress] It is to me!

[exit XENA, tossing aside VILLAGER in her haste]

Xena frequently faces the everyday obstacles that plague us all with the same aplomb as she does the fantastic foes more befitting an action series, making her even more of a role model for the Electronic Present. As in *Ulysses,* in which Joyce brought the heroic epic into everyday life, XWP makes surmounting everyday obstacles a heroic act. To further illustrate, Xena spends much of season five pregnant (making her what may be the world's first and only pregnant action hero), bringing this eminently natural but awkward state into the realm of the heroic.

TRANSCENDING SEXUALITY

However, it cannot be forgotten that Xena is a woman, and an attractive one at that. This simple fact allows for a wide range of interpretations of XWP, as will be explored below. Firstly, she is more than attractive enough to draw the young and middle-aged male audience. She is a stunning, imposing figure of woman, towering above most other characters (the actress, Lucy Lawless, stands nearly six feet tall), with dark hair, piercing blue eyes, and showing a great deal of skin. What passes for her armor is little more than brass wire accentuating her voluptuous features, worn over a leather miniskirt and tube top, prominently displaying legs, arms, and cleavage. In a word, for the heterosexual male viewer, what's not to like? Yet, those looking for a fantasy 'dream girl' are quickly disappointed. Any advances by male characters are met with Xena's aloof scorn (at best) or a merciless and unbeatable barrage of Xena's lethal combat skills (at worst). She is so uninterested in men that her sexuality is a matter of fierce speculation, as will be further addressed below; but, in short, there is nothing to titillate the heterosexual male viewer apart from Xena's physical attributes and penetrating stares. And yet, that seems to be entirely sufficient.[13] Secondly, the viewer will notice that, in contrast to virtually all previous examples of the female action hero,[14] Xena never relies on a male character to bail her out of even the toughest situations. Almost without exception, the male characters on the show are either the villains or buffoons (the most frequently recurring male 'good guy,' Joxer, is a sort of secondary sidekick of Xena's and provides comic relief). Trinidadian literary critic Kenneth Ramchand typified the male unease this causes by commenting,

> As a man, I can't like Xena. All she does is thump the men. And the men she doesn't thump, she doesn't even respect enough to thump.[15]

Xena is an obvious feminist role model because she is one of the very few leading female action heroes. She never relies on a man to get her out of a situation she can't handle, and this alone sets her apart from all other female action heroes before her. She is physically unmatched and dispatches all adversaries, both male and female, in close physical combat. But at the same time she is far from the stereotypical feminist icon for several reasons. Firstly, the fact that she is attractive to the heterosexual male calls the notion of the feminist heroine into question (Innes 1999; Morreale 1998). She is, to put it bluntly, ogled by men, both on-screen and off. The feminist viewer questioning whether a truly feminist heroine should be so scantily clad and so obviously attractive to men is comforted only by the fact that Xena spends most of her time ruthlessly and effortlessly laying waste to male opponents, as described above. And yet, just when one would expect the show's message to turn to one of simple male-bashing, Xena hands the viewer a message that confounds the pure feminist reading. One example takes place in the episode 'The Dirty Half Dozen,' in which Xena, imprisoned in a cell with the man-hating woman warrior Glaphyra, who is berating Gabrielle for trusting a man:

GLAPHYRA: Check the arrangement. Do you see any men in this cell?

GABRIELLE: I'm not a little girl—and I have met some good men. I married one.

GLAPHYRA: Yeah? And how long was he good? I notice he's not with you now. Maybe he lost interest? Or maybe he decided to find another conquest!

GABRIELLE: [coldly] Maybe he was murdered.

XENA: By Callisto—a woman.

[exit Gabrielle]

GLAPHYRA: She hasn't seen much of the world, has she?

XENA: Gabrielle's been through more than you'd think—yes, more than you. And, despite everything, she doesn't carry hatred toward others. Good people don't.

GLAPHYRA: And the bad people?

XENA: The bad people are us, Glaphyra—who I was; who you are. You know, you're so quick to blame everything on men, you have never once looked inside yourself for the answers. It's something that I had to learn. Gabrielle is a good teacher. Who knows? If—if I had met her back when I met you, maybe it'd be me who changed.

Again, those seeking a 'monolithic message' of feminism are frustrated.

As noted above, XWP is also able to transcend expectations of the heroine's sexuality by deliberately toying with the issue. At a very early stage in the series, Xena and Gabrielle's sexuality was gradually called into question, and since then there has never been any shortage of innuendo to support the lesbian reading of the show. Lesbian innuendo is known to the fans of the show as 'subtext,' and, as alluded to above, is the single most studied aspect of XWP.[16] The friendship between Gabrielle and Xena is the centerpiece of each episode, and sometimes there are indications that that friendship extends to sexual intimacy: apart from the occasional longing glance, double entendre, thinly veiled symbolism, and the like, there are coyly ambiguous kisses and alluring physical contact, to name a few examples. The show's producers have stated that they do intend to 'blur the lines' of the characters' sexuality and that 'the underlying homosexual subtext of the show is not unintentional.'[17] Indeed, when seeing episodes such as "A Day in the Life" (for the picture of the ins and outs of a long-term relationship) or "Destiny" (for what is known among fans as 'The kiss' between Xena and Gabrielle), to name just a few, it is hard to reach any other conclusion than that Xena and Gabrielle are a lesbian couple. Yet those seeking security in a heterosexual heroine also find ample evidence: Xena has an ex-boyfriend (Mortal Beloved) and a son (Hooves and Harlots); Gabrielle has an old flame, Perdicas, whom she marries (The Return of Callisto). Still, for those seeking the lesbian reading, these indicators of heterosexuality can, to some degree, be explained away by the fact that, at least in the early part of the series, they all take place in the context of the supernatural.[18] In the same way as in the film *Ma vie en rose,* in which Ludovic's homosexuality is confined to the magical realism of his imagination, Xena's heterosexuality is largely confined to the realm of the supernatural. Ultimately, the show never offers any definitive answer to the question of 'are they or aren't they?' and here, too, the viewer is free to take away the desired interpretation.

TRANSCENDING GEOGRAPHY

As mentioned above, the characters on XWP challenge our perceptions of how characters on a pseudo-historical drama should behave by speaking in modern, idiomatic American English. While XWP makes no pretences whatsoever at historical accuracy, it is nonetheless worth noting that Xena further challenges our notions of the classical world by transcending the boundaries of the world known to the ancient Greeks. It has been speculated[19] that Alexander the Great served as a historical model for Xena, because, among other reasons, at least in the early part of the series, her travels parallel the journeys of Alexander the Great: she is seen traveling to the same places as Alexander in the same order. Later in the series, Xena ranges far outside of Alexander's empire and she is seen visiting far-flung locations, which Alexander never dreamed of: Britain, Scandinavia, Siberia, China, and, ultimately, Japan. Yet, wherever she travels, among strange cultures, customs and peoples, Xena never seems out of place; on the contrary, she always knows how to handle herself and to give a few well-placed instructions to Gabrielle. Here, too, she serves as a role model for those trying to cope with a shrinking world. In the Electronic Present, one must adapt to new situations at a moment's notice and, for the successful, there is little or no 'break-in' period.

In a discussion of colonialist space and the process by which it was appropriated, Raman (2001) notes that, in the quest to demystify the unknown and thereby make it less terrifying, the discovery and demystification of these territories is attributed to Alexander the Great: where one has gone before, others can surely follow.

> Indeed Alexander the Great was the one exceptional individual who had apparently embarked on that terrifying journey to the eastern limits of the world. Often interpreted in terms of the Herculean legends, the figure of Alexander regularly takes on . . . a quasi-mythic function in the course of its long history, especially productive at times of intense imperialistic activity (Raman 2001, 91).

Xena can be seen in exactly this same context: increasing globalization brings with it a necessary demystification of alien cultures. Xena's ability to handle herself with aplomb in all kinds of situations and all kinds of cultures is a consequence of her heroic status within the tradition of the Herculean legends. But, as with Alexander, she provides a role model for the nonheroic population of the Electronic Present: where one has gone before, others can surely follow.

In most cases, Xena's ability to blend seamlessly with alien cultures is explained by the fact that 'she's been there before' (through the aid of on-screen flashbacks). In one particularly telling sequence ('The Debt,' when Xena is seen first traveling to China), Xena's face is juxtaposed over a map of the Old World as her path across Asia is traced in a blood-red line. She explains:

> XENA (voiceover): With shattered legs and crippled soul, I went east . . . to lose myself in vengeance . . . not against Caesar, but the entire human race . . .

Raman has theorized that, in expanding his latter-day Mongol empire, Tamburlaine's (Timur) true conquest was not in warfare but in mapping his world, and thus making it his own, assimilating it, absorbing it. In the poem Tamburlaine the Great, Christopher Marlowe has the dying conqueror feasting his eyes on a map. Raman writes:

> The map allows Tamburlaine to experience the distance between the space he commands and the space he wishes to command as real (Raman 2001, 93).

Just as Tamburlaine (and others) 'mapped' their world through conquest, Xena can be seen to be mapping a strange and terrifying world by conquest and travel. The image described above from 'The Debt' shows a clear spatial parallel to the image of Tamburlaine feasting his eyes on a known world.[20] If Xena once 'maps' a place she can then move freely there and apply her warrior way, adjusting to local conditions but remaining consistent in her approach.

In the episodes immediately preceding 'The Way,' Xena is tormented by the question of whether she has followed, and is following, the right path in her life. In 'The Way,' she learns from Hanuman that for each person there is only one 'way,' but, once found, that way can be applied to be successful in any situation. By the episode 'Endgame,' Xena realizes that her way is the way of the warrior, which she has applied in her life and must continue to do to be successful (by contrast, Gabrielle must follow the way of peace, and we see the characters apply their two seemingly opposed 'ways' to the same situations). As has been outlined above, Xena's 'way' transcends the viewer's notions of heroism, gender, sexuality, and locality. What makes Xena successful is her ability to transcend any essentialist notion of identity (as a hero, a feminist, a lesbian, etc.), supplanting it with the nonessentialist capacity for following a 'way.' This makes Xena a role model ideally suited for the Electronic Present, in which 'one thing' (the essentialist notion of identity) is no longer sufficient for success.

CONCLUSION

Appadurai (1996, 9) has demonstrated that the crisis of identity in the Electronic Present is distinguished from previous sociological theories of modernity because it is linked to an unprecedented level of globalization and electronic-mediated communication. This crisis of identity, in turn, provokes a new sense of agency, which Appadurai calls the 'agency of the imagination': the new and critical interface between the individual (the focal point of agency) and a globalized construction of identity. In this chapter, we have argued that the emerging agency of the imagination requires a new heroic figure, and that Xena is perhaps the first manifestation of that ideal.

Inness (1999) describes Xena as "a tough girl for a new century," and this description is perhaps the most apt. At the time of XWP's debut, it had become apparent that the contemporary heroic figure of the mass media was proving inadequate for the Electronic Present.[21] Increasing globalization calls for increasing capacities for dealing with transnational situations; increasing reliance on new media requires an aptitude for adapting to new technologies. Neither of these are virtues exemplified by the conventional action hero. Xena, in contrast, is able to exemplify both. XWP is thus the first heroic figure for the Electronic Present. It is, then, not coincidental that identity and the construction of identity are so explicitly thematized on the show.[22] Previously, conventional heroic figures were always assured of their essentialist identities; Xena is a hero searching for a nonessentialist construction of identity, which she finds in her 'way.'

Xena's ability to transcend an essentialist construction of identity is reflected in the show in several ways, not least of which is the heterogeneous fabric of the show's structure, but, more pertinently, in the character's own nonessentialist construction of identity. Xena transcends the heroic by making the mundane adventurous; she transcends gender by virtue of her role as a masculine action hero; she transcends sexuality through her ambiguous orientation, allowing the viewer to decide.

For these reasons, Xena can be seen as a new type of action hero, one created in response to changing notions of identity construction dictated by the transition to the Electronic Present. Since the appearance of XWP, more recent action heroes have emerged who seem to be cast in the same nonessentialist mold[23] and it can be speculated that the conventional, essentialist action hero may already be a thing of the past.

NOTES

This paper is based on a talk given as part of a workshop on *Cultural Identities and Media Representations*. We would like to thank the organizers Stefan Kramer and Natascha Gentz, as well the conference participants, for some valuable feedback. Thanks go to Beate Binder and Tatjana Eggeling for a number of discussions and helpful comments both before and after the talk and thanks also go to Ulrich Lutz for technical assistance in producing the video clips we used to accompany the talk. Finally, we would like to thank Irene Wolke for providing some of the necessary creature comforts.

1. The term 'Electronic Present' is defined in chapter 4 of Appadurai, *op cit.*

2. The fact that virtually all action heroes in printed and film media are flat characters should not be subject to dispute, but has nonetheless prompted some discussion. During the development of this paper, the authors have frequently faced the question of why some other particular favorite action hero is not just as 'complex' as Xena. What about James Bond, for example? Or Batman? Or Spiderman? What makes such characters flat is that they consistently draw on a static set of skills and never respond to a situation dynamically; these characters are all but incapable of genuinely surprising their audience. James Bond has an impressive arsenal of skills at his disposal, but they are all applied in the same way to essentially the same situation. The viewer knows that before the end of the film, he will sleep with the two female leads, outwit the bad guy, and, with the help of his outlandish gadgets, save the world. His sexuality will never be even slightly called into question. He is 'pure' good (he has a lifetime of self-sacrificing service to Her Majesty's government and has never done anything else) and his opponents are always pure evil; and his arena is always the same 'real' world of high-tech international espionage (in contrast to Xena who must act in many different arenas, both natural and supernatural).

The same could be said of Batman, although it has been argued that Batman's sexuality is also ambiguous because of his close relationship with his sidekick, Robin. As early as 1955, Fredric Wertham wrote in 'Seduction of the Innocent' (London) that "Only someone ignorant of the fundamentals of psychiatry and the psychopathology of sex can fail to realize a subtle atmosphere of homoeroticism which pervades the adventure of the mature 'Batman' and his young friend 'Robin.'" There is, however, no evidence to suggest that this reading is intentional on the part of any of the writers who have been involved in the large number of comic book and on-screen incarnations of Batman (with the possible exception of the film 'Batman Forever,' which was released in the same year that XWP debuted), while that is the case with XWP (see Section II of this chapter). Like James Bond, Batman, too, having no intrinsic superpowers, can always be expected to rely on his array of gadgetry to get him out of a tough spot and save the day. Finally, in reference to comparisons with comic book heroes in general, who often lead 'double lives,' it should be noted that simply having a secret identity does not entail multi-identity.

3. See Susanne Romaine's book on bilingualism for a comprehensive summary (Romaine, *Bilingualism*).

4. As alluded to above, the subtext is probably the single most talked-about and written-about aspect of XWP; a large number of papers on the subject can be found on www.whoosh.org, the 'International Association for Xena Studies.' The Subtext FAQ found on that site explains succinctly, "The relationship between Xena and Gabrielle is extraordinarily close and is a vital aspect of everyone's enjoyment of the show. The producers/writers are trying to leave it an open question so that viewers can see the relationship however they want."

5. See Diane Esparza, 2000. "Is there a correlation between the explosive growth on the Internet and the XenaVerse?" *Whoosh* #50 (http://www.whoosh.org/esparza3. html), among others.

6. In this context, it is also interesting to note that of the around 6,500 languages currently spoken in the world, a third are likely to be extinct by 2050 (figures supplied by the German Society for Endangered Languages, the *Gesellschaft bedrohter Sprachen*).

7. XWP is a spin-off of a series called *Hercules: The Legendary Journeys*. In an episode of the latter series, as a prelude to the former, the evil warlord Xena is confronted with Hercules. In that confrontation, Xena begins to realize the error of her ways and in response sets out to travel a path of good.

8. One could argue that Xena undergoes the transformation identified as 'The Hero's Journey' by Joseph Campbell in *The Hero with A Thousand Faces* (Princeton, 1949) each and every time she overcomes the dynamic obstacles she faces, instead of just once as exemplified by the action heroes that precede her.

9. XWP debuted at 94% national coverage and with a two-year commitment, and was quickly given a two-year renewal; this level of success far overshadows *Hercules: The Legendary Journeys* and even surpasses the monumental *Star Trek* franchise. The ratings of XWP were consistently higher than those of *Hercules*. Kim Taborn, "Mysteries Surrounding the Creation of the Syndicated Television Show *Xena: Warrior Princess*." *Whoosh* #3 (http://www.whoosh.org/issue3/kym1.html).

10. This quote is reminiscent of Ien Ang's *Watching Dallas: Soap Opera and the Melodramatic Imagination* (1986), but note that Xena had an even wider appeal than the show *Dallas* since it manages to cross sexual and age boundaries as well as racial and class boundaries. For example, XWP appealed to 6-year olds as much as it did to people in their 70s, something which cannot be said for *Dallas*, a TV show in the soap opera genre.

11. An extensive survey of the Hong Kong influence on *XWP* can be found at http://www.slip.net/redbedan/xena/xena_hk. html

12. This seems to span hundreds of years; obviously the show makes no pretensions of historical accuracy. For example, Xena was present when God calls on Abraham to sacrifice his son Isaac (ca. 2000 BC), was an instrumental figure in the siege of Troy (1183 BC?), was involved in the assassination of Julius Caesar (44 BC), and met the Greek physician Galen (129–199 AD); clearly the makers of *XWP* do not shirk from rewriting history.

13. In her analysis of XWP as feminist camp, Morreale points out that, while the story content of the show is unmistakeably feminist, the visual presentation moves squarely within the established male-dominated conventions of Hollywood (Morreale, "Xena: Warrior Princess as Feminist Camp"), thus rendering the show accessible to the hetereosexual male gaze.

14 Innes notes that previous examples such as *Wonder Woman,* the *Bionic Woman, Cagney & Lacey,* etc. all had a male character as a 'safety net' to rely on when the female hero was in a situation too difficult to handle, thereby reinforcing the notion that a woman must 'naturally' be rescued by a man in the end. Innes, *op cit.*

15. Ramchand, pc. personal communication, December 1997.

16. A good place to start for references is the "Sapphic Subtext FAQ" at http://members.aol.com/daxwtesq/FAQ/FAQ.htm

17. Executive Producer Rob Tapert in Melissa Meister. "The Importance of Sapphic Subtext in *Xena: Warrior Princess*" (http://www.whoosh.org/issue17/meister1.html). This paper also cites producer Liz Friedman as saying, "I have no interest in making [Xena and Gabrielle] heterosexual."

18. Xena's ex, Marcus, is in Hades when we first hear of him, and Xena must travel to the Underworld to meet him; her long-lost son Solan has been raised by centaurs, supernatural creatures, in her absence. Gabrielle's betrothed Perdicas is promptly (and conveniently) killed as soon as they marry.

19. Swenson, Gregory. "Alexander the Great: Blueprint for Xena?" Whoosh #4, 1996 (http://www.whoosh.org/issue4/richan.html).

20. *XWP* plays with the charting of unknown territory in other ways as well. The episode 'Here she comes . . . Miss Amphipolis,' for example, features a beauty contest for the title of 'Miss Known World.'

21. As further evidence of this claim, consider Arnold Schwarzenegger's 1993 film *The Last Action Hero.* In this film, Schwarzenegger, whose name is synonymous with the conventional action hero, plays a caricature conglomeration of all his previous roles who is magically brought into the real world, and is then seen to be completely unable to cope with the everyday realities that we all face. As the film title literally suggests, this movie was meant to destroy the notion of the contemporary action hero, in much the same way as Cervantes intended to destroy the notion of the knight of chivalry with his 1605 master work *Don Quixote.* Note that XWP debuted in 1995, shortly after Schwarzenegger's film.

22. Karen Pusateri. "*Xena: Warrior Princess:* An Analytical Review." Whoosh #1, 1996 (http://www.whoosh.org/issue1/ pusateri.html); Richard LaFleur. "Quest Update." Whoosh #13, 1997 (http://www.whoosh.org/issue13/lafleur3.html), and others.

23. The first and most obvious example of a television action hero following in the wake of Xena is *Buffy the Vampire Slayer,* although a direct comparison of Xena and Buffy is, regrettably, beyond the scope of this paper.

REFERENCES

Ang, Ien. *Watching Dallas: Soap Opera and the Melodramatic Imagination,* New York, Methuen 1986.

Appadurai, Arjun. *Modernity at Large: Cultural Dimensions of Globalization.* Minneapolis: Univ. of Minnesota Pr. 1996.

Campbell, Joseph. *The Hero with A Thousand Faces.* Princeton, Princeton Univ. Pr. 1949.

Cherny, Lynn. *Conversation and Community: Chat in a Virtual World.* Stanford, CSLI Publications 1999.

Dickinson, Chris. "For the Love of Lucy." *St. Louis Post-Dispatch,* 5 September 1996.

Esparza, Diane. "Is There a Correlation Between the Explosive Growth on the Internet and the Xena Verse?" Whoosh #50, 2000 (http://www.whoosh.org/esparza3.html).

Goddard, H. H. "Mental tests and the immigrant." *Journal of Delinquency* 2 (1917), 243–277.

Inness, Sherrie. *Tough Girls: Women Warriors and Wonder Women in Popular Culture.* Philadelphia, Univ. of Pennsylvania Pr. 1999.

Jespersen, Otto. *Language.* London, G. Allen & Unwin 1922.

LaFleur, Richard. "Quest Update." Whoosh #13, 1997 (http://www.whoosh.org/issue13/lafleur3.html).

Meister, Melissa. "The Importance of Sapphic Subtext in Xena: Warrior Princess." Whoosh # 17, 1998 (http://www.whoosh.org/issue17/meister1.html).

Morreale, Joanne. "Xena: Warrior Princess as Feminist Camp." *Journal of Popular Culture,* no. 32 (1998), 79–86.

Pusateri, Karen. "Xena: Warrior Princess: An Analytical Review." Whoosh #1, 1996 (http://www.whoosh.org/ issue1/ pusateri.html).

Raman, Shankar. *Framing 'India': The Colonial Imaginary in Early Modern Culture.* Stanford, California, Stanford Univ. Pr. 2001.

Romaine, Susanne. *Bilingualism.* Oxford, Blackwell 1995.

Smith, M. E. "Measurement of Vocabularies of Young Bilingual Children of the Same Family." *Child Development* 6 (1949), 19–25.

Swenson, Gregory. "Alexander the Great: Blueprint for Xena?" Whoosh #4, 1996 (http://www.whoosh.org/issue4/richan.html).

Taborn, Kim. "Mysteries Surrounding the Creation of the Syndicated Television Show *Xena: Warrior Princess.*" Whoosh #3, 1996 (http://www.whoosh.org/issue3/kym1.html).

Wellman, Barry. "Computer Networks As Social Networks." *Science* 293 (14 September 2001), 2031–34.

Wertham, Fredric. *Seduction of the Innocent.* London, Museum Press 1955.

Woodward, Kathryn, ed. *Identity and Difference.* London, Sage 1997.

Literature/Identity:
Transnationalism, Narrative and
Representation

ARIF DIRLIK

When I suggested the title above for this chapter, my intention was to further pursue a question I had raised in earlier writings: that of the relationship between narrative form and the construction/reception of cultural identity as it appears in Asian-American writing. I will still address this question, but from a perspective that foregrounds the relationship between literature and history. The discussion is restricted to issues thrown up by the appropriations, denials, and subversions of history in literary work, most importantly in the blurring of distinctions between fiction and history. The question of the relationship between history and literature, I argue below, is not an academic question of disciplinary boundaries, a question of scholarly versus creative work, or an abstract question of culture; it is most importantly a political question, as it compels attention to the fundamental issue of the implication of writing in configuring the boundaries between the public and the private.

Ethnic or transnational literatures present a challenge, not only to historical ways of thinking, but also to the ways in which we have organized the study of the world in terms of nations, areas, and regions. While the challenge is to be welcomed for forcing a rethinking of history and its complicity in power, those who would dismiss history, celebrate the blurring of the boundaries between fiction and history, or simply privilege literary over historical constructions of identity, often overlook the indispensable critical insights compelled by a consciousness of historicity. The blurring of boundaries between fiction and history, moreover, calls into question, not only the identity of history, but also the identity of literature. As literature has been placed at the service of exploring ethnic and transnational (or diasporic) identities, the construction of identities in literary work has been confounded with the ethnography of culture, subjecting the writer to pressures that subvert the autonomy of creative work. Compounding this confusion is the question of the cultural belonging of literature as it is divorced from earlier associations with nations and national languages.

This is especially important when it comes to questions of cultural identity and representation, which are a primary concern here. There has been a renewed tendency over the last decade or so toward the reification of cultures in the equation of cultural with national, regional, or civilizational boundaries. While the goal of most ethnic or transnational writing has been to break down such boundaries, is it possible that dehistoricization of the explorations of identity in such writing, and the language in which such exploration is articulated, contribute to the reification of cultural identity, however contrary that may be to the intentions of its authors? The question is evident in the controversies among writers and critics over the status of history in fiction. It is necessary, I think, to place these discussions in a broader social and ideological context, and to relate the issues they raise to a broader field of discourse, of which they are both constituents and beneficiaries.

The Chinese American writer and poet Russell Leong remarks in an interview that

> there's the view of history as grandiose, the 'sweep of history,' but most history is made up of the lives and actions of ordinary people and really not the 'heroic' in the sense that it's even recorded ... The grand sweep of history is for traditional historians, and that presupposes that history is linear, and that it's going someplace, and that there's a beginning and an end, a goal located within a master narrative. But many times, when you're just living life, you're not sure of its end point, or its beginning, or the middle (Ito 2000, 237).

Leong is a historically minded writer, and what he has to say about history is not so much a rejection of it as an insistence on incorporating history in literary work to bring to the understanding of the past and the present elements that are left out of history, or may be impossible to contain within historical categories. Likewise, for Karen Tei-Yamashita, a Japanese-American writer, the preference for literature grows out of a sense of the insufficiencies of history:

> With straight history, you . . . couldn't express the emotion. You couldn't express those extra things that illustrate history . . . I also wanted to bring in a feeling for the sense of place, that scene, the smell (Murashige 2000, 343).

In the case of these two authors, history and literature complement one another, each making up for the lack in the other. If, in the process, the boundary between history and literature becomes blurred, it is to the enrichment of both. Such is not always the intention underlying the questioning of history. The Burmese-American writer Wendy Law-Yone asserts that "history, after all, is the version of the victors . . . Literature, on the other hand, documents the version of the conquered. I'm on the side of literature" (Law-Yone 2000, 301–302).

While none of these statements may be taken as representative or typical of Asian-American writers, together they represent a range of attitudes toward history that extends from a desire to bring history and literature together to the benefit of both, to the repudiation of history for its complicity in hegemony, oppression, and erasure of ethnic pasts and sensibilities, in which case literature has to take over in the construction of the past. This privileging of literature in the case of ethnic and diasporic populations in general is evident in the following lines from Azade Seyhan in her *Writing Outside the Nation:*

> As cultures collide, unite, and are reconfigured in real and virtual spaces in unprecedented ways, postcolonial, migrant, and border-crossing theorists and artists fine-tune received critical traditions in order to safeguard historical and cultural specificities. Ultimately, every theory of postcolonial, transnational, or diasporic literature and art is most convincingly articulated and performed by works of literature and art themselves. Literature as an institution and literary fiction as an expression of human experience predate their theoretical articulation, a truism perhaps best exemplified by Aristotle's *Poetics*. Literature as social document resists the erasure of geographical, historical, and cultural differences (Seyhan 2001, 7).

What happens to literature when it is converted into a "social document" is a problem, which the author conveniently overlooks. It is a point to which I will return below, as it is crucial to the plight of the ethnic writer. Here I would like to note that there is something puzzling about this privileging of literature (if we overlook the vulgar objection of institutional self-interest, which is not to be dismissed for its vulgarity, but distracts from more important questions), and charges, as in the case of Law-Yone, that history speaks for power while literature provides a voice for the oppressed and marginalized. I do not share some professional historians' reluctance to recognize the important ways in which literature contributes to voicing experiences erased or simply ignored in historical ways of knowing and representing, or find objectionable the blurring of the boundaries between literature and history. It seems necessary to note, nevertheless, that there is a profound confusion in such statements of the conditions that attended the emergence of modern historiography as we know it (so-called historicism) and the actual practice of history—which is a confusion that is common to certain tendencies in postcolonial criticism, to the point of having become a cliché. Such charges seem to speak to a past historiography that set the standards for contemporary historiography where issues of fact and fiction are concerned, but they otherwise overlook the very significant ways in which contemporary historical practice has broken with its origins, in many ways paving the way for postcolonial criticism. Gender, ethnic, and social histories, as they have unfolded since the 1960s, could hardly be charged of complicity with power, as they led the way in challenging inherited assumptions concerning history and have been charged by conservative historians with undermining "Western civilization." It is arguable that any work of history that makes claims of significance needs to attend to questions of politics, power, and public consciousness. But that is not the same thing as a categorical assertion of history's complicity in power and oppression. If historians do anything these days, it is to call into question the relationship of their disciplinary legacy to power, and to bring into history those who were excluded from it by virtue of race, culture, and gender. The more important problem, it seems to me, lies elsewhere.

To elucidate this problem, I would like to turn here to the discussion of the problem of narrative by Hayden White, whose work lies at the origins of much of the contemporary discussion of the relationship between history and literature. In a discussion of narrative in nineteenth-century European historiography, White observes that

> Hegel . . . insisted that a specifically historical mode of being was linked to a specifically narrative mode of representation by a shared "internal vital principle."

This principle was, for him, nothing other than politics. He then goes on to quote Hegel to the effect that,

> We must suppose historical narrations to have appeared contemporaneously with historical deeds and events. Family memorials, patriarchal traditions, have an interest confined to the family and the clan. The uniform course of events that such a condition implies is no subject of serious remembrance . . . It is the state that first presents a subject matter that not only is adapted to the prose of history, but involves the production of such history in the progress of its own being.

What is of interest here is White's brilliant invocation of Hegel to deconstruct the problem of narrative in nineteenth century historical thought. As he puts it,

> Hegel's views on the nature of historical discourse had the merit of making explicit what was acknowledged in the dominant practice of historical scholarship in the nineteenth century, namely, an interest in the study of political history, which was, however, often hidden behind vague professions of an interest in narration as an end in itself. The doxa of the profession, in other words, took the form of the historical discourse—what it called the true story—for the content of the discourse, while the real content, politics, was represented as being primarily only a vehicle for an occasion of storytelling . . . It is in this respect, rather than in any overt espousal of a specific political program or cause, that nineteenth-century professional historiography can be regarded as ideological. For if ideology is the treatment of the form of a thing as a content or essence, nineteenth-century historiography is ideological insofar as it takes the characteristic form of its discourse, the narrative, as a content, namely, narrativity, and treats "narrativity" as an essence shared by both discourses and sets of events alike (White 1987, 29–30).

What White has to say accords closely with current criticisms of the European historical tradition to which contemporary historiography is heir; this is not very surprising, as he was one of the first to point out the relationship between ideology and historical narrative. We may add also that the reference to politics in Hegel's statement is not just to any kind of politics, but to the politics of the state, which informs critiques of history for its complicity with power. We need also to remember that this was the basis for Karl Marx's critique of Hegel and his insistence that it was civil society and not the state that was the ultimate location of politics.

What is more to the point, however, is the relationship White points to between narrative-form and ideology which, read reflexively, has much to tell us about contemporary forms of narrative, that, concerned with narrative as an end itself, also disguise the relationship between narrative form and politics. There is more than meets the eye in the contemporary rejection and suspicion of history and the valorization of fictional forms of representation, which may have less to do with history and literature as alternative forms of narrative than with alternative forms of politics. The appropriation of history for literature implies also the privatization of history—and of the political function history has served; thus, politics conceived as public activity is replaced by politics conceived as identity politics, privatized and yet fraught with implications for our understanding of what is public and what is private. Where Hegel, and nineteenth-century historians, pointed to the state and the public realm (identified with the state) as the location for history, the privatized literary version of history locates it in what Hegel regarded as the private realm ("the family and the clan"). The argument that it is literature rather than history that fulfills the needs of the oppressed and marginalized perpetuates the Hegelian prejudice that history belongs to the state, while it also privatizes the political needs of those who are left out of state-centered histories. In the process, it yields the public realm to the state. This is often accompanied, in the case of ethnic groups, by a displacement of political questions to the realm of culture. Cultural politics, moreover, easily lends itself to the reification of cultural identity as culture is evacuated of history.

The confounding of politics and cultural narrative is apparent in Azade Seyhan's identification of the distinctive feature of what she describes as "diasporic narratives":

> In the broadest sense, then, "diasporic narratives" discussed in this study represent a conscious effort to transmit a linguistic and cultural heritage that is articulated through acts of personal and collective memory. In this way, writers become chroniclers of the displaced whose stories will otherwise go unrecorded. Literature tends to record what history and public memory often forget. Furthermore, it can narrate both obliquely and allegorically, thereby preserving what can be censored and encouraging interpretation in the public sphere. Through the lens of personal recollection and interpretation, the specificity of class, ethnic, and gender experiences gains a stature that is often erased (Seyhan 2001, 12).

It is not at all apparent to this reader why history cannot undertake the task of recovering what has been forgotten or "censored" in public memory, or force a reinterpretation of "the public sphere." It seems to me that this is what gender and ethnic historiography has been all about. The question, moreover, is not merely a question of forgetting, suppression, or censorship in memory, but of the very real historical denial of citizenship and, therefore, political participation to certain groups on the basis of gender, ethnicity, race, and culture; the result was that they could be excluded without much ado from any history, written as a celebration of the state's progress in time, which conveniently overlooked the suppression of difference that was an inextricable part of this progress. In the case of so-called diasporic populations, they could find a place in history only to the extent that they were assimilated and could be seen to have contributed to such progress, which, again, was impossible so long as they were denied political participation. The recovery of the historical presence of these groups is a challenge not only to state-centered conceptions of politics, but also to history written around the state. It adds the challenge of transnationality to a challenge first mounted in the name of citizenship. The challenge does not indicate the impossibility of history, but calls for a different kind of history.

All this, however, may be irrelevant to the agenda implied by Seyhan, which does not only privilege literature over history, but also the private over the public, while easily glossing over the question of "personal and collective memory" by throwing them together, in the process erasing the contradictory relationship between the two. Seyhan is quite right to stress the importance of personal memory in "diasporic" writing. But her celebration of personal memory, and reification of the "ethnic" or "diasporic," obviates the need to explore further the contradiction between the personal and the collective, as well as between history and memory. The appropriation by literature of the social and the historical may be celebrated as a blurring of the boundaries of conventional categories, but it also burdens literature with tasks that may undermine the autonomy of the individual writer, just as the conflation of the personal and the collective raises the question of the public (and, therefore, political) responsibility of the literary work in the representation of collective consciousness.

It may be argued that literature has been endowed all along with such responsibility in its association with the nation. Timothy Brennan writes that,

> It was the novel that historically accompanied the rise of nations by objectifying the 'one, yet many' of national life, and by mimicking the structure of the nation, a clearly bordered jumble of languages and styles. Socially, the novel joined the newspaper as the major vehicle of the national print media, helping to standardize language, encourage literacy, and remove mutual incomprehensibility. But it did much more than that. Its manner of presentation allowed people to imagine the special community that was the nation (Brennan 1990, 49).

Brennan's reference in the last line is to Benedict Anderson, who, in his *Imagined Communities,* pointed to the correspondence between "the 'interior' time of the novel" and the "'exterior' time of the reader's everyday life," which "gives a hypnotic confirmation of the solidity of a single community, embracing characters, author and readers, moving onward through calendrical time" (Anderson 1995, 27).

Where there is some assumption of cultural and linguistic homogeneity, as in the case of national culture, the individual work of literature may still claim a unique voice. The situation is somewhat different in the case of minority and transnational literatures in a heterogeneous cultural and linguistic context, heterogeneous not only in the composition of the transnationalized national society, but in the constitution of the minority group itself. In such a context, the very affirmation of diversity burdens the unique creative voice with the additional task of social and cultural interpretation, of mediating not only between different spaces but different times, where "the characters, the author and readers" do not belong in the same spatiality or temporality, and "the interior time of the novel" does not confirm but challenges "the exterior time" of "the reader's everyday life"—where the very language in which the novel is written, while it is seemingly the very same national language, nevertheless calls for translation because its idiom now includes the legacies of many other languages.

This burden of translation, which transnationalization imposes upon the writer, has been recognized by Asian-American writers and critics alike. One such critic, King-Kok Cheung, writes that,

> Like most artists of color, authors of Asian ancestry in the United States face a host of assumptions and expectations. Because their number is still relatively small, those who draw inspiration from their experiences as members of a minority are often seen as speaking for their ethnic groups. Because their work is frequently treated as ethnography by mainstream reviewers, many in the Asian American communities hold them accountable for an authentic "representation" (Cheung 2000, 1–2).

The most dramatic illustration of Cheung's observation is the celebrated controversy occasioned by Maxine Hong Kingston's *The Woman Warrior,* published in 1976, which remains alive after two decades. Submitted by the author as a work of fiction, the book was marketed by the publisher as autobiography—bringing the author no end of grief and distracting from what is a powerful meditation on growing up as a Chinese-American woman in Stockton, California. The mere naming of the genre converted an imaginative piece of work into a "social document," raising fundamental questions about personal and collective memory, fiction and history, the relationship of Chinese Americans to their society of origin, and even the nature of Chinese society itself. Kingston herself has queried, in total frustration, "Why must I 'represent' anyone besides myself? Why should I be denied an individual artistic vision?" (Kingston 1998, 101) But, as another critic, David Li, points out:

> Once *The Woman Warrior* is labeled as nonfiction, it is understood by convention to be a real narrative of real events. The consequence is actually twofold. On the one hand, it invites the audience to identify it as an account of real life. On the other hand, it dissuades the possibility of interpreting it as a symbolic act. Therefore, the generic definition can have the effect of depriving Asian American expression of its credibility as imaginative art and reducing it into some subliterary status, serving the role of social scientific data, an encompassing reflection of Asian American totality (Li 1998, 189–190).

Li's point is well taken, and many participants in the discussion of this work have pointed to the publisher's labeling of the book as a major factor in its "misreading," which, to more uncompromising critics, also appears as evidence of Kingston's complicity in the mis-representation of her work. This is a serious problem that has not stopped with Kingston's work. Publishers in recent years have repeatedly classified fictional or semifictional works by Asians under "Asian Studies," thrown together in catalogs of Asian and Asian American writers, and placed writings on Asian America among "Asian peoples." How such labeling affects the reading of these works is not self-evident, but we must suppose that it plays some part in the reading, where the works are placed in bookstores and libraries, and how it may influence decisions in course adoption.

And yet it is worth pondering if the reading of *The Woman Warrior* by critics or readers would have been affected substantially had it been labeled fiction. Amy Tan's works are marketed under fiction/literature, and yet that has not stopped readers from treating them as accounts of "Chinese" life and etiquette. She says in a 1999 essay that

> I am alarmed when reviewers and educators assume that my very personal, specific and fictional stories are meant to be representative down to the nth detail not just of Chinese-Americans but, sometimes, of all Asian culture (Tan 1999, 11).

Autobiography is a problematic genre. Li is correct to point out that, by convention, autobiography suggests real events and historicalness. After all, autobiography is personalized history, and is expected, for that reason, not only to tell us something about history but also to comply with historiographical rules of evidence. This is what we expect, at any rate, of autobiographies by public personages, as when a Henry Kissinger writes his memoirs.

But it would be wrong to place a work such as *The Woman Warrior* in the same category as public autobiography, because that is not what it strives to be; it does not take for granted a historical subjectivity that then acts to make history, but rather relates the construction of identity out of social and cultural fragments. That may be the reason why, as autobiography, it has lent itself to readings that find in it a narrative of Asian-American history and an ethnography of Chinese culture, but has been vulnerable also to accusations by Chinese-American critics of hijacking Chinese-American history and grossly distorting "the facts" of Chinese society.

It seems to me that autobiography, writing the self, can also include self-exploration, the point of departure for which is not necessarily the outside public world, but the construction of the self's interiority, which may include stories, fantasies, perversions, and assorted deployments of the imagination which may not stand the empirical test of history or ethnography, but are no less real in the construction of the self. *The Woman Warrior* is evidently this kind of autobiography, one that explores the inner world and self-construction of a young Chinese-American woman as she sorts through fantasies, stories, and a variety of social and cultural encounters.

Viewed in this perspective, we may include among Kingston's questions cited above another, perhaps more fundamental, question: is the ethnic writer permitted to have an autonomous interiority, or is s/he condemned to represent the ethnic collectivity in the senses, in David Li's terms, both of "standing for" and "acting" or "speaking for" (Li 1998, 193). Phrased differently and less abstractly, what mode of expression best offers the greatest hope of escaping the ethnic prison-house? While the phrasing here foregrounds the personal and the subjective, I would like to underline its political implications, because the question presupposes the separation once again of the personal and the collective, the private and the public, in other words, a move away from identity politics toward a politics informed by public consciousness.

It would be pretentious for me to try to answer this question, and somewhat contrary to my premises here, as so-called ethnic writers differ immensely from one another and must face the problem from different situational perspectives. On the other hand, it is somewhat easier to identify the circumstances and narrative strategies that reinforce identity politics and facilitate appropriations of individual for collective consciousness, while obstructing the formulation of a publicly informed politics. Crucial in either case is the way culture comes into play in the articulation of identity.

Some of these circumstances are products of the racialization and culturalization of the ethnic writer in the dominant ideology of the larger society. In her study of the concept of representation, Pitkin tells us that in its earliest usages, representation conveyed the sense of embodiment, "as when a virtue seems embodied in the image of a certain face" or as "church leaders [were] seen as the embodiment and image of Christ and the Apostles" (Pitkin 1967). This sense of representation has not quite disappeared, as the racialized body, or any other marker of race or foreignness, such as names, is taken to authorize the writer (or anyone else for that matter) to stand or speak for the group of which s/he is allegedly a member by virtue of physical appearance or some other trait, regardless of how remote the connection of the author to the society of origin, or how complicated the composition of the group. In the case of a Chinese American such as Kingston or Tan, the writer is taken as the "embodiment" of an abstract "Chineseness" that defies historicity, in which Orientalist notions of a dehistoricized and desocialized Chinese culture are blended imperceptibly with supposedly racial traits, producing a notion of culture that is "almost biologized by its proximity to 'race'" (Gilroy 1996, 263). The identification justifies the qualification of the author to speak for something called Chinese, but also the containment of what s/he has to say in an originary Chineseness, where it is no longer clear whether ethnic identification is a cultural privilege or a cultural prison-house. This is also where an oppressive and hegemonic culturalism becomes barely distinguishable from a liberal and benign multiculturalism, which may valorize "Chineseness" differently, but is otherwise subject to the same conceptual protocols; most importantly in the abstraction of the idea of culture and in the failure to define its boundaries.[1]

The racialization and culturalization of Chinese Americans is not new, but a legacy of Orientalism with a long history. On the other hand, it derives additional force from recent developments, which have created an ideological environment that favors ethnicization. The emergence of multiculturalism in response to ethnic self-assertion is itself one of these new developments. Equally important is the part multiculturalism plays in the commodification of culture and ethnicity. I have referred already to the marketing of books, and how that affects the labeling of literature. In recent decades, ethnicity (and culture) have become major concerns of marketers and corporate management. As one sociologist observes wryly,

> in an age that celebrates diversity and multiculturalism, it has become almost a civic duty to have an ethnicity, as well as to appreciate that of others.[2]

Unlike in an earlier period of hegemonic Orientalism, in other words, ethnicity appears in contemporary United States society as a desirable trait, and ethnics themselves participate freely in the promotion and marketing of the cultures of their societies of origin. Contemporary migrations, moreover, nourish the reethnicization (or reaffirmation of cultural roots) of populations that only a few decades ago were concerned mostly to assert their places in United States society and history, which is especially pertinent in the case of Asian Americans, whose increasing prominence was fueled by Pacific Rim discourse. At the broadest level, the ideology of globalization extends multiculturalism globally, reviving the reification of cultures as civilizations in an earlier modernization discourse, though with some ambiguity now over its consequences: clash of civilizations versus peaceful coexistence in mutual recognition of difference.[3]

My immediate concern here is with ethnic complicity in cultural reification. The reception of ethnic writing in the dominant culture, and the contribution to it of the ideological environment, are crucial questions, but they do not exhaust the problem. One of the most astute critics of Asian-American literature, Sau-ling Wong, has observed that there is a history in Asian-American literature of autobiography as guided tour of China and Chinatown, in which "the individual's life serves the function of conveying anthropological information" (Wong 1998, 156–157). The most prominent beneficiary of the contemporary valorization of ethnicity may be Amy Tan, whose writings have enjoyed phenomenal success, been placed among American classics, and invoked exuberant comparisons with the likes of Leo Tolstoy. Whatever merit Tan's writing may have, there is good evidence also that she has benefited immensely from the ethnic touch. In a brilliant analysis of Tan's novels, the same critic, Sau-ling Wong, writes with reference to Tan's deployment of "Chinese" details:

> Are the reviewers simply misguided when they laud Tan's "Convincing details"? Not at all. The details are there, but their nature and function are probably not what a "Commonsense" view would make them out to be: evidence of referential accuracy, of the author's familiarity with the "Real" China. Rather, they act as gestures to the "mainstream" readers that the author is familiar with the kind of culturally mediated discourse they have enjoyed, as well as qualified to give them what they expect. I call these details "markers of authenticity," whose function is to create an "Oriental effect" by signalling a reassuring affinity between the given work and American preconceptions of what the Orient is/should be (Wong 1995, 187).

Wong observes shrewdly that anti-Orientalist gestures in Tan's writing do not undermine, but further contribute to the impression of her authenticity as cultural mediator. I referred above to Tan's own complaint about being placed in this role, which is less than convincing in light of what we must assume to be her compliance in the marketing of her works. Her name and the very "Chinese" cover of her latest book, *The Bonesetter's Daughter,* now grace the tins of "Mandarin Orange Spice Green Tea" complete with a recipe, marketed by *The Republic of Tea* in bookstores such as Borders, an honor never accorded the likes of Leo Tolstoy.

Chinese-American critics of the manipulation of literary work by publishers, reviewers, readers, and tea-peddlers themselves are not immune to complicity in the reification of Chineseness. The criticism of *The Woman Warrior* for its representation of things Chinese, and its representation to the reading public as autobiography and, therefore, history, quickly spilled over into a discussion of "Chineseness"—what was or was not authentically Chinese, whether or not Chinese myths were immune to historical and social interpretation, and questions of masculinity and femininity in Chinese culture. The very invocation of "China" in a discussion of a work of Chinese-American literature was indicative of the erasure of the spatial and historical distance that separated Chinese Americans from the society of origin, rendering competing Chinese-American visions of China into alternative visions of a China without history, in the process reifying Chineseness at the risk, not only of denying Chinese differences, but also of bracketing their own histories.[4]

The question of ethnic complicity in cultural reification may be a product ultimately of the language of writing and representation within its social and political situation. In a critical evaluation of *The Woman Warrior*, Amy Ling refers to "the dialogic dilemma" of Asian-American writers. As she puts it,

> In applying Bakhtin to *The Woman Warrior*, one may read the entire text as an extended exploration of the internal dialogism of three words: Chinese, American, and female. Each term carries a multitude of meanings in dialogue, if not open warfare, with each other ... The entire book is devoted to an exploration of these words in an attempt at a self-definition that, finally, is never definitive in the sense of complete, conclusive, static (Ling 1998, 172).

Ling's analysis is perceptive and to the point, but in spite of its recognition of the overdeterminedness of the very terms of the dialogue, remains trapped in the limits set by those terms, possibly because of an unwillingness to look beyond a social situation in which a self/other confrontation sets the stage for cultural and political imagination. A question worth raising here is whether it is the culturally fragmented self that finds expression in the dialogue she analyzes, or whether it is the insistence on such a dialogue that fragments the self, making for the "dialogic dilemma" to which she refers. Ling's point of departure in the discussion is similar to the problem indicated in the statement by King-Kok Cheung, which I cited above: the predicament of Asian-American writers

> writing of the cultural specificities of their own cultural backgrounds [who] are forced into the language of anthropological ethnography and thereby partake of the hierarchical binaries of Same and Other, Normal and Exotic, Advanced and Backward, Superior and Inferior (Cheung 2000, 1–2).

In other words, Cheung refers to the predicament of the creative writer as "native informant." While the analysis that follows denies the "conclusive, complete and static," the role she assigns to the Asian-American writer and critic seems to be premised upon the static—as when she writes that the role

> of all minority writers in this society, if we wish to be understood by a majority audience, cannot help but be that of cultural explainers until such time as everyone is informed of the myriad cultures that make up the United States ... We have no choice, except of course, if we choose to speak only to others exactly like ourselves (Ling 1998, 168–169).

The "myriad cultures" apparently do not refer to myriad divisions within each sphere of cultural ethnicity, as her analysis of Kingston's work would suggest, but to different ethnic cultures defined by a space of "others exactly like us." Hence, once again, the writer and critic appears as cultural interpreter or bridge, foregrounding, in the very act of interpretation, the intelligibility and, therefore, the internal coherence, if not homogeneity, of the culture to be interpreted. Ling underlines the importance of unequal power in creating this situation, which may hardly be doubted, but she ignores the equal importance of a social situation in which hybridity has become a valuable social asset as "it has become almost a civic duty to have an ethnicity." It is interesting that it is the language of the cultural rather than the social that stands out in her analysis, as it does in much critical analysis these days. Unlike the social, which stresses the here and now, the cultural facilitates the connecting of the experience of the here and now with some originary point of departure somewhere, drawing attention away from the historically concrete unfolding of identity (its dialectics) to its entrapment in confrontations of abstract cultural belongings (its dialogics). The two versions speak to different historical circumstances with different social and political expectations. But they are not mutually exclusive, at least I do not think they are. But closing the gap between them requires a different kind of language than the one that has dominated cultural discussion in recent decades, a language that is more cognizant of the historicity of the cultural, which in turn is premised on a politics driven, not by questions of cultural identity, but by questions of social and public responsibility.

A transnational perspective on the identity of Chinese American literature may help elucidate the problem I have in mind here. In a fascinating examination of the reception of Kingston's work in China, the Hong Kong literary critic K.C. Lo has analyzed efforts in Taiwan and the People's Republic of China to appropriate Kingston for the Chinese national cultural sphere. Lo writes that

> the claim of cultural particularity is not only confined to the writing of national literature but also closely associated with the translation of other literatures into its cultural code. The recent scholarship and translation of Chinese American and Chinese diaspora literatures in Mainland China and Taiwan always highlight the appeal to the cultural origin or cultural commonality of these "Chinese" literary works written in English. The affirmation of cultural nationalism in the translation constitutes a means of reinventing the Chinese nation and the unified Chinese self in the changing environment of the twentieth century. If the Western reader of Chinese literature in English is more interested in politics than in literary work itself, the Chinese translations of Chinese American novels are also prone to stressing more their cultural and ethnic identification than their artistic achievement or creativity . . . While asserting the continuity of Chinese cultural tradition in a trans-national setting and prolonging the myth of national unity, the Chinese translations of the Chinese American fictions could contain and diffuse the cultural hybridity and hetero-geneity of the "homeless" Chinese immigrants and their descendants. Cultural distinctiveness and difference found in Chinese American literature could be neutralized, or even erased in translation (Lo 2000, 78–79).

In light of charges brought against her by Chinese American critics of distorting Chinese culture and history, it must have been heartening for Kingston to read in the introduction to the Mainland translation of *China Men* that this work of Kingston has dealt with the suffering of Chinese immigrants in America relatively well. If it can be called a fiction, I would prefer to call it a history of Chinese written in blood and tears (Lo 2000, 87).

While these same critics alleged, moreover, that the autobiography form of *The Woman Warrior* placed her in the tradition of Euro-American missionary writing on China, she was more than pleasantly surprised by being placed by Mainland writers in a Chinese canon. As she put it in her interview after her first visit to China in 1984,

A poet told me that I was the only Chinese that was writing in the tradition of the Dream of Red Chamber because here is Wittman [the protagonist of her then new work, *Tripmaster Monkey*] as the effete, young man battling to keep his manhood among the matriarchy, the twelve women of that book. And, in part of the conference, they were telling us that there was a "roots" literature movement in China—because during the Cultural Revolution they cut off the roots. So they had cut off their ties to the West, and cut off the bindings of feudalism, the imperial arts and all that. But then they weren't left with anything . . . And I spent this lifetime working on roots. So what they were saying was that I was their continuity . . . But, God, I felt so terrific. Because they were telling me that I was part of a Chinese canon. And here I was writing in English.[5]

It is a statement of redemption, as with those Chinese Overseas who go to China to awaken all of a sudden to their slumbering Chineseness. It appears, from what Kingston was told by Chinese writers, that the Chinese literary canon, having lost its connection to its past at home, took a detour through California to discover its continuity through a Chinese-American writer. Here is literature deterritorialized in order to establish cultural continuity of sorts, but at the price of the abstraction of culture from place and time. What is also interesting is that Kingston ignores the anti-feminist implications of the reference to the Dream of the Red Chamber, and finds invigorating her identification as quintessentially in "Chinese," which, within a United States context, constitutes a in "mis-reading of her book."

What is equally interesting, where the identity of literature is concerned, is the reinterpretation of the form and content of literature in order to sustain a sense of national cultural belonging. A pioneer translator into Chinese of Chinese-American works (and a long time professor of Chinese in the United States who has relocated to Hong Kong) writes that

Although Chinese American literature is written in English, its content is— no matter it is positive or negative—a resonance of Chinese memory since its writers are Chinese descendants. Therefore I see it as part of my research field . . . What determines the "nationality" of literature is not its language, but its content . . . So I consider Chinese American literature a branch of Chinese literature.[6]

Lau's statement is reminiscent of Salman Rushdie's argument that Indian literature is as Indian as Indian literature in any other Indian languages (Rushdie 1997, 53–61).

But the two cases are different. Whether a legacy of colonialism or not, English in India has a long history. In the case of China, English is the language of Chinese with their own histories outside of China, and requires translation back into Chinese. Here, claiming English language literature for Chineseness requires a different kind of rupture in the national narrative where not a continuing legacy but "descent" provides the recuperation of memories written elsewhere as Chinese, foregrounding once again a cultural unity that can be sustained by racializing Chineseness in the language of nation and culture. Language and history, in other words, no longer serve as markers of the identity of literature, as they did in the case of national literatures.

Migrants writing in the language of the place of arrival need to be translated so that their works may be comprehended both in the place of departure and the place of arrival. In the former case the translation is literal, from one language into another. But translation is necessary even within the same language. An interesting illustration of this is to be found in the case of Emine Sevgi Ozdamar, a German writer of Anatolian origin. Ozdamar writes in German, and the Germanness of her writing has been recognized in the literary prizes that she has been awarded. On the other hand, her German is so loaded with Turkish idiom and references to the Turkish past that it requires translation to make it comprehensible to the German reader.[7] In a case such as this one, language does not serve as a marker of belonging, either in the place of departure or the place of arrival, but becomes an object of investigation itself.

This may be a problem of all ethnic or diasporic literature. Transnationalization has created a new kind of literature that is not easily identifiable by the earlier terms of national literature. On the other hand, transnationality is itself haunted by its origins in nations, and transnational literature faces the predicament of serving as the site for a new politics of literature. National claims on literature have not disappeared, but now take the form of the racialization and culturalization of the writer in both the society of departure and the society of arrival. Ironically, the very diversity and contradictoriness of such claims (what constitutes an authentic national or cultural identity) may be taken as evidence of the vacuity of such claims. As David Li has observed, the literary works of writers such as Frank Chin and Maxine Hong Kingston, taken as articulations of Chineseness, represent instead different ways of constructing Chineseness and, therefore, point to differences among the populations so named (Li 1992). As Lo puts it,

> The dialectic of control and resistance occurs in the translation of Kingston's stories. If dialectic is understood as the grasping of the opposites in a wholeness, then the Chineseness asserted in the translation of Chinese American literature can only actualize itself by alienating itself, and restore its self-unity

by recognizing this differentiation as nothing other than its own manifestation. The only possible way to weave or reweave the Chinese cultural tapestry
in the transnational era, I believe, is to recognize the multiple differences in
its culture's worldwide peregrination (Lo 2000, 92–93).

These terms are the legacies of the struggles of the 1960s, which brought
Chinese Americans, as well as other groups, into cultural and political recognition in the United States. A term such as Asian American first appeared,
not as a term of cultural, but of political identity. As far as we know, the term
was coined by the distinguished Japanese-American historian Yuji Ichioka in
the heat of political struggles in Berkeley/Oakland sometime in 1968. It is
not that cultural identity was not important for those such as Ichioka, but
rather that cultural identity was not conceived to be detachable from politics.
And the goal of politics was transformative, transformative both of the constitution of the public in the United States, and of public consciousness, including the consciousness of those who were encompassed by the term Asian
Americans.[8] History was deemed essential to this goal, as is evident from the
titles in a bibliography by Ichioka of Japanese-American history (A Buried
Past) and a comparable one by Him Mark Lai (A History Reclaimed).

The privatization of history in literature enriches our understanding of
the diversity of the historical experiences of Asian Americans, or any other
group for that matter. The substitution of the private for the public is another
matter, because it runs the risk of substituting for a socially and historically
informed idea of culture one that is deterritorialized and abstract, which may
make it more manipulable in the expression and exploration of identity, but is
also more amenable, for the same reason, to appropriation for culturalist practices of one kind or another beyond the intentions of the author. This is quite
evident in the painful recognition by ethnic writers of the treatment of their
work as ethnography, which erases individual and social complexity.

In a situation of transnationalism, we might note, conceptualization of
ethnic groups in terms of, not their social standing and social differences, but
in terms of some imaginary cultural unity, is also the first step toward their
reappropriation into reified cultural claims of nations and civilizations. The
term transnational itself is not without problems. If it captures the contradictions created by the coexistence of globalizing tendencies with continued
claims to national and civilizational cultural homogeneity, it also conceals the
importance of viewing contemporary social, political, cultural, and even economic processes translocally—which is crucial to deconstructing the claims of
abstract cultural entities with the concrete practices of everyday life. This may
be the key not only to "rescuing history from the nation," as the title of a
recent study goes, but perhaps, more importantly, to rescuing the nation from
history (Duara 1995). History has served to bolster the claims of the nation-
state, as literary critics argue, but the converse is also true. Nations, having created imaginary histories in their legitimation, also find themselves trapped by

their own creation, unable to conceive of themselves in ways other than what that history will permit. If literature may be of help in rescuing the nation from history, history, in turn, may be indispensable in guarding against the entrapment of literature in culture.

NOTES

1. For three important, and personalized, discussions "Chineseness," see Ien, "On Not Speaking Chinese;" Ien, "Can One Say No to Chineseness?;" Chow, "Introduction." For a more light-hearted discussion, see Duke, "Representing China."

2. Robert Wood, cited in Halter, *Shopping for Identity*, 2000, 9.

3. For further discussion of these problems, see Dirlik, "Modernity as History," and Dirlik, "Markets, Culture, Power."

4. Kingston's critics are many (and they are not all male) but among them, Frank Chin has been the most persistent. For his comprehensive criticism of Chinese-American writers, including Kingston and Tan, see "Come all Ye Asian American Writers of the Real and the Fake." In *The Big AIIIEEEEE!*, ed. Chan, Chin, Inada and Wong.

5. Marilyn Chin, "Writing the Other: An Interview with Maxine Hong Kingston," In *Conversations with Maxine Hong Kingston*, ed. Paul Skenazy and Tera Martin Jackson, Jackson, MI, 1998, Quoted in Lo, 82.

6. Joseph Lau, quoted in Lo, 81

7. See her *Life Is a Caravanserai—Has Two Doors—Came in One—Went Out the Other*, tr. Louise Von Flotow (London, 2000). Ozdamar's Turkish idiom has been captured successfully by the translator in the English translation as well. For a perceptive analysis of Ozdamar's work, see Seyhan, *Writing Outside the Nation*, chapters 4 and 5.

8. Yuji Ichioka's recollections are available in his "A Historian by Happenstance," *Amerasia* 26, no. 1 (2000): 33–53. For comparable recollections of Chinese-American struggles, see Him Mark Lai, "Musings of a Chinese American Historian," *Amerasia* 26, no. 1 (2000): 2–30.

REFERENCES

Anderson, Benedict. *Imagined Communities: Reflections on the Origins and Spread of Nationalism.* London, New York, Verso 1995.

Brennan, Timothy. "The National Longing for Form." In *Nation and Narration*. Edited by Homi Bhabha. London, New York, Routledge 1990, 44–70.

Chan, Jeffrey Paul (et. al) ed. *The Big Aiiieeeee! An Anthology of Chinese American and Japanese American Literature.* New York, Meridian 1991.

Cheung, King-kok. "Introduction." In *Words Matter: Conversations with Asian American Writers.* Edited by King-kok Cheung. Honolulu, Univ. of Hawaii Pr. 2000, 1–17.

Chow, Rey. "Introduction: On Chineseness as a Theoretical Problem." *boundary 2* 25, no. 1 (1998), 1–24.

Dirlik, Arif. "Markets, Culture, Power: The Making of a 'Second Cultural Revolution' in China." *Asian Studies Review* 25, no. 1 (2001), 1–33.

Duke, Selina Li. "Representing China." *Quadrant* 42, no. 6 (1998), 62–66.

Duara, Prasenjit. *Rescuing History from the Nation: Questioning Narratives of Modern China.* Chicago, Univ. of Chicago Pr. 1995.

Gilroy, Paul. "'The Whsiper Wakes, the Shudder Plays': Race, Nation and Ethnic Absolutism." In *Contemporary Postcolonial Theory: A Reader.* Edited by Padmini Mongia. London, Arnold 1996, 248–74.

Halter, Marilyn. *Shopping for Identity: The Marketing of Ethnicity.* New York, Schocken 2000.

Ien, Ang. "On Not Speaking Chinese: Postmodern Ethnicity and the Politics of Diaspora." *New Formations* 24 (1994), 1–18.

———. "Can One Say No to Chineseness? Pushing the Limits of the Diasporic Paradigm." *boundary 2* 25, no. 3 (1998), 223–42.

Ito, Robert B., "Russell Leong." In *Words Matter: Conversations with Asian American Writers.* Edited by King-kok Cheung. Honolulu, Univ. of Hawaii Pr. 2000, 233–50.

Kingston, Maxine Hong. *The Woman Warrior: Memoirs of a Girlhood Among Ghosts.* New York, Vintage International 1989.

———. "Cultural Mis-readings by American Reviewers." In *Critical Essays on Maxine Hong Kingston.* Edited by Laura E. Skandera-Trombley. New York, G. K. Hall 1998, 95–103.

Law-Yone, Wendy. "Interview by Nancy Yoo and Tamara Ho." In *Words Matter: Coversations with Asian American Writers.* Edited by King-kok Cheung. Honolulu, Univ. of Hawaii Pr. 2000, 283–302.

Li, David Leiwei. "The Production of Chinese American Tradition: Displacing American Orientalist Discourse." In *Reading the Literatures of Asian America.* Edited by Shirley Geok-lin and Amy Ling. Philadelphia, Temple Univ. Pr. 1992, 319–31.

Li, David Leiwei. "Re-presenting *The Woman Warrior:* An Essay of Interpretive History." In *Critical Essays on Maxine Hong Kingston.* Edited by Laura E. Skandera-Trombley. New York, G. K. Hall 1998, 182–203.

Ling, Amy. "Maxine Hong Kingston and the Dialogic Dilemma of Asian American Writers." In *Critical Essays on Maxine Hong Kingston.* Edited by Laura E. Skandera-Trombley. New York, G. K. Hall 1998, 168–81.

Lo, Kwai-Cheung. "Reaffirming 'Chineseness' in the Translation of Asian American Literature: Maxine Hong Kingston's Fictions in Taiwan and Mainland China." *Translation Quarterly* 18 & 19 (2000), 74–98.

Marx, Karl. *The Eighteenth Brumaire of Louis Bonaparte.* New York, International Publishers 1963.

Murashige, Michael S. "Karen Tei Yamashita." In *Words Matter: Conversations with Asian American Writers.* Edited by King-kok Cheung. Honolulu, Univ. of Hawaii Pr. 2000, 343.

Pitkin, Hannah F. *The Concept of Representation.* Berkeley, Univ. of California Pr. 1967.

Rushdie, Salman. "Damme, This is the Oriental Scene for You!" *The New Yorker,* 23 & 30 June 1997, 53–61.

Seyhan, Azade. *Writing Outside the Nation.* Princeton, Oxford, Princeton Univ. Pr. 2001.

Tan, Amy. "Why I write." *Literary Cavalcade* 51, no. 6 (1999), 10–13.

White, Hayden. "Narrative in Contemporary Historical Theory." In *The Content of the Form: Narrative Discourse and Historical Representation.* Edited by Hayden White. Baltimore, London, The Johns Hopkins Univ. Pr. 1987, 26–57.

Wong, Sau-ling Cynthia. "'Sugar Sisterhood': Situating the Amy Tan Phenomenon." In *The Ethnic Canon: Histories, Institutions, and Interventions.* Edited by David Palumbo-Liu. Minneapolis, MN, Univ. of Minnesota Pr. 1995, 174–210.

———. "Autobiography as Guided Chinatown Tour? Maxine Hong Kingston's Woman Warrior and the Chinese-American Autobiographical Controversy." In *Critical Essays on Maxine Hong Kingston.* Edited by Laura E. Skandera-Trombley. New York, G. K. Hall 1998, 146–67.

How to Get Rid of China:

Ethnicity, Memory, and Trauma in

Gao Xingjian's Novel *One Man's Bible*

NATASCHA GENTZ

Gao Xingjian has become one of the most prominent "Chinese" writers because he received the Nobel Price for Literature in 2000. This award implies the integration of an author's oeuvre into the canon of "world literature," a concept which has been criticised for its imperialist implications or praised as an avenue for breaking the confines of national boundaries in literary creation.[1] In both views, the ethnic background of the author is the central element determining his identity and position in the transnational literary economy. Gao's novel *One Man's Bible*[2] (Gao 2000) is an explicit statement against such ascriptions of national identity, and his attempt at escaping from ethnicity involves a complex process of negotiating notions of history, private and collective memory, and the construction of identities. In this chapter, I will analyze the way in which Gao Xingjian solves his problem of claiming an autonomous identity devoid of ethnic definitions although narrating a historical account so closely related to a specific politically and nationally defined environment: Gao presents a biographical account of a man's life in China and abroad from the 1950s to the late 1990s, focusing on one of the most historiographically contested and politically sensitive periods of modern China, the Great Proletarian Cultural Revolution (CR), 1966–1976. Emphasizing time and again in his novel and his interviews that he wants to get rid of "China," the label of a "Chinese writer," and also of politics, in choosing this content for the novel, Gao is nevertheless joining a transnational conversation about exactly these topics.[3] Moreover, Gao's personal interpretation of the protagonist's experiences are informed by paradigms of a collective memory present in numerous other accounts on this specific period as well. Still, his account is a deviation from previous narratives, as Gao consciously attempts to avoid any application of essentializing categories through a complex—and, to some of his book reviewers, rather confusing—merge of narrating historical events and reflection upon the process of narrating itself.

An intertextual reading will therefore help to clear out the distinct position Gao takes in this multivocal dialogue with other literatures from China and abroad, but also, to bring to the fore those aspects that make his novel a truly transcultural endeavor. What seems to be singular in this novel and what sets it apart from previous accounts of this period in China, is that the author himself is well aware of all these theoretical problems, even if he is not always able to solve them.

CONTENT AND STRUCTURE OF THE NOVEL

The protagonist in the novel shares many biographical details with the author Gao Xingjian. Born in 1940 in the remote Jiangxi Province, Gao received his education in French language and literature at the Foreign Language Institute in Beijing and was then (1962) assigned to work in the Foreign Language Press as translator. In his student years, his mother died in a state farm and he was sent to the countryside after having been involved in political activities in the factional fights between revolutionary and rebellious Red Guards. Having spent five years (1970–1975) in a small village, Gao was able to return to Beijing and started to publish his first books in the early 1980s, among them a controversial much-debated collection of essays on modern literary techniques in which he fundamentally breaks with the most basic assumptions of a politicized literature of socialist realism.[4] In 1980, Gao started his career as a playwright at the Beijing People's Theatre and wrote a number of innovative and, again, controversial plays, which were criticized as "spiritual pollution" by the Chinese government. Escaping political harassment, Gao first undertook a long journey along the Yangzi river in 1983 and left China in 1987 to seek residence in France, where he still lives now.[5] Except for his journey through China's countryside, which resulted in his more famous novel *Soul Mountain*,[6] all these and more similar features appear as biographical elements of the protagonist in *One Man's Bible*.

As in his other writings, in this novel Gao makes use of a variety of modern literary techniques and includes different narrative modes in his story about a life in the CR. The general story of the novel has a linear temporal line and a teleological direction—which is a common feature of the biographical genre—yet the specific segments of the story are not presented in a chronological order and are interrupted by numerous reflections on the process of writing itself. For this reason, and also because many historical details are not explained but only alluded to, the story was sometimes judged as confusing and incomprehensible to readers unfamiliar with the specific political background of China's twentieth-century history.[7] The segments in the novel do not, however, appear in an arbitrary mixture, but follow a distinctively elaborated structure of two lines, which each, when set apart, reveal a logical and, to a large part, chronological narrative.

Most parts of the sixty-one chapters of the novel are presented in a realistic setting, defined by space and time, and can be divided into four groups: the protagonist's childhood and youth in his hometown (early 1950s), his student years and life before, during and after the Cultural Revolution in Beijing (late 1950s to 1976), his years on the countryside in a village in the southern parts of China (1970–75), and his later life as an exile author, which leads him to Hong Kong (mid-1990s) and makes him move around between Paris, Sweden, Australia, New York, Toulon, and finally Perpignon (mid-1990s–1996).

The first part of the narrative (chapters 1–16) consists of memories of his childhood and life in Beijing, alternating in a regular A-B pattern with a chronological narrative of his encounter with a German-Jewish woman, Margarete, in Hong Kong. Margarete had studied in China in the early 1980s and met the protagonist there. Their coincidental encounter in Hong Kong leads to a short love affair. The dialogues with Margarete confront the protagonist with his own past and evoke arbitrary memories of his mother's death; his escape from China and farewell to his Chinese lover in 1987; his first love affair in the 1960s with a girl named Lin, an offspring of a high cadre family; his later unhappy marriage to a wife, who attempts to denounce him; the beginnings of the Cultural Revolution in his work organization; first childhood experiences in the early 1950s; and his flight from the May Seven Cadre School in 1970 and an encounter with a former schoolmate, a frustrated and desolate poet who has resettled in the protagonist's hometown. The dialogues between Margarete and the main protagonist are presented in direct speech. After Margarete has left Hong Kong in chapter 16, the protagonist finally decides to write down his history and continues a dialogue with himself by addressing himself as "you." Again, this section is presented in an alternating A-B pattern of recollections of events and reflections by the writer (chapters 16–39). In this second section, the historical A part gives a chronological account of the protagonist's involvement in the factional fights during the CR. The B part interrupts this narrative with discussions of historiographical problems, how to present a truthful picture of the events, the status of literature, his own position and psychological state of mind under a fascist system, dreams from his childhood, and parables about the structure of this inhuman system. The third section sets out with his courageous escape from the labor camp and final settlement in a small village in the countryside (chapters 40–48). This period is narrated in an about sixty page-long linear chronological pattern without any interruption. It is contrasted by the following fourth section, which suddenly leads the reader to Sydney in the late 1990s and again takes up the alternating A-B pattern (chapters 49–55). Descriptions of the fates of the people he had encountered after the CR as well as his life abroad in the A line are again interrupted by dreams and reflections on his spiritual escape and liberation. The last six chapters of the novel (56–61) are set in the present, in which the writer contrasts his sexual encounters with a "liberated" woman in the West in the A line with an almost hymnic and triumphant conclusion about the individual freedom he finally had achieved in the West in the B line. These seemingly arbitrary shifts between the two narrative modes are thus deliberately chosen, even if this is not visible to the reader at first sight.

HISTORY, HISTORIOGRAPHY AND AUTOBIOGRAPHY

Because there are so many congruencies between the life of Gao and the story of his protagonist, this book is mainly regarded as an "autobiographical" novel, and his account is taken as an authentic representation of his experiences in China as a "native informant."[8] Such an assumption implies two problematic premises.

The first problem with applying this genre categorization is the identification of Gao's story with "Chinese" realities. Such identification is in tune with a general tendency in Chinese literary criticism to regard "realism" as the only and dominant form of modern Chinese literary creation. This might be due to the fact that an indigenous Chinese literary theory has emphasized realism as the main and mandatory literary technique since the beginnings of modern literature in China, which resulted in the extreme formulations of "revolutionary" or "romantic realism" in the socialist political literary theory. Being aware of this prejudice, Gao has opposed this literary theory of realism in all of his many theoretical writings on literary creation by formulating programmatic statements like "the writer is not the consciousness of society nor is literature the mirror of society."[9] Yet, the identification of Chinese literature as "realistic" touches upon the larger issue of the reception of non-Western literature in the West, that is, the position of the ethnic writer. Because the author is a Chinese writing about his own experiences, Gao's account is easily understood as an authentic description of the situation in China. That the reception of non-Western literature is largely dominated by a nationalist or ethnic perspective leads Arif Dirlik, in this volume, to provocatively pose the question of whether the ethnic writer may have an autonomous interiority at all, which does not merely reflect ethnic collectivity in a "truthful" and "authentic" manner. Gao opposes such an ethnic essentialisation of non-Western literature from a literary point of view by claiming that literature has no national boundaries. Quite to the contrary, Gao sees the most fatal distortion of modern Chinese literature in its increasing concentration on the nation, the victimization of the authors by the myth of the nation, and their subsequent tendency to act as spokesmen for the masses motivated by patriotism (Lee 2002, 31–32). With such statements the author is writing against the still largely prevalent assumption of the Chinese writer's "obsession with China," which was identified by C.T. Hsia many decades ago and meant the Chinese writers' inherent sense of duty to save the nation (Hsia 1971). It might seem paradoxical if Gao then chooses such a dramatically important part of recent Chinese history as the novel's central focus. Yet, in this novel, the author is neither interested in political explanations of the disastrous events in the CR, nor in any possible solutions for the future of China.

His narrative of specific events more often than not lacks broader explanations of policy shifts in the background, which is another reason why this book sometimes appears incomprehensible to uninformed readers. To depict the events in this manner is a strategic choice by Gao, as he does not intend to explain the politics of the day, but is merely interested in the individual psychological reaction toward the concrete realizations of these policies in daily life ("You want to tell about an individual who was contaminated by politics, without having to discuss the sordid policies itself," 182).

Thus, the criticism of Wu Han, the emergence of middle-school Red Guards, the work team period, the split of the Red Guard movement on the basis of the blood line theory, the takeover by the Rebellious Red Guards, the shifting targets of political persecution from class enemies or capitalist roaders to the Seventh May Clique, the dismissal of Kuai Dafu, and other specific political contexts are all mentioned as historical markers for the background story but not explained or even interpreted in their political significance. It is instead taken for granted that they form a part of the collective memory shared by the readers. This would suggest that the book is aimed at a Chinese readership familiar with these specific political events. But, more importantly, it underlines Gao's intention, not to depict a specific historical event, but to describe a political catastrophe devoid of a specific temporal or political background as a universal human experience ("It is best that you do not try to write a history, but only to look back upon your own experiences," 151).

The protagonist in the novel is very direct in expressing his disintegration from his Chinese past ("What you want is precisely to remove the China label from yourself," 61), rejecting any national prescription of his literature ascribed to him ("[A friend saying to the protagonist:] You're really writing for the people of China. You said you are writing only for yourself," 280) and declaring that he is using the Chinese language only for pragmatic reasons ("The only thing in his past he didn't break with was the language. He could, of course, write in another language, but he didn't abandon his language, because it was convenient and he didn't need to look words in a dictionary," 419.) Any further discussion about the nature of his literature is rejected as belonging to the realm of politics, not literary creation:

> . . . can Chinese literature communicate? Communicate with whom, the West? Or communicate with the Chinese on the Mainland, or with the Chinese living abroad? And what is Chinese literature? Does literature have national boundaries? And do Chinese writers belong to a specific location? Do people living on the Mainland, Hongkong, Taiwan, and the Chinese-Americans all count as Chinese people? This, again, brings in politics, let's talk just about pure literature. But does pure literature really exist? (296)

The problematization of the existence of a pure literature which is not linked to "politics," the question of the possibility of writing "nonattached" history, is pursued further, not in explicit deliberations, but through narrative technique, which is linked to a second, more theoretical problem inherent in the category of "autobiography."

Although biographies had been written centuries before, the notion of "autobiography" was invented in Europe only in the nineteenth century, being a most fashionable trend in the romantic literature of the time. The concept emerged together with questions about the relationship of truth and fiction, the possibility of truthful accounts of lived events and concerns of proper literary forms, all of which were reflected by the authors of these new works (Levin 1998). In the 1960s, Roy Pascal observed that distortion of truth through the act of memory is even a fundamental feature of autobiographies, although the notion of an autonomous subject remains intact in his writings (Pascal 1965). Only after poststructuralist studies emphasized the strong relationship between subjectivity and language were autobiographical writings understood as a constant process of constructing identities through language.

Apparently well aware of these historiographic problems, the author approaches these theoretical problems of writing about oneself when he reflects upon the possibility of exploring the interior world of his main protagonist(s). In his novel, this dilemma is solved by a refined technique of introducing different pronouns for the main protagonist, the "you" of the present (B line) and the "he" of the past (historical A line). Much has been written about Gao Xingjian's innovative usage of the pronouns "I," "you," and "he/she" in different contexts for the same person. Gao elaborates on this technique in many of his theoretical writings and had experimented with it already in his early short stories of the 1980s. A major function of this dissection of a person into different pronouns is to open different perspectives on this person by the person him/herself. Yet, in this semiautobiographical novel, the dissolution of the author gains another dimension because of the fact that the actual narrator, the "I," is missing. By presenting the self of the present as a "you," Gao elucidates the dialogical character of his explorations: the "I" is of course present as the actual narrator of the autobiography, since somebody must be in dialogue with the "you." Through this construction Gao imagines a confrontation of the reflecting, writing self (absent "I") with the reflected self of the past ("he") in a dialogue with the (seemingly authentic) "you" (of the present) discussing the "he." This segmentation of the subject into different pronouns is yet more than a split of selves, which enables the reader to "see the subject from the subjects other points of view," as Kwok-Kan Tam has observed (Tam 2002, 308). Gao makes a qualitative distinction between the different subjects: the "he" is invented as a fictional protagonist by the "I" who addresses "you," whereas the "you" of the present, in contrast, evokes the impression of an "authentic" self. That this self is constructed is revealed through the absent "I."

You seek only to narrate your own impressions and psychological state of that time, and to do this, you must carefully exercise the insights that you possess at this instant and this place, as well as put aside your present thoughts.

His experiences have stilted up in the creases of your memory. How can they be stripped off in layers, coherently arranged and scanned, so that a pair of detached eyes can observe what he has experienced? You are you and he is he. It is difficult for you to return to how it was in his mind in those times, he has already become so unfamiliar. [. . .] While observing and examining him unmasked, you must turn him into fiction, a character that is unrelated to you and has qualities yet to be discovered. It is then that writing is interesting and creative, and can stimulate curiosity and the desire to explore (182–83).

Between the narrating self and the experiencing self of the past lies a chasm, a temporal rupture which even obstructs the narrating self's identification with the experiencing self of the past. He is constructed as a stranger, who can only be approached through literary techniques—fiction. What might seem a confusing mixture of subjective perspectives to some readers is instead a deliberate narrative technique to approach a historical subject through present reflections, a translation and actualization of the past self in the present through a hermeneutic dialogue.

Gao did not use a term related to (auto)biographies to label his novel, but chose the word "*shengjing*"—in modern Chinese usually rendered as "bible,"[10] which can easily be misinterpreted by simply understanding it as a reference to the Christian canonical text. "*Shengjing*" is composed of the two elements "holy" (sheng) and "classic, canonical writing" (jing), and, in its earlier usage, referred to all scriptures of major world religions, such as the Buddhist, Jewish, and Christian canon as well as the Confucian writings. In combination with other words it is even used for the writings of the sages in general, handed down to posterior generations.[11] To translate it as "bible" or "the holy scripture" would therefore imply a reduction to a Christian cultural context, which is somewhat misleading. In the author's own words, "*shengjing*" has to be understood as the following:

You have written this book for yourself, this book of fleeing, this *One Man's Bible* [trsl. of *yige ren de shengjing* by Mabel Lee], you are your own god and follower, you do not sacrifice yourself for others, so you do not expect others to sacrifice themselves for you, and this is the epitome of fairness. Everyone wants happiness, so why should it all belong to you? However, what should be acknowledged is that there is actually very little happiness in the world (198–99).

This description is quite the opposite of what is understood as the basic elements of the bible: a canonical text handed down by God, written down by his disciples to be followed verbatim by all true believers. This shows, on the one hand, that Gao employs the label "bible" in an ironic fashion. On the other hand, seen in the light of his constructions of identities, it opens possibilities for a more profound interpretation that brings to the fore his understanding of his constructions of the self. Taken verbatim in a religious context, the bible is the revelation of God, just as the Chinese classical texts are revelations of the unspeakable, transported into the medium of language. This process necessarily distorts the original "meaning" of the divine: "Words do not exhaust meaning" (*yan bu jin yi*), is a locus classicus in Chinese literature for expressing this problem inherent in language, which permeates the Daoist and Buddhist literature.[12] The bible we are confronted with in Gao's novel is the revelation of an invisible and unspeakable "I," transmitted to the "you," who, by writing it down, already corrupts the true meaning of the "I." Thus, already through the title, Gao addresses the fundamental problem of the authority of the writer. The struggle with language and the impossibility of exhausting meaning through words is a topic which runs through the whole novel, and it is Gao's construction of separating the narrating and the experiencing self, the former being in dialogue with "I" (the "truth" of God), which transcends this linguistic and methodological problem into a spiritual one.

HISTORY AND MEMORY

Emphasizing the individual aspect of his interpretation of life and history by this title, Gao is yet writing and speaking in a real environment. With his choice of subject he is taking part in a transnational discourse on this period of the Cultural Revolution, which is informed by several layers of communicative and collective memory.[13] This becomes visible by comparing his narrative with other histories from officially sanctioned PRC literature, banned publications in the PRC as well as so-called "dissident" literature of other exiled authors. To situate his version of the historical past within this context is necessary in order to clarify his singular position within this discourse.

The author is again well aware of the dangerous traps involved in the recollection of historical memories and their connection to language usage. The first indirect dialogue between the "I" and "you" is thus devoted to a debate of the question of how history can be written without falling prey to current ideological terminology and without explaining the implications of the basic words and notions of the period. For Gao, it seems more important to know the political and psychological implications of words like "party," "learning," "rebellion," or "revolution," or even "history" rather than the actual events described by these words. Earlier descriptions of the atrocities in the CR, as for instance Yang Jiang's short (and mild) account on her life in a cadre school, have dealt with this language question implicitly by, for instance, putting the political notions into brackets and thereby alluding to their shallow content.[14] The possibility of arbitrary interpretations of these words leads the protagonist ("you") to deny any significance to any theory or ideology. Instead he attempts to unmask them as mere tools for fooling, manipulating, and oppressing people (chapter 18). Moreover, these reflections reveal the author's constant struggle with language. On a contextual level, his search for a new and nonpartisan language is part of a collective struggle to overcome the "Mao style" (*Mao wenti*), which dominated Chinese language in its most extreme form during the CR.[15] On the personal level it represents the individual struggle of an author to find his "own" language, a language that is able to reflect the interior of his self. What he explored is an almost hyperrealistic, plain and simple style, full of grammatical shifts and sometimes even mistakes, at times evoking the impression that he has been transcribing a speech, thereby substantiating the hermeneutical dialogue through language. Even more literary descriptions of the landscape or different people recur in almost identical phrases—again a deliberate choice by the author:

> You must find a detached voice, scrape off the thick residue of resentment and anger in your heart, then unhurriedly and calmly proceed to articulate your various expressions, your flood of confused memories, and your tangled thoughts. But you find this very difficult. What you seek is a pure form of narration. You are striving to describe in simple language the terrible contamination of life by politics, but it is very difficult. You want to expunge the pervasive politics that penetrated every pore, clung to daily life, became fused in speech and action, and from which no one at that time could escape (181–82).

From a superficial look at the content, Gao's "fictional" creation of the life experiences of his "he" is in tune with many other narratives of exile memoirs published outside China. The protagonist shares many biographical elements of other exile memoirs which were identified by Peter Zarrow in his analysis of exile memoirs of the CR (Zarrow 1999): the protagonist started as a promising young student in a peaceful childhood in the 1950s—and this "Golden Age" of Chinese communism during the 1950s is not only epitomized in the protagonist's memories of an extremely happy childhood, but also in the high expectations his parents and friends held for the communist liberation. The first fundamental breach of trust by the party came with the Anti-Rightist movement in the late 1950s. Later he was caught up in political factional fights during the first phase of the CR (ch. 19), realized the shallowness of these struggles, and volunteered to leave Beijing only to land in a Seventh May Cadre School labor camp, where he was soon to be persecuted because of his rebellious background. Knowing that this political investigation would mean his death, he managed again to escape with a courageous trick, and intended to settle in the countryside for life (ch.13). During the political struggles in Beijing, he also sided with brutal and ruthless rebellious Red Guards, but he always attempted to deescalate the conflicts and remain conciliatory toward his enemies (chs. 23, 29, 32). His attacks were a mere act of self-defense (ch. 29) and all in all he managed to maintain his inner moral integrity.

In many interviews and writings Gao articulates his attempts to escape this predicament of being entrapped by ideologies and their languages by placing himself at the margins of society as a neutral spectator. In the novel, this role of an outside observer is taken over by the experiencing self of the past ("he"). The sceneries are filled with a large number of people from different social strata, through which Gao gives a panoramic picture of the Chinese society of those days. Yet none of the characters are developed as individuals.

Gao has been criticized for this lack of individual voices of his other protagonists, especially Margarete, who is described in the fullest length in the novel, and (in other writings) women in general. His stereotypical presentation of woman as naïve and emotional rather than rational, and mainly sex-oriented, was interpreted as a misogynist and male-chauvinist attitude.[16] But this reduction of persons to stock characters again appears as a specific strategic device to fully develop the protagonist and his character as the main hero. Moreover, it is not restricted to women alone. The different backgrounds of the people he encounters, such as poets, painters, philosophers, entrepreneurs, or lovers, reveal different aspects of the personality of the protagonist, they only function to convey these aspects in their dialogues with the main character.

In looking at the overall depiction of Chinese society through these characters, we find an astonishingly mild verdict of the author. Except for Lin, a privileged high cadre daughter who had a risky love affair with the protagonist, all persons introduced experience a tragic fate, in one way or another. They can be divided into two groups: those who actively attempt to change their situations (a.o., his superior, the cadre Liu Ping, his schoolmates, the poet Luo, the mathematician Datou, his colleague Liang Kuan and a friend, the painter Dong Ping) and those who are passive and subjected to their inevitable destinies (e.g., his elder colleague Tan Xinren, his father, his father's cousin Fang, his schoolmate Rong, Xiaoxiao, a former Red Guard, and his disciple Sun Huirong in the village). Some among the first group are, like the protagonist, able to get away by escaping from China (Datou, Liang Kuan, Dong Ping and a Hong Kong entrepreneur), or by escaping from the political center, like the village cadre Lu who withdrew to a small hut in the mountains. There is only one truly negative figure in the novel: Danian, a brutal and ruthless blood-line Red Guard, who is the concrete enemy of the protagonist in their Red Guard struggles, and is sentenced to confinement after the CR. Another villain, the local cadre Zhao, only gradually reveals himself as a coward when it is disclosed that he raped a school girl. Yet, the actual villains responsible for the national catastrophe remain abstract, represented by nameless masses following the orders from above like a mass of sheep or an obscure political leadership giving those orders as anonymous agents. Even the responsible cadres at the highest political level, are, when mentioned, depicted as persons full of moral integrity who deserve the protagonist's respect.

This mild diagnosis of Chinese society seems, to a large part, to be indebted to a flow of a literature of humanism, widespread in China in the early 1980s, a reaction to the dehumanization of the individual in the CR and an attempt to restore the value of human dignity. Especially the degraded local cadre Lu, the only thoroughly positive figure in the entire novel, and a person the protagonist clearly admires, is imbued with the virtues of fairness, cleverness, and leniency and presented as a model party cadre under whose rule and protection the protagonist feels ultimately happy and content. The mild voice of the author reminds of conciliatory attempts to restore the image of a harmonious society, which had only been disturbed for a while during the turbulences of the CR but was not essentially fractured, alienated, or sick, an image actively promoted by the PRC leadership in the early 1980s; this is rather surprising, given the general tone of contempt for the political oppression that occurred.

If other previous accounts of former Red Guards followed a strategy of emphasizing their political blindness, which prevented them from recognizing the manipulation of the masses and of denying any true authenticity in their political actions (Zarrow 1999, 172), the protagonist's perspective allows him to remain authentic.[17] He was never blinded, but always able to figure out the necessary tactical moves. Because of this ability, he was never a concrete victim subjected to cruelties by others, but suffered only from the general aggressive and restrictive climate. As an observer he was not only able to detect the false and shallow behavior of his contemporaries, but also to scrutinize and analyze his own behavior during the events, yet this scrutinization does not imply any specific sense of guilt felt by the protagonist.

Such a seemingly heroic story is, however, undermined by the fact that the protagonist is entirely alienated from his environment and not able to survive in it, fleeing constantly. Escape is one of the major themes in Gao Xingjian's writings, not only physical escape from one place to another, but also escape from a mental perspective, from any philosophical territory that could restrain his intellectual freedom. Escape, as a leitmotif of his life, is the only possible way to maintain individual integrity and autonomy against political authorities, public opinion, social morals, or commercial interests.[18]

This trope of escape runs through the whole novel. Yet, there is one sequence in which it does not appear; this is during the protagonist's life in the village. Also, the narrative structure of this part underlines the protagonist's apparent feeling of relief and the redemption of an unfractured self, as it is the only sequence in the novel which is not interrupted by metareflections. Instead, the countryside was the ultimate destiny of salvation. When able to finally settle down in small village for the rest of his life, the protagonist rejoiced in happiness and the author gives an extremely romantic and seemingly naïve picture of his bucolic life on the countryside (ch. 41). Thus, at first, the protagonist experiences the countryside in a romantic tradition, highlighting the purity, simplicity, and naturalness of a peasant life (and thereby follows a stereotype of the traditional Chinese literati). Here, the author deviates form other standard narratives of the sent-down youth, for whom the point of disillusionment with CR politics came with the death of Lin Biao or their relegation to the countryside (Leung 1994). In contrast to most sent-down youth narratives, which emphasize ideological disillusionment in the face of hardships and the corruption and feudal practices in the villages, Gao's protagonist is only slowly exposed to the cruelties of rural life through the lessons taught by the above-mentioned party secretary Lu, the secret "king of the mountains" in this area (ch. 47). Before this, he constantly nourishes his hope to become "one of them," and at times even feels accepted as an ordinary peasant. It is the only—although short—phase in his mature life in China, when he identifies with his surrounding and overcomes the overall feeling of alienation—even if only to recognize that this identification was an illusion as well.

Lu explains the farmers' ruthlessness, unreliability, and selfishness in a historical perspective, as the essential character of the ordinary peasants in China, drawing a line from the Taiping rebellion to the liberation wars and finally to the Cultural Revolution. Yet, with his protagonist, Gao refuses any reference to a Chinese cultural tradition or a Chinese particularity. The confrontation of the protagonist's past in China with present his life in the West is never explained in terms of cultural difference. In his descriptions of events in China there are not even hints of residues of a feudal Chinese tradition in human relations or of sociopolitical habits of strict obedience to the ruler, as, for instance, are found in Liang Heng's *Son of the Revolution*.[19] Neither is there any attempt to explain a culturally defined Chinese character or to provide broader historical perspective on the course of Chinese history, as found in other writings after the Cultural Revolution.[20] If he generalizes, he speaks of human beings, mankind, or—in social terms—the masses. Even when reflecting upon his own identity as a Chinese, he merely emphasizes his fundamental radical break with this identity without ever touching upon questions of what qualitative features these "Chinese" elements would have.

However, as a matter of fact, the protagonist takes cultural and ethnic differences for granted, as revealed in his dialogue with Margarete: "You are not like other women of the West, you are much more like a Chinese girl."[21] Such statements again testify the common phenomenon, that cultural and ethnic essentializations are much more easily applied to the "other," even if they are explicitly rejected for oneself.

In his analysis of exile memoirs on the CR, Zarrow discovers a common linear narrative structure from tragedy (the experience of Maoist China as a pure nightmare) to triumph over the troubles (recognition of realities) and actual accession to freedom in the West.[22] He argues that this triumphant arrival in the West as the final destination and only place in the world allowing for individual freedom and true subjectivism caters to a Western readership by reinforcing the common assumptions of a Orientalist despotic East against a free democratic West and that this makes up for the common success of such descriptions outside China. In Gao's case, this is substantiated by many reviews of his recently published English translation as well as the publisher's promotion, which all emphasize exactly this point, describing the book as "a profound meditation on the essence of writing, on exile, on the effects of political oppression of the human spirit, and how the human spirit can triumph."[23]

Indeed, the protagonist's experiences in the West are presented in the same romantic fashion as his life on the countryside, evoking images of bucolic landscapes and indulging in his own feelings of an achieved personal freedom to live his own independent life. Ironically, reminding almost of CR propaganda narrations of "remembering the bitterness of the past and rejoicing in the sweetness of the present," the West serves as the final point, where the teleological narrative of a process of maturing (by learning to understand realities), resulting in the achievement of a true and independent position, comes to an end. Yet, in the case of *One Man's Bible*, the image of a free West is exaggerated to an extent that suggests that the author is producing a (contrasting) image rather than intending to present "Western realities." The protagonist praises the freedom in the West in hymnic verses: this environment not only provides political freedom (as he is able to articulate whatever opinion he has) or individual freedom (as he is able to sleep with any woman without thereby infracting social or moral norms) but also economic freedom (as he is not forced to rely on writing for his income).

> You're light, and float up as if you were weightless. You wander from country to country, city to city, woman to woman, but don't think of finding a place that is home. You drift along, engrossed in savoring the taste of the written language, and, like ejaculating, leave behind some traces of your life. . . . You simply live in this instant, like a leaf on the brink of falling from a tree. . . . sooner or later it has to fall, but while it's fluttering in the breeze, it must strive for freedom (426).

This image of his free and careless life in the West, evoked by these comments, might appear naive, yet it is an image painted by the protagonist, and thus a narrative technique which serves as a negative foil to poignantly contrast the heavy psychological burden of the dictatorial system of the past. It also expresses the articulation of the "you"'s insurmountably strong and ultimately essential desire for freedom as a consequence of his experiences in the inhuman system of his past. It is thus necessary only in order to provide a counter-image to the unbearable conditions of the past.

Moreover, this individual perception of the protagonist's own freedom is contrasted with anecdotes and scenes from the West, which subvert this positive image. This technique of juxtaposing tragic fates of individuals he observed in China and in the West is most clearly applied in chapters 48–52, which narrate his encounters with student girls in the Chinese village alternating with scenes of his love affair with a French girl Sylvie. In the A line, the protagonist meets two sent-down girls who live alone in a school in a deserted area, teaching the children during the day and catering to the village population at night. Spending a night in their house, he notices the lack of door locks (ch. 48). In the next scene, the protagonist of the present is in Sydney together with his current lover, Sylvie, searching a primordial forest area. Sylvie is introduced as a sexually and ideologically liberated woman who frequently changes partners regardless of their ethnic background (which is emphasized). However, this life does not bring full happiness to her, as she frequently sinks into deep depressions—partly because this life is the result of a former unhappy alliance which had lead to pregnancy and a subsequent abortion (ch. 49). Back in the village in the following chapter, the protagonist discovers that his former student Sun Huirong has been raped by the local party official. Reading through all the files of the case he learns that she had become pregnant, was accused of having seduced the man, and has therefore been transferred to a remote production brigade. Her mother had helped her settle the abortion in a hospital, and finally, Sun became the whore of the village (ch. 50). In France, Sylvie tells the story of her intimate girlfriend Martina. Martina also had an active sex life with changing partners, yet this was not accepted by Martina's mother, who sent her to a mental hospital, anxious that society would regard her daughter as a whore. Martina became an alcoholic and finally committed suicide. Sylvie then reveals the grievous story of her own full "sexual liberation," experienced during a holiday trip with Martina, during which Martina had seduced Silvie's first boyfriend and arranged a sexual encounter of all four partners, which caused Silvie's inner moral disillusionment. Gao does not compare these events in China and the West, but juxtaposes them without any comment. The reader is forced to draw his or her conclusion, or, just to let this image evoked by the juxtaposition take effect. The protagonist's escape to the West is therefore not an arrival but the continuation of a permanent state of fleeing (in) the world.

Thus, his choice of a voluntary exile from his homeland is not perceived as a preliminary state of existence which had to be overcome, but as the ultimate source of joy and happiness.

> He had no leader, because he was not controlled by the Party or some organization. He had no hometown, because his parents were dead. And he had no family. He had no responsibilities, he was alone, but he was free and easy, he could go wherever he wanted, he could drift with the wind (419).

By fully appreciating the good fortunes of his exile life, the protagonist is ardently speaking against the assumption expressed by Edward Said that "the essential sadness of exile can never be surmounted. . . . The achievements of exile are permanently undermined by the loss of something left behind forever" (Said 1990, 357).[24] This sets him apart from the real exile poets of the present, such as Bei Dao, Yang Lian, and Duo Duo, who reflect

a melancholic longing for their distant homelands. In contrast, the protagonist does not feel rootless and depressed for having been culturally deprived,
but evokes the impression of having stepped into a cosmopolitan space from
which he is able to pick and choose the raisins out of the international con-
fectioner—at least there is no single word of a miserable feeling about this
state of life in the novel.

In tune with those exile writers is Gao's detest for political statements. A
surprising feature of most of these exile writers is their common rejection of
the political implications of their writings and a strong defense of the concept
of "art for art's sake," instead of calling for political action.[25] This withdrawal
from social and political responsibility might be a reaction toward their common experience of the consequences of an extreme political reading of Chinese literature in China. By maintaining that he is only writing for himself
and by establishing this realm of internal exile, the protagonist mainly con-
firms the reachievement of his human dignity. This means keeping a private
mental space isolated from social or political interference and nourishing this
space in times of darkness.

> A person cannot be crushed if he refuses to be crushed. Others may oppress
> him, and defile him but, as long as he had not stopped breathing, he will still
> have the chance to raise his head. It is a matter of being able to preserve his
> last breath, to hold onto his last breath, so that one does not suffocate in the
> pile of shit. A person can be raped, woman or man, physically or by political
> force, but a person cannot be totally possessed; one's spirit remains one's own,
> and it is this that is preserved in the mind (446–47).

The overall story of the experiences during the CR narrates a heroic account
of a protagonist who is able to overcome all difficulties through his cleverness, wit, and mental superiority. In all cases, the protagonist is able to escape
from persecutions because he can foresee them and thus prepare against
them by escaping from the dangerous environment: from Beijing he sets out
to inspections tours, from the cadre school he flees to a village in the South,
after the CR he escapes to the West. This hero apparently also feels no need
to develop a "sense of shame" as articulated in Qian Zhongshu's remarkable
foreword to his wife's account of her life in the state farm, describing himself
as belonging to those persons who are "feeling ashamed of their own cow-
ardice, people who lacked the courage to protest that which they believed
unjust, but whose most courageous act was 'passive' participation in the campaign."[26] This self-scrutinizing perspective is, admittedly and as far as I can
see, unique in the current literature on the CR. The few self-accusing
instances in the novel are restricted to descriptions of the protagonist's passive attitude, for instance, for passively watching an old lady being beaten to
death on the street. At the same time, the subsequent remarks on that
instant, that the police were inactive as well, place responsibility on the state
instead of on the individual.

MEMORY AND TRAUMA

The possible acknowledgment of a sense of guilt and a thorough reflection on traumatic experiences faced during the CR on the side of the victims is limited by the fundamental problem that such a discourse on the CR is still tabooed in the People's Republic of China.[27] Yet, "to hold traumatic reality in consciousness requires a social context that affirms and protects the victim and that joins victim and witness in a common alliance" (Herman 2001, 9). This social context is not given and makes it so difficult for most of authors writing on the CR to sincerely overcome the past in a more reflected and rational fashion. The crucial question for an official reevaluation of the CR lies in a new evaluation of the role of Mao Zedong and Jiang Qing (or the "Gang of Four"). Plays or literary and academic pieces which attempt to approach this sensitive question by a more neutral perspective are still banned in China.[28]

In Gao's novel the question of how to deal with this period in a sincere and proper way is the central question. The whole issue of recovery from the traumatic experiences is approached through a comparison between the CR and the Holocaust, while at the same time the possibility of this comparison is made a topic of discussion. Apart from the fact that such an analogy is largely rejected in academic scholarship, it nevertheless prevails in popular descriptions of the CR.[29] In academic discussions, the question is posed of whether the experiences of the CR victims can be regarded as "traumatic" at all. Ann Thurston affirmed the traumatic character of the experience as she observed a general sense of loss generated by an extreme situation that lacks possible explanations (Thurston 1988). Lucien Pye has argued against this by referring to the quick return to normal life after the fall of the "Gang of Four," which would contradict the fact of a traumatized society.[30] More recently, Vera Schwarcz has approached this topic by comparing the modes of recollection of Jewish and Chinese victims by highlighting the fundamental relation of individual memories to cultural memories.[31]

In Gao's novel, this comparison is directly addressed, when the "you" is confronted with Margarete, the German girl with a Jewish family background, who suffers from transgenerational traumatic syndroms. Because of her own loss of a sense of safety, still being fearful of persecution by remaining Neo-Fascists in Germany, Margarete involves the "you" in exhaustive discussions about the necessity "to remember": in order to avoid letting history repeat itself, on the one hand, but more importantly, in order to gain relief through communicating the experienced suffering (ch. 8). The protagonist ("you") refutes her arguments one by one, unwilling to see himself as suffering from any posttraumatic syndrome. Time and again he emphasizes that he had cut off all links with the past and only thus had acquired his new happiness and freedom.

Margarete slowly deconstructs this self-image of the protagonist as a content and happy citizen of the world. She serves to exemplify the traumatized person with whom the protagonist "you," who regards himself as "untraumatized" and as free person, has to be forcefully confronted. Also here, there is no sense of shame, which restrains the "you" in the beginning from retelling the stories of the past, shame about the indignity suffered or the violation of bodily integrity, which often prevents the traumatized from recollecting their experiences. The only reason why the "you" at first refutes approaches is because of his conviction that forgetting was the only way of relief, thus repeating his trope of "escape" as a device of survival.

This attraction of amnesia appears repeatedly in the novel through the metaphor of flowing water. As Vera Schwarcz has explored, the metaphor of water is linked with the benefits of amnesia in Chinese folklore, and it seems significant that water, small ponds, rivers, or the seaside are the most common features in the landscapes painted in the novel. Most obviously, the largest part of the scenes from the protagonist's exile life takes place at the seaside in Sydney (ch. 49) and Toulon (ch. 59), or at a lake in Sweden (ch. 17), and the Hong Kong scenes are full of descriptions of the sea, too. Diving into water in order to forget or free oneself is a trope, which Gao has extensively elaborated in his short story "Haishang" (Out at Sea), whereas in "Choujin" (Spasms), the attractiveness of the sea (in a metaphorical reading: of amnesia) is a real threat to the life of the protagonist.[32] The cadre Lu, who retreated into the mountains to break with his past, built his house beside a small pond, which the protagonist hears murmuring while lying on bed at night (ch. 52). It is this oscillation between painful memory and sedative amnesia that directs the mode of narration in the novel and defines the fundamental condition of the narrator(s).

The protagonist's desire for amnesia is successfully crushed when Margarete explains in what respect the Holocaust fundamentally differed from the Cultural Revolution. Only then the protagonist feels so provoked that he flares up to state:

> "Fascism was not only in Germany, you never really lived in China. Fascism was no worse than the Cultural Revolution," you said coldly. "But it wasn't the same. Fascism was genocide, it was simply because one had Jewish blood in one's body. It was different from ideologies and political beliefs, it didn't need theories." She raises her voice to argue. "Your theories are dog shit! You don't understand China at all, and haven't experienced the Red Terror. It was an infectious disease that made people go mad!" You suddenly lose your temper (66–67).

The protagonist begins to recall his sufferings, which come into the picture first and foremost as nightmares ("You say that memories might give her strength but for you they are the same as nightmares," 60). An experience is defined as traumatic if the victim is suffering from posttraumatic stress disorders, nightmares, stress symptoms, and nervous anxieties. Traumatic moments become encoded in forms of memory which break spontaneously into consciousness, as flashbacks or nightmare, and they are not encoded in a verbal, linear narrative, but in vivid sensations and images (Herman 2001, 37–38). Also, this is clearly reflected in Gao's structural arrangement of the novel. After this outbreak, the "you" who had denied any traces of trauma beforehand, begins to explain that he can find relief only through sexual intercourse with woman.

> She needs to search for historical memories, and you need to forget them. She needs to burden herself with the sufferings of the Jews . . . , but you need to receive from her body a confirmation that you are living at this instant (67).

The many sexual encounters narrated in this novel are presented as a vehicle to overcome the traumatic experiences inscribed into the body of the protagonist. As their dialogues continue, it is revealed that Margarete's actual trauma was that she had been raped in her early youth. Margarete's physical manifestation of her trauma is her masochistic desire for sadist sexual practices and the experience of physical pain, as she discloses to the "you" in their last sexual encounter (ch. 16). For the protagonist the only way of relief was his ejaculation into a female body. The connection between the political and the physical is taken further by the "you" when he compares his political experience to being raped.

> You say that you have experienced the feeling of being raped, of being raped by the political authorities, and it has clogged up your heart. You can understand her, and can understand the anxiety, frustration, and oppression that she can't get rid herself of. Rape was no sex game. It was the same for you, and it was long afterward, after obtaining the freedom to speak out, that you realized it had been a form of rape. You had been subjected to the will of others, had to make confessions, had to say what others wanted you to say (121–22).

The traumatic experience of the protagonist was not physical persecution, but a spiritual one. The leniency in his verdict about most of the people involved in the struggles in his homeland, and also in his overall evaluation of the good and bad in his life (repeating that he has no enemies and even expressing a general gratitude for his after all still lucky fate), is contrasted with his fundamental traumatic suffering from oppression of freedom. And there is only one person responsible for this trauma, whom he cannot forgive:

> What he wanted to say was, you could kill people at your will. What he wanted to tell Mao was, you made every single person to speak your words. He also wanted to say that history would fade into oblivion, but, back in those days, he had been forced to say what Mao had dictated, therefore, it was impossible for him to eradicate his hatred for Mao. Afterwards, he had said to himself that as along as Mao was revered as leader, emperor, god, he would not return to that country (405).

The interpretation of his experience as a physical rape emphasizes the sense of being the victim of a criminal act rather than of a tragic political development. It also emphasizes the senselessness of the occurrences. The protagonist's reevaluation of the role of Mao is therefore one of a criminal who raped people at will. Although this political rape is part of the past, it is still actually present in the protagonist's subsequent rejection of articulating anything political and in his final solution of seeking relief only in the depths of a female body. Metaphorical analogies between ejaculating and writing, both presented as the ultimate modes of decreasing his psychological pressure, recur time and again. According to Herman "traumatic events have primary effects not only on the psychological structures of the self but also on the systems of attachment and meaning that link individual and community" (Herman 2001, 51). Given the fact that there is yet no outside support for the CR traumatized to recover by communicating their experience to a trustworthy community, the protagonist's solution out of his psychological dilemma is a kind of solipsism, a rejection of any outside influence and ultimate concentration on himself and physical—sexual—sensations, which he ultimately defines as an "awareness of life." For his artistic life, this means gracefully sublimating the frustrations of life into art (p. 445).

CONCLUSION

In his account of the history of an individual life during the CR, Gao has obviously no intention to give a new interpretation of the historical past in his description and (unwilling) analysis of the political and social background of the Cultural Revolution. Instead, he presents a mosaic of ostensibly unrelated scenes filled with a wide range of various people, which are most convincing in their capacity to convey the general sense of tragic disillusionment behind seemingly trivial events. The novel presents a genuine mixture of approaches in an individual's attempt to localize himself in historical, social, and ethnic terms. It addresses the fundamental problems in this process of localization, trying to solve them partly expressively, by theoretical explorations, but mainly implicitly through literary techniques. His attempt to integrate reflections on identity and self-construction, the human conditions of remembering, the self-positioning in a transnational literary economy, and the process of writing into the literary creation itself is certainly a unique approach to the complex problem of the role of the Cultural Revolution in Chinese history and in individuals' lives, which has up to now been dominated by stereotypical accounts and shallow political or psychological explanations.

Gao's complex construction of the protagonist's self in the novel is another attempt at escape from collective memory and, from a theoretical point of view, a very interesting approach to the complex issue of history, historiography, and language. The superficial teleological narrative of an individual arriving at a state of ultimate happiness by voluntary withdrawal is subverted by the simultaneous disclosure of the illusionary character of this happiness and freedom of the protagonist when pointing at the traumatic stress he is actually suffering. The protagonist's various attempts to overcome his traumatic past certainly make up for the strongest parts of this novel, although the presented solution is full of contradictions. Claiming to have overcome all the horrors of the past and having achieved an ultimately independent and freed state of mind, the protagonist is still caught by his powerful need and desire to vent his psychological pressure through unattached sexual activities. This contradiction is taken further at the end of the novel, where he ponders the question of where he could find a woman who was independent and solitary like him, yet would be willing to fuse his "solitude with hers in sexual gratification" (439), and thus expresses his still fundamentally present desire for psychological attachment.

To understand this contradictory image of the protagonist, it has to be kept in mind, that the "you" who is speaking with a seemingly authentic voice about his freedom and happiness is also a figure, developed through the hermeneutic dialogue with the absent "I." If, at the final point of his biographical journey the protagonist seems to have regained an intact identity, this is presented as an illusion as well. It is in this particular respect that Gao's elucidation and stress of the extreme anxieties, difficulties, and contingencies a self-stated nonethnic writer faces is successful. His novel is the testimony of an attempt to dissolve the "subject of culture" by situating it within a terrain of contested sites and by making these contestations visible.

NOTES

This paper is a by-product of my translation of Gao Xingjian's novel *One Man's Bible* into German (*Das Buch eines einsamen Menschen,* Frankfur a. M.: Fischer Verlag, 2004). I wish to thank Irmy Schweiger for her critical remarks and helpful suggestions.

1. For a critical discussion of the ideological and economic implications of this concept see Jones, "Chinese Literature in the 'World' Literary Economy." Torbjörn Lodén, who also took issue with Stephen Owen's essay discussed by Jones, takes a more positive stance emphasizing the creative possibilities opened up through a transnational literary intercourse. Cf. Lodén. "World Literature with Chinese Characteristics."

2. Gao started writing this book in 1996 in France; it was first published in Taipei in 1999. For an English translation see Gao Xingjian, *One Man's Bible,* translated by Mabel Lee, London: Flamingo, 2002, which is used in this paper for reasons of stylistic coherence, if not indicated otherwise.

3. In an interview with Jean-Luc Douin Gao said: "I think of me as a citizen of the world. A frail man, who has managed not to be crushed by authority, and who speaks to the world with his own voice." Label France, April 2001. In another interview at Harvard University he defined his Chinese identity as entirely personal: Asked how he views his cultural identity, and whether he misses China, Gao gives a typically internal definition of self. "I am China," he says, tapping his chest. Wo jiushi Zhong-

guo. "China is inside me, and that China," he says, gesturing to encompass the world of politics and pain, of fallibility on a systematic scale, "has nothing to do with me." Shen, "Nobel winner affirms the 'self.'"

4. Gao Xingjian, *Xiandai xiaoshuo jiqiao chutan* (A Preliminary Exploration of the Techniques of Modern Fiction), Guangzhou, 1981. The book incited a polemic discussion on modernism in Chinese literature.

5. More biographical details can be found in the various contributions to the monograph on Gao Xingjian edited by Tam, and especially Terry Siu-Han Yip's chronology of his life and writings in this volume. Tam, *Soul of Chaos*.

6. Gao Xingjian, *Lingshan* (Soul Mountain), Taipei, 1990. For an English translation see Gao Xingjian, *Soul Mountain*. Translated by Mabel Lee, London, 2000.

7. E.g. W.J.F. Jenner, in *The Guardian*, 30 November 2002; Peter Gordon, "Cure for Bitterness," *Asian Review of Books*, 24.10.2002; see also the reviews under: http://btobsearch.barnesandnoble.com/booksearch by Shirley N. Quan, Library Journal; Kirkus Reviews.

8. The identification of the protagonist with Gao is either taken for granted in most of the reviews of *One Man's Bible* mentioned above, or the distinction between the fictional account and his biography is regarded as insignificant.

9. Gao Xingjian, *Meiyou zhuyi* (Without isms), Hong Kong, 1996, 23, which is a collection of such essays. For an analysis of his literary reflections see Mabel Lee, "Gao Xingjian on the Issue of Literary Creation for the Modern Write," in Tam ed., loc. cit., 21–41.

10. The term was—together with many other optional translations—integrated into the Chinese language as a translation for "bible" in the early-nineteenth century, yet only in the early-twentieth century did it become the standardized translation word.

11. *Hanyu dacidian* (Great Chinese Dictionary), Shanghai: Hanyu dacidian chubanshe, 1991.

12. "Xici shang," in *Shisanjing zhushu*, ed. Ruan Yuan, Beijing: Beijing daxue chubanshe, 1999, vol 1: *Zhouyi Zhengyi*, 82.3. "As for the Way, the Way that can be spoken of is not the constant Way. As for the names, the name that can be named is not the constant way" is another well-known passage from the *Daodejing*, which immediately comes to mind in this regard. Cf. *Lao-tzu Te-Tao-ching. A New Translation Based on the Recently Discovered Ma-wang-tui Texts*. Trsl. By Robert G. Henricks, New York: Ballantine Books, 1989, 188.

13. Communicative memory is a term coined by Jan Assmann in his studies on the cultural memory, and ecompasses memories which are related to the recent past (in contrast to a cultural memory which refers to fixed points in the past represented in symbolic figures). Assmann, *Das kulturelle Gedächtnis*.

14. Yang Jian's "Ganxiao liuji" (Six Notes from a Cadre School) was first published in *Guang jiaojing* (Wide Angle) 103 (April 1981). For an English translation see Yang Jiang, *Six Chapters From My Life "Downunder."* Translated by Howard Goldblatt, 1983.

15. On a brief analysis of this *Mao wenti* see Kong Jiesheng, "Xishuo yuyan" (Playful words on language), *Zhengming* 10 (October, 1993), 78–81.

16. On stereotypical descriptions: E.g. Bradley Winterton, *Taipei Times*, October 20, 2002. Roger Gathman. *http://www.csmonitor.com/2002*; for a more balanced analysis of Gao's treatment of woman in *One Man's Bible* see Rojas, "Without [Femin]ism." I wish to thank the author for making the article accessible to me before its publication.

17. Zarrow argues that the conventional narrative of individual triumph excludes the possibility to depict a sense of freedom or intellectual incitement or the righteousness of beating political victims during the CR.

18. See his essay collection *Meiyou zhuyi.*, Gao Xingjian, 1996, loc.cit. "Escape" is also the title of one of his plays: Gao Xingjian., "Taowang" (Fugitives), *Jintian* 1990. 1. See also Gao Xinjian, 1990.

19. Liang Heng and Judith Shapiro. *Son of the Revolution*. New York, Vintage, 1984.

20. E.g. Sun Longji, *The Deep Structure of Chinese Culture*, published in Hongkong in 1983. Excerpts from this much debated book are to be found in Barmé and Minford, *Seeds of Fire. Chinese Voices of Consciousness.* In the literary realm the authors of the "New Historicism" as Mo Yan, Su Tong or Yu Hua would be examples of choosing a broader historical perspective to explain the underlying paradigms of the Chinese culture.

21. Mabel Lee translates this passage as "You're not like a Western woman, you're more like a Chinese woman," p. 95 in her translation, but the Chinese text distinguishes between the Western woman as *"xifangren"* (Westerner) and the Chinese as "Chinese girl" (*Zhongguo guniang*), which I think is significant.

22. Zarrow, 1999, esp. 170–73. Most explicitly this theme runs through the prominent biographical account of Nien Cheng in Cheng Nien, *Life and Death of Shanghai*, New York 1988.

23. Barnes & Noble Review. From the publisher. *http://btobsearch.barnesandnoble.com/booksearch*.

24. In contrast to Gao's novel, this situation is dramatized, for instance, in Nien Cheng's account on her final departure from China. Cf. Cheng Nien, 1988.

25. For a very interesting and lively discussion of literary activities inside and outside China after the Tiananmen massacre see the website of the China Symposium '89, Bolinas, California, 27–29 April, 1989 edited and annotated by Geremie R. Barmé, especially Leo Ou-fan Lee's contribution under http://www.tsquare.tv/film/Bolinas7lee.html. A short description of the exile writers situation can be found in Oliver Kramer, "No Past to Long For? A Sociology of Chinese Writers in Exile."

26. Qian Zhongshu, Foreword in Yang Jiang 1983, 8.

27. On the current political evaluation of the CR in the PRC leadership see Dittmer, "Rethinking China's Cultural Revolution amid Reform."

28. For instance, Sha Yexin's play "Jiang Qing and Her Husbands" (Jiang Qing he tade zhangfumen), written in 1991 and published in Hong Kong, can still not be performed on PRC stages. For an analysis and translation into German see Natascha Vittinghoff, *Geschichte der Partei entwunden—Eine semiotische Analyse des Dramas Jiang Qing und ihre Ehemänner (1991) von Sha Yexin*, Bochum, Projekt Verlag 1995.

29. E.g. Sheng-mei Ma, "Contrasting Two Survival Literatures; Vera Schwarcz, "The Burden of Memory: The Cultural Revolution and the Holocaust."

30. Without attempting to engage in this discussion it should be noted, that trauma theories stress the point, that between the traumatic event and the post traumatic disorder lies a period of latency, during which no direct effects of the experience can be observed. Pye, "Reassessing the Cultural Revolution," 605–6.

31. Yet she also firmly maintains that there was a fundamental difference between the Cultural Revolution and the Holocaust. Schwarcz, *Bridge Across Broken Time*, ch. 4.

32. Gao Xingjian, "Haishang" (Out at sea) and "Choujin" (Spasms), in *Gei wo laoye mai yugan* (Buy my grandfather a fishing rod), 1989, 87–94, resp. 236–40.

REFERENCES

Assmann, Jan. *Das kulturelle Gedächtnis. Schrift, Erinnerung und politische Identität in frühen Hochkulturen.* München, Beck 1999.

Barmé, Geremie and John Minford. *Seeds of Fire. Chinese Voices of Consciousness.* Hong Kong, Far Eastern Economic Review Ltd. 1986.

Dittmer, Lowell. "Rethinking China's Cultural Revolution amid Reform." In *China's Great Proletarian Cultural Revolution. Master Narratives and Counternarratives.* Edited by Woei Lien Chong, London, Rowman and Littlefield 2002, 3–26.

Gao Xingjian, *Xiandai xiaoshuo jiqiao chutan* (A Preliminary Exploration of the Techniques of Moden Fiction). Guangzhou, Huacheng Chubanshe 1981.

———. *Gei wo laoye mai yugan* (Buy My Grandfather a Fishing Rod). Taipei, 1989

———. *Lingshan* (Soul Mountain). Taipei, Lianjing Wenxue 1990.

———. "Taowang" (Fugitives). *Jintian* 1 (1990).

———. *Meiyou zhuyi* (Without isms). Hong Kong, Tiandu tushu youxian gongsi 1996.

———. *Soul Mountain.* Translated by Mabel Lee, London, Flamingo 2000.

———. *Yige ren de shengjing* (One Man's Bible). Taipei, Cosmos Books Ltd. 2000.

———. *One Man's Bible.* Translated by Mabel Lee. London, Flamingo 2002.

———. *Bibel eines einsamen Mannes.* Translated by Natascha Vittinghoff. Frankfurt a. M., Fischer 2003.

Hanyu dacidian (Great Chinese Dictionary). Shanghai, Hanyu da cidian chubanshe 1991.

Herman, Judith Lewis. *Trauma and Recovery. From Domestic Abuse to Political Terror.* London, Pandora 2001.

Hsia, C. T. *A History of Modern Chinese Fiction.* New Haven and London, Yale Univ. Pr. 1971, 533–609.

Jones, Andrew. "Chinese Literature in the 'World' Literary Economy." *Modern Chinese Literature* 8, nos. 1&2 (Spring/Fall), 171–90.

Kong Jiesheng. "Xishuo yuyan" (Playful Words on Language). *Zhengming* 10 (October 1993), 78–81.

Kramer, Oliver. "No Past to Long For? A Sociology of Chinese Writers in Exile." In *The Literary Field of Twentieth Century China.* Edited by Michel Hockx. Hawaii, Univ. of Hawaii Pr. 1999, 161–77.

Lao-tzu Te-Tao-ching. *A New Translation Based on the Recently Discovered Ma-wang-tui Texts*. Translated by Robert G. Henricks. New York, Ballantine Books 1989.

Lee, Mabel. "Gao Xingjian on the Issue of Literary Creation for the Modern Write." In Kwok-Kan Tam ed., loc. cit., 21–41.

Leung, Laifong. *Morning Sun: Interviews with Chinese Writers of the Lost Generation*, Armonk, N.Y., M. E. Sharpe 1994.

Levin, Susan M. *The Romantic Art of Confession. De Quincey, Musset, Sand, Lamb, Hogg, Frémy, Souliè, Janin*, Drawer, Camden House 1998.

Liang Heng and Judith Shapiro. *Son of the Revolution*, New York, Vintage Books 1984.

Lodén, Torbjörn. "World Literature with Chinese Characteristics: On a Novel by Gao Xingjian," *The Stockholm Journal of East Asian Studies* 4 (1993), 17–39.

Ma, Sheng-mei. "Contrasting Two Survival Literatures: On the Jewish Holocaust and the Chinese Cultural Revolution." *Holocaust and Genocide Studies* 2, no. 2 (1987), 81–93.

Nien Cheng, *Life and Death of Shanghai*. New York, Penguin 1988.

Pascal, Roy. *Die Autobiographie*. Stuttgart, Kohlhammer 1965.

Pye, Lucian W. "Reassessing the Cultural Revolution." *China Quarterly* 108 (1986), 597–612.

Rojas, Carlos. "Without [Femin]ism: Femininity as Axis of Alterity and Desire in Gao Xingjian's One Man's Bible." *Modern Chinese Literature and Culture* 14, no. 2 (2002), 163–206.

Said, Edward. "Reflections on Exile." In *Out There: Marginalization and Contemporary Cultures*. Edited by Russell Ferguson, Martha Gever, and Trinh T. Minha. New York, The Museum of Contemporary Arts 1990.

Schwarcz, Vera. "The Burden of Memory: The Cultural Revolution and the Holocaust." *China Information* 11, no. 1 (Summer, 1996), 1–13.

Schwarcz, Vera. *Bridge Across Broken Time. Chinese and Jewish Cultural Memory*. New Haven and London, Yale Univ. Pr. 1998.

Shen, Andrea. "Nobel Winner Affirms the 'Self': Gao Remains Apolitical in his Approach to the Creative Enterprise." *Harvard University Gazette*, 8 March 2001.

Shisanjing zhushu. Edited by Ruan Yuan. Beijing, Beijing daxue chubanshe 1999.

Tam, Kwok-Kan. *Soul of Chaos. Critical Perspectives on Gao Xingjian*. Hong Kong, Chinese Univ. Pr. 2002.

Yang Jiang. *Six Chapters From My Life "Downunder."* Translated by Howard Goldblatt, Hong Kong, Chinese Univ. Pr. 1983.

Thurston, Anne. *Enemies of the People: The Ordeal of the Intellectuals in China's Great Cultural Revolution*. Cambridge, MA, Harvard Univ. Pr. 1988.

Vittinghoff, Natascha. *Geschichte der Partei entwunden—Eine semiotische Analyse des Dramas Jiang Qing und ihre Ehemänner* (1991) von Sha Yexin, Bochum, Projekt Verlag 1995.

Zarrow, Peter. "Meanings of China's Cultural Revolution: Memoirs of Exile." *Positions* 7, no. 1 (1999), 165–91.

Film and Music, or

Instabilities of National Identity

ROGER HILLMAN

INTRODUCTION

Time was when classical music knew its place, or places. Largely immune to cultural wars till the onset of jazz between the wars, it occupied the concert hall as a bourgeois institution, the opera house as a greater social melting pot, the drawing room as a social grace, and so on.

Classical music was drawn on by film from the outset of its history, a history of just over one hundred years, embracing nothing less than a new art form, a new technology, and a prime source of images for a century progressively dominated by the visual. Not least was the case with live accompaniment in the 'silent' era. Indeed, without the competing elements of dialogue and sound effects, music was both more exposed and more readily manipulated by the demands of the images. Reduced to a set of emotional stimuli in the cue books of Rapée and others, certain set pieces from the classical repertoire functioned as a kind of acoustic animation. Others found new moorings, which were to be highly influential in the history of the cinema (e.g., Wagner's *Ride of the Valkyries* in Griffiths' *Birth of a Nation* and its afterglow in Coppola's *Apocalypse Now*).

Largely overlapping the advent of the talkies, radio brought new possibilities of disseminating all kinds of music. And still early in the history of this new medium, Nazi propaganda left indelible fetishized imprints on chosen vehicles, as when Liszt's *Les Préludes* interrupted regular programs with announcements from the Eastern front. Such ideological demonization of particular music in turn proved a rich resource for historical allusion in the New German Cinema (see below), or in that of formerly occupied countries (e.g., the same Liszt devastatingly accompanying the central figure's own 'victory' in Forman's *Closely Watched Trains*, when he conquers premature ejaculation).

This brief overview is simply designed to establish the cultural mediation of classical music, which occurs, often in veiled form, in film. It is further veiled in scholarship; there are very few works that document this symbiosis (Flinn 2004; Hillman 2005). Yet it is clearly a key area where cultural identities are at stake in media representations. Without realizing it, the first exposure of many people to classical music now comes through sound bytes arresting attention to mobile phones. Here, the music itself barely retains any identity, as a digitalized melody without tonal or any other color, far from any cultural signifiers attaching to the music and/or its reception. What might cultural authenticity mean in such a case?

The prime focus of what follows in the 1970s and early 1980s then consciously invokes a historical stage in the use of classical music in film. In films discussed, such music is still used with national resonances, long after the excesses of chauvinism have been discredited. In retrospect this can be read as an anticipatory gesture of defiance toward three phenomena which were to proliferate in the 1990s: a) globalization (the phenomenon of the three tenors, or an Andrea Bocelli); b) the technological usurping of our choice of music; and c) an attendant increasing powerlessness over whether to have music in the first place (mobile phones; *muzak;* acoustic padding to make telephone answering machine queues endurable).

IDENTITY ISSUES: IMAGE AND MUSIC

The mix of national identity, cultural memory, and classical music can be a potent combination in film. Unlike originally composed film scores, classical music of course comes from another era, usually an era predating film as an art form, when national identity was often a burning issue. At some stages—just think of Wagner or Verdi—the music was often equated with national identity. The gradations of the music's reception are then often appealed to via the cultural memory of the cinema audience, creating an inbuilt historical dimension which is lacking, by definition, with originally composed film scores. Contravening classical Hollywood's notions of music as an accompaniment to dominant images, music both in and beyond Hollywood has attained far more independence as an integral part of the narrative, not just its adornment.

Concentrating on classical music, Royal S. Brown writes of "music's movie-like status as a major cultural provider of images" (Brown 1996, 564). When that music comes from a tradition where music itself has enjoyed cultural hegemony, as with Germany, citing music from that canon ensures a highly charged narrative device on the soundtrack of a film. At one point in Kluge's *Die Patriotin,* the viewer sees the Reichstag building but hears Haydn's *Emperor Quartet,* that is, the melody but not the orchestration of the *Deutschlandlied.* This is the vast challenge the film sets itself in looking for a positive version of Germany's past. It seeks to restore the original cultural significance of 'absolute' music, by a composer not sharing the historical baggage of a Wagner, but music nonetheless appropriated as its national anthem by a nation which came to betray its own classical tradition. In purely dramatic terms the challenge lies in moderating the apparent lack of ambiguity of the image (seat of Nazi power) through the 'positive,' original version of a melody whose acoustic significance seems hopelessly yoked to such visual domination. Is it possible, or was it in the late 1970s when the film was made, to reinvest the beauty of this music without being (perceived as being) historically revisionist? Could this melody be heard primarily as Haydn, above all in the considerable expanses of Europe once occupied by Germany?

To approach such complexity, let us first consider less fraught examples of music accompanying significant moments portraying national identity. In Peter Weir's *Gallipoli*, the Australian soldiers finally embark for their nation's rite of passage. From darkness and then floating mist emerges the procession of small boats about to land on the coast of Gallipoli, the whole mise-en-scène pointing toward this being a transition from life to death. The music to accompany this Charon-like effect is the Albinoni Adagio for Strings, and it is highly effective dramatically. Its measured rhythm and sustained minor key lend dignity to these soldiers and lift them into the realm of the mythical. Rather than historical reconstruction, this depiction is in keeping with Weir's primary concern with a myth—and not least how that myth might look after Australia's involvement in Vietnam.

By the time of Weir's film this was world music. It clearly carries none of the Italian overtones of a Verdi, so often invoked as patriotic icon in postwar Italian films. In that capacity the Albinoni matches perfectly Weir's depiction of these men as universal soldiers, whose fate transcends their historical function in the forging of Australian national identity. It may well be that no preexisting Australian music could have combined a similar dramatic mood with overtones of recognizable nationality. Weir's choice is a highly effective example of classical music used as drama/mood, without national overtones. This particular film has played a significant part in shaping Australian perceptions of a historic event (commemorated in the only Australian public holiday tied to a battle). It filtered this event through a version that is strongly anti-British: a reflection of rupturing the colonial umbilical cord that flavors many 1970s films, especially Weir's. But perhaps yet more revealing of cultural identities is the tacit acceptance that the nation was still without identifiable musical markers of that identity in its transition from British allegiance to national independence, both in retelling the historical past and in asserting the cultural present. The dilemma for expressions of German identity in the Kluge example above is here a gap in the text.

A similar mood function, but now *with* national overtones, is served by the Samuel Barber Adagio for Strings which appears throughout Oliver Stone's *Platoon*. In terms of the images it accompanies, most memorably the torching of a village, the music functions at one level as a generalized lament, focusing neither on the fate of the occupied nor the progressive bestialization of the occupiers, but incarnating both. There is a significant element going beyond the *Gallipoli* example above, and that is the overlap between the national identity of film director, music composer, and primary subject matter of the narrative. Beyond a more universal lament, this music also resonates at a domestic level, as a mid-1980s reappraisal of a turning point in the psyche of the twentieth century U.S. The musical commentary of the Barber achieves a synchronicity of a historical verdict on the soundtrack overlaid upon a visually evoked historical event. So the Adagio in *Platoon* matches in dramatic intensity the Albinoni in *Gallipoli,* but introduces a further element with its national dimension.

In European films, at least until the 1980s, German or Italian classical music has a cultural validation reserved for very few comparable examples of American music, with the Barber Adagio a notable exception. Furthermore, this status alone provides an impenetrable defence against Americanization. "The Yanks have colonized our subconscious," observes a figure in Wenders's *Kings of the Road:* images can usurp identity. But the Yanks alone could never colonize the final non-American layer of German or Italian classical composers. That conquest was reserved for global music, not an exclusively U.S. phenomenon.

In André Téchiné's *Wild Reeds* (1994), the narrative is concerned, at the public level, with France's painful withdrawal from Algeria at the beginning of the 1960s. The same Barber piece is used as background to, and commentary on, this narrative. It functions dramatically in very much the same way as in *Platoon,* and, for an Anglo-American audience, undoubtedly evokes the earlier film. Whatever the director's intentions with this choice of music, the dramatic similarity spills over (again, for an Anglo-American audience) into a political parallel. For, alongside its own Vietnam earlier in the 1950s, France's agony in withdrawing from Algeria was every bit the equivalent of the U.S.'s with regard to Vietnam. Téchiné's use of Barber evokes the historical reckoning of Stone's earlier film in his own, suggesting a further frame of cyclical world history, beyond a view of the Algerian crisis as a purely domestic issue.

Mise-en-abíme via the soundtrack is treated all too rarely in film studies. Visual allusions to earlier films are acknowledged as a powerful means of creating an additional layer of reference, both to broader history as well as cinema history, but the phenomenon just observed can be at least as powerful, perhaps more so for being 'hidden' on the soundtrack. A similar phenomenon can operate indirectly too. The composition on which Julie's late husband was working in Kieslowski's *Three Colours: Blue*—one in which she too had a hand, perhaps a major hand—was designed for a single simultaneous performance in twelve European cities. Music, supposedly functioning across national boundaries, then is viewed as crowning the new unity of the EU-member states. For Kieslowski's film music composer Preisner this would seem a nigh impossible task, as it was for the comparably weighted "Prize Song" in Wagner's *Meistersinger* (but with national rather than transnational ballast). Greater than this aesthetic challenge, however, is the shadow cast by what must be the profilmic cultural event, the *Ode to Joy* from Beethoven's Ninth. Part of a symphony appropriated by the Nazis, the *Ode to Joy* has become the supranational anthem of the European

Community, (Clark 1997, 789–807) barely half a century after its territorial-ization as a national cultural treasure. At an earlier stage of the Community's evolution, this alone would have raised fears of German domination. Preis-ner's utopian assignment is outstripped by the ideological path of his histori-cal model. A salutary reminder of how "the specific constructions of identities [. . .] are always evolving in response to changing political, ideological, and economic conditions" (Cornwell and Stoddard 2001, 2), this is an extreme example of the flexibility of cultural memory.

CLASSICAL MUSIC AS
(WESTERN) CULTURAL IDENTITY

Kubrick's *A Clockwork Orange* employs classical music as nothing less than (Western) cultural memory. The film exhibits a wide range of classical music used in various ways. The most prominent musical example is of course Alex's adoration of Beethoven's Ninth. Alex's bedroom is the setting for a demoni-cally choreographed Scherzo. The 'joke' of the movement's tempo designation has become the untamed energy of Alex's gang, the droogs, its pounding ket-tledrum beats almost an antiestablishment gesture. In this, Kubrick's use of Beethoven is on a par with Godard's use of the Rolling Stones (*Sympathy for the Devil*). Nonetheless, it is Beethoven's Ninth which Alex is subjected to in the course of his 'cure,' and its combination with concentration camp images he deems a 'sin,' the first time in the film he uses moral language without satire. However much the particular constellation of Beethoven and Leni Riefenstahl is meant to exemplify Nazi propaganda and the misappropriation of art, the symphony seems to be operating as a sort of generalized cultural memory of the West, stripping the work of those acquired nationalistic over-tones to which Kubrick is also undoubtedly alluding. Kubrick provides an unsettling amalgam of Germanic and generalized European connotations of the Ninth, all of them championed by an otherwise amoral Englishman on the margins of his own society.

Once embedded with overtones from its appropriation by the Nazis, the *Ode to Joy* melody from the Ninth became, within Kubrick's lifetime, the official anthem of the European Union. Halfway along this shift from the exclusivist national to the supranational, from German(ic) music to world music, German directors of the 1970s used this final movement of Beethoven's Ninth Symphony as a key to their core quest for identity. Even had they wanted to essay a film as idiosyncratic as Kubrick's, it is hard to conceive of a freedom such as Kubrick creates being available to their musical signifiers. For the same reason they largely avoided Wagner, of whom the history professor Rossini in Marco Leto's 1973 film *La Villeggiatura* says: "Too many irrational myths, but Verdi was ours." He thereby established an opposition that is crucial for postwar perceptions of Italian identity. The very different status of these two key composers in the cul-tural history of their respective lands is to be borne in mind as we approach.

VERDI IN ITALIAN CINEMA

When Verdi operas are used in film, past events can function as a gloss on the present. A fictionalized, heroic narrative is merged with 'real' history, which often has to be transmuted into mythology to make it heroic. Postwar Italian films in this category have a multilevel time structure. To oversimplify, the Risorgimento to which Verdi belonged functions as historical allegory for the immediate postwar situation of Italy. This second Risorgimento is in turn viewed retrospectively by directors of the 1970s and 1980s. Verdi's music, originating in the first timeframe and carrying a similar political message in the second, becomes a powerful device for cultural and historical commentary.

Independently of the treatment of the music, the Verdi myth is used in Italian cinema as a provider of national unity. Inasmuch as World War II and its aftermath are reassessed from an ever more distant perspective, the same process of image and after-image is at work in the notion of a second Risorgimento. Part of Verdi's suggestiveness evokes the myth of the Italian Resistance, an element which would not necessarily stand up to historiographic scrutiny, but which defies such scrutiny on a film soundtrack. Verdi then as reinvoked myth partly filled the void of a lacking sense of national unity and provided an uncomplicated icon of national signification, before the three tenors furthered Verdi's transition into world music.

By elevating the Resistance "into a 'Second Risorgimento' whose chief legacy was patriotism" (Bosworth and Dogliani 1999, 7), Italian cinema had the potential to manipulate public memory still further when citing Verdi on the soundtrack. Even the plots of the opera's libretti made for a convenient elision of historical ambiguities in the twentieth-century afterimage. On the one hand stood the historical Verdi's appeals for the eviction of the Austrian occupiers as the first stage of national unification (e.g., in *Attila* or *Nabucco*). On the other, the wounds of post-World War II reconstruction could be camouflaged by evoking a similar unified purpose in the wake of the eviction of an Austrian-born leader, the occupier who had also, of course, been an ally. Prominent among those Italian directors showing a nuanced approach to the dramatic, political and culturally resonant possibilities of Verdi's music have been Visconti, in *Ossessione* or *Senso*, and Bertolucci, in *Before the Revolution* or *The Spider's Stratagem*. The use of Verdi in these films clearly informs his appearance in *The Night of San Lorenzo* (Night of the Shooting Stars) (Taviani Brothers, 1982).

THE NIGHT OF SAN LORENZO
(NIGHT OF THE SHOOTING STARS)

This film continually both circles back to an Italian context and opens out that context through the use of Verdi's *Requiem*, a more open-ended cultural marker than purely operatic examples. The very nature of the text of the *Requiem* is, after all, both universal and egalitarian, and with this work Verdi bade farewell to more incendiary Risorgimento tendencies.

Other works quoted are "O Star of Eve" from Wagner's *Tannhäuser*, and the *Battle Hymn of the Republic*. Heard but once, each is nevertheless counterpointed against Verdi's *Requiem* by virtue of its implications. The *Battle Hymn* evokes another Civil War, while *Tannhäuser* traces a different path of pilgrimage and penitence. In their own *Star of Eve* scene, the Tavianis draw an analogy to the opera plot of *Tannhäuser* which extends to history, operatic history, and German-Italian history on Italian soil. The filmmakers' design undoubtedly intends the parallel between *Tannhäuser's* failure to gain absolution in Rome, and the German eviction from Rome in World War II and their retreat home up the peninsula in defeat.

The *dies irae* from Verdi's *Requiem* appears in the wheatfields sequence, the battle between the blackshirts and partisans, which engulfs a wandering group under no political banner. Under extreme duress, the little girl recites the childhood poem meant to ward off anxiety. To accompany the switch in registers to the realm of fantasy released by this acoustic talisman, a blaze of trumpets bursts forth, accompanying surreal images. A row of gladiators miraculously appears, hurling their spears at the blackshirt who has just killed the old man. The cinematic reference seems to be Kurosawa's *Throne of Blood*. The Japanese Macbeth figure succumbs to a hail of arrows from his own men, enabling the Taviani Brothers to evoke both a Macbeth other than Verdi's, and the end of Fascism executed by its former followers, the 'ideal' version of Italian history.

With the Americans and Germans having been reduced to bit parts in the course of the film, the final struggle remains an internecine affair, with brother pitted against brother. Historically, it had indeed been the case that coexisting in different parts of the north were the Germans in retreat, the advancing Allies, the blackshirts of the Republic of Salò, and the partisans. The Tavianis reduce the combatants in the decisive struggle to a confused blend of the Italian factions, for which Verdi, as an icon of Italian unification, is particularly apt. The actual battle, however, is portrayed in mythological images, for which Verdi's *Requiem* is equally appropriate—particularly the *dies irae*, the day that brings the ultimate classless society.

In this film Verdi functions as a synthesis of earlier postwar approaches, reflecting the indirect call by the Tavianis for a historical truce. Thus, the Verdi they enlist is no longer a figure of Risorgimento pathos or righteous nationalistic fervor, but rather a Baroque *memento mori*. In the pivotal battle sequence, the theatricality of the music is matched by the camerawork, as documentary is inverted into surrealism. This parallel between visual and acoustic depiction is apt for conveying the malleability of postwar Italian cultural identity. Most tellingly, the time levels evoked in this sequence transcend the all too neat first and second Risorgimento parallel, and return us to gladiatorial battles of classical legend. The Verdi myth is thus exposed as timebound after all, and indeed seems to reach something of an endpoint with this film: Daniel Schmid's *Tosca's Kiss* converges with the Tavianis's contemporary film in its leavetaking from the myth.

CODA

The amalgam of nineteenth-century German music in late 1970s German cinema frequently embodies cultural and historical discourses, in particular of the Nazi era, within films addressing contemporary issues of national identity. Viewed this way, music, once the greatest glory of the German *Geist* and a vindication of the apolitical, becomes an intensely social sign within the cultural and political concerns of these films. In an article exploring the aural "spaces of Jewish absence and memory in Germany," Leslie Morris demonstrates how

> ... by exploring the repetition of sound and the echo of memory in texts (poetic, filmic, visual) we can find, in the interstices between sight and sound, additional layers in the production and creation of memory (Morris 2001, 368 and 377).

Those interstices serve the powerful function of filtering cultural memory through multiple layers of historical reception. And this, beyond any reception of the history of such music, is confined to purely musical performances.

In German cinema of the late 1970s the *Ode to Joy* made frequent appearances on the soundtracks of films exploring issues of national identity, where its fluctuating reception enabled a further layer of historical referentiality.[1] The other work featured most prominently in these films was the erstwhile German national anthem, the *Deutschlandlied*. Filmmakers drew on its polyphonic connotations, from its origins with Haydn as a hymn to the emperor, through to its martial arrangement as "Deutschland, Deutschland über alles." (One particularly effective use was seen in the Kluge example at the beginning of this chapter.) As markers of very different aspects of German national identity, such works (not to mention Wagner's) exemplify an aspect of German cultural history of almost obsessive interest to Germans themselves, but barely approached from this angle by film studies or musicology.

Questions of cultural hegemony are also raised. Within German history the notion of a *Kulturnation*, a nation defining and representing itself through culture, survived well beyond belated unification in 1871. Within culture, music, through its supposed nonrepresentational quality, occupied the highest rung ("*die deutscheste Kunst*," "the most German art," according to Third Reich cultural politics). How do these issues look with regard to other European cultures and histories? What are the implications of Martin Jay's assertion (Jay 1993, 265) of a hierarchy of the senses whereby hearing is favored in the German hermeneutic tradition, while the French battle with a controversial interpretation of vision? Film studies has repeatedly approached scopic regimes, the issue of the cultural boundedness of visual images. Acoustic regimes are surely equally as crucial in their cultural specificity. The challenge for both disciplines, musicology and film studies, is to approach cultural identities through media representations of the acoustic. These issues have barely been theorized, and of those which have even been addressed, none has been exhausted.

NOTES

1. For the case of Beethoven's Ninth (third movement) in Fassbinder's *Marriage of Maria Braun,* see Hillman, "Narrative in Film, the Novel and Music," 188–89.

REFERENCES

Bosworth, R. J. B. and Patrizia Dogliani. *Italian Fascism: History, Memory and Representation.* London, Macmillan 1999.

Brown, Royal S. "Modern Film Music." In *Oxford History of World Cinema.* Edited by Geoffrey Nowell-Smith. Oxford, Oxford Univ. Pr. 1996, 558–66.

Clark, Caryl. "Forging Identity: Beethoven's 'Ode' as European Anthem." *Critical Inquiry* 23 (1997), 789–807.

Cornwell, Grant H. and Eve Walsh Stoddard. "Introduction: National Boundaries/ Transnational Identities." In *Global Multiculturalism: Comparative Perspectives on Ethnicity, Race, and Nation.* Edited by Grant H. Cornwell and Eve Walsh Stoddard. Lanham, Rowman and Littlefield 2001, 1–28.

Flinn, Caryl. *The New German Cinema: Music, History and Matter of Style.* Berkeley, Univ. of California Pr. 2004.

Hillman, Roger. "Narrative in Film, the Novel and Music: Fassbinder's 'Marriage of Maria Braun.'" In *Fields of Vision: Essays in Film Studies, Visual Anthropology and Photography.* Edited by Leslie Devereaux and Roger Hillman. Berkeley, Univ. of California Pr. 1995, 181–95.

Hillman, Roger. *Unsettling Scores. German Film, Music and Ideology,* Bloomington, Indiana Univ. Pr. 2005.

Jay, Martin. *Downcast Eyes: The Denigration of Vision in Twentieth Century French Thought.* Berkeley, Univ. of California Pr. 1993.

Morris, Leslie. "The Sound of Memory." *The German Quarterly* 74, no. 4 (2001), 368–78.

The Cinematic Support to

National(istic) Mythology:

The Italian Peplum 1910–1930

IRMBERT SCHENK

I.

Italy's national unification was realized in 1861 under the auspices of the king-dom of Piemont, but Rome could become the Italian capital only in 1871 when it fought off the Vatican state. (This liberation of Rome in the famous battle of Porta Pia is the subject of the first Italian 'historical film' and one of the first fictional films, *La presa di Roma*, in 1905.) The state is institutional-ized as a monarchy, not as a republic, as it was intended by the decisive bour-geois forces of the Risorgimento and the 1848 revolution. But this is only one of the problems starting with the unification. On a larger scale its date corre-sponds with the beginning oppositional split in the country, leading to an increasingly asynchronous social development in the North and South of Italy. This made the development of a unified national identity on the basis of actual conditions of life very difficult. More easily, it could be constructed by referring to a common great past, for example the antique Roman Empire, or by trying to engage in a colonialist or imperialistic expansion outside Italy. For both purposes the term *"Mare Nostrum"* became a central slogan, claiming the Mediterranean as the original hegemonic sphere of Italy in the past—and the present.

The history of cinematography in Italy starts, as in other European coun-tries, in 1895 with the *"Kinetografo"* of Filoteo Alberini. For about ten years the production is dominated by documentary and actuality films under a strong French influence. The production of fiction films is rather retarded—nearly until *La presa di Roma*. In 1907, we find nine cinema manufacturing companies, consolidating prevalent family-level organized production. In 1915 there are eighty firms producing films (centered in Turin, Rome, Milan and Napels) and 1,500 movie theaters. These numbers show the rapid increase of the Italian cinematografic economy between 1907 and 1915, which was nevertheless not based on a real industrial organization but on a more anarchic-speculative finance system with small units and with less monopolistic concentration. Due to this not very stable, but very flexible economic status, from 1908 to 1809, Italian cinematography had a greater ability to master the international crisis of the movie economy than other national cinematographies. One of its outlets consisted in the enlargement of the film length (leaving the 1-2-roler) and the concentration on the historical and monumental film genre (reaching 4,500 meters with Pastrones *Cabiria* in 1914). This facilitated its central place, not only in the Italian, but in the worldwide market, with a summit in the period from 1912 to 1915 (until Italy entered World War I in May, 1915). The other main genre was the melodrama with stories situated in aristocratic or bourgeois salons (with exquisite and decadent passions and without any realistic dimension), which generated the first kind of star system, the *divismo* (with male '*divi*' and especially with female '*dive*'). The third genre of high importance, both for the national and international markets, were the short comic sketches, the "*comiche*" (whose main comedians astonishingly came from France).

The world success of the historical and monumental genre started in 1908 with *Gli Ultimi Giorni di Pompei* by Luigi Maggi. As this picture (and the large number of its successors with the same title) was based on the worldwide popular novel "*The Last Days of Pompeii*" by Edward George Bulwer Lytton (1834), so the many *Quo Vadis?* were related to the book by Henryk Sienkiewicz (1896).[1] Other sources for these films were the legends about Roman emperors like Nero and Caesar; female rulers like Agrippina, Messalina, and Cleopatra; or figures out of popularized literature or other antique or Christian popular narrative and mythology, completed by strong men like Ursus, Spartacus, Maciste, Hercules, Saetta, Samson, and Goliath. Each film surpassed its forerunner by length, number of sensational sets, and costumes and extras in the mass scenes.

In this chapter, I will discuss the monumental-historical films of the tens, the "peplum" or "colossal," under the special interest of their support of mythology and ideology in Italy before and during Fascism. A second aspect of interest has to do with the fascination non-Italian audiences had with this genre. Even if we consider the fact that Italian cinema and the "peplum" film declined after 1918, when U.S.-American cinema took over the genre, we can nevertheless recognize that the historical saga still had a central role in cinema until today—or at least until the fifties and sixties, when the various *Quo Vadis?*— *Spartacus, Nerone, Cesare* and *Gli Ultimi Giorni di Pompei*—produced in Italy and the U.S., were projected in full cinemas as they are today on television screens in all continents.

II.

Why is it that this genre was "invented" in Italy, a genre which exerted such a strong attraction on audiences all over the world, not only during a short period, but for decades? Answers to this question unite a lot of stereotypes about Italy in general and the peplum in particular. Consisting of comments on a tendency to mere rhetoric and showiness by "the" Italians or a fundamental musicality by "all" Italians, who generate Italian opera and great spectacles, we find no statements of analytic value for our discussion (even if the indication of the opera can at least open a formal trace of tradition when looking at the spectacular *mise-en-scène* both of opera and peplum). Some stereotypes about Italy were already presented by contemporaries like the frequently quoted French director of the Eclair company, Victor Jasset, who stated in 1911 that the expansion of the Italian colossal can, on the one hand, be explained by the Italian sun and the climate in general, and, on the other, by the low cost and widespread availability of work—a far more reasonable idea because it deals with economic factors.[2] Others suppose the historical monuments spread all over Italy to be a source of inspiration for this genre. Yet, another point of view has been scarcely reflected: the fact of the incredibly vast migration from Southern Italy to Northern Italy and subsequent emigration northwards to Europe and to Northern and Southern America. Apart from the fact that film export is highly important for the amortization of the peplum production costs, to the emigrants abroad, these films could convey a sense of a unified origin as Italians (and not only as Sicilians, Apulians, Calabrians, etc.) and even a certain pride about those 'own' glorious ancestors—both a welcome support for identity construction of persons scattered over the world and normally situated in rather difficult conditions of life.

But let us return to what we can know for certain, that is, the aesthetic contributions these Italian films have made to cinematography worldwide and to the language of cinema in this period of important changes in cinema history after 1911. These films are, at first glance, "monumental" because of their length and because of the large number of actors and extras that are put in motion. Another novelty lies in their quantity and the quality standards of the scene setting. Filming so many people and so many plots needs space. A few painted sets in small studios is no longer sufficient, but stable architectural structures, large open spaces, and natural landscapes are necessary. This also requires a new idea of framing and of depth. It is the time for the invention of a real deep focus and the beginning of a more complex story structure connecting the foreground and the background. This is true for the first films, when the camera is still subjected to the rules of the central perspective of the viewer and even more so when the camera is set in motion, for example in the "Cabiria movement" (Salt 1983, 297 and 1991).[3]

The success of these films can also be called "monumental" all over the world. It is for this reason that these films are presented at inaugurations of the increasingly grand and luxurious cinema theatres from Paris to London and New York, being accompanied by large symphonic orchestras, choirs, water, and light effects.

Synthesizing the aesthetic contribution of these films to international cinema, it could be said that, in these films, for the first time the visual aspect of the cinema gains its own autonomous status and gains independence from its earlier reliance on literature and theatre. The viewer seems to be able to enjoy a new type of *Schaulust* [visual pleasure] by looking at big open spaces, and to find pleasure in these monumental stories or mythological tales which are estimated as great and magnificent, being timeless and linked to a distant past at the same time. In this process, the details and the logical progression of the plot become less important than the epic nature and the grandeur of the film representation. Nevertheless, these films are still linked to an old fixed relationship between images and textual presentation: the narration of the story unfolds in a still very static fashion, being carried out through a simple succession of pictures (like in an illustrated book), in which the action is theatrical and two-dimensional, with the main actors set in the foreground (Mitry 1967, 400).[4]

I think that the great fascination these films exert with the Italian and world public is related to these aesthetic contradictions. Apart from the epic visual expansion of the story, the fascination is, above all, grounded in the particular "realism" of the outdoor and mass scenes. Among the new mass media, cinema is particularly suitable to represent a great number of "real" men in "real" locations with "real" décors. I think that it is for this reason that the reviewers of the time, at Rome, Berlin, London, or New York, regarded *Quo Vadis?* (1913) by Guazzoni or *Cabiria* (1914) by Pastrone as a phenomena which had "never been seen before," and equate it to the "construction of a new world." Under the headline "World's Greatest Film is Screened," *Motography* portrays *Cabiria* as the most marvellous film beyond all description (Turconi 1963, 53).[5]

This realism is based on stories which are historical and mythological and thus leave plenty of space for the viewer's imagination. This also opens up the possibility of filling this space with ideological contents related to specific historical and social conditions. The pleasure of capturing wide spaces and grand stories in the darkness of a cinema can stimulate and reinforce the ideological and political receptivity of the viewer. Anticipating a point I will take up later, I would argue that here an antimodern point of view is being communicated with the most modern use of cinema, which itself is an expression of modernity.

Before focusing on my initial question (why the peplum was created in Italy), I will present some reflections about the effect it had on international audiences and the reasons for the great popularity these films enjoyed. The visual conquest of space and of history via both realistic and fabulous images inculcates a kind of unique promise to the psychology of the viewer. Dreams about force, power, and goodness incite an illusion, leading the infantile part of the ego to an adult-like matured state in which the person is capable of real actions. (It is clear that all this happens in a regressive process stimulated by cinema and by the whole cinematic apparatus.) A large part of the spectacular marvelousness of these films is therefore linked to the infantile and dreamlike mythologization of history, by which the visual "colossal" fuses with the fantasy of individual (and collective) grandeur in the head of the viewer. It is in these processes that cinema and popular culture appear so strongly linked with each other.

III.

A first approach to the question about the Italian origin of this genre should start with some considerations about ideological developments, that is to say about possible "collective fantasies of collective grandeur" and their links to concrete historical ideologies. Refering to the social and historical situation in Italy around 1900, I will restrict myself to a few synthetic notes.

As soon as Italy was unified the country began to fall apart. It was divided into a North, in which a quick industrialization took place, beginning in the 1880s (rather late in European comparison), with most significant developments occuring from 1900 until 1913 (beyond the European average level); second part, the South, was stuck in an agriculturally-based economy with very low production rates and tied to feudal structures, with large parts of the population suffering from poverty. In 1914, fifty-five percent of the Italian population was still working in the agricultural sector and only twenty-eight percent in industry (which for the most part was divided into small units). Emigration figures (mainly from the South) reached an annual average of 650.000 units between 1909 and 1913; in 1911, half of the population was still illiterate.

Such data, which I have elaborated in detail elsewhere, (Schenk 1991 and 1994) is necessary here only to remind us of the enormous social and political tensions and contradictory conditions under which these films came into existence. Contradictions not only existed between North and South, but also within each of the two areas—and among the same people. How are these conditions that dominated peasant and provincial life related to the life conditions of modernization and urbanization in a modern industrial society? How can the elements of an agricultural economy of latifundia be linked to those of industrial and productive capitalism? Given these striking inequalities in the historical formation of Italian society, taking place in an extreme synchronicity, how can one formulate a common system of norms and values and common processes of identification for the construction of a common national and historical identity?

In view of this historical situation, the explanation given by Sadoul (and many others) that *Cabiria* is the result of the colonial wars of 1911/12, which ended with the conquest of Libya and Dodecaneso, seems too simplistic. Unfortunately, these commentators neglect the fact that the earlier history of Italian colonialism and imperialism is far less glorious, the catastrophic defeat of Adua in 1896 (for which Fascists sought "reparations" in 1936) being but one example. From this we can see that heavy contradictions and uncertainties about historical identity existed.[6]

Numerous other examples for this could be found until the "lost victory" or "mutilated victory" of 1918/19, but what is important to stress here is that Italy too often was disappointed in its attempts to join the modern world powers. The approach via cinema, with its ability to convert fiction and dream into realistic images, could perhaps offer some insights into the process of negotiating these contradictions and the profound splits in the society. In the production and diffusion of ideology, cinema plays a role equally important to other agents, like the magazines *Mare Nostrum, La Grande Italia, L'Idea Nazionale,* or architectural schemes like those of the Law Courts in Rome or of the monument to Vittorio Emanuele II, as well as more symbolic cultural phenomena of the period under discussion. Notions like Mare Nostrum, the Magna Grecia, the Roman Empire, Latin civilization, Christianity, and the Italic culture, from the antique period to the late-medieval period to the Renaissance, are evoked to demonstrate historical greatness and serve as rhetorical and ideological constructions of a contemporary unity and identity—in an attempt to seal up the deep fractures and real contradictions within the individuals and in society.

This attempt initiates the creation of a new category of cinematographic mythology: the peplum, a genre in which a contemporary type of mythology is formulated and communicated by film. That this genre emerged within the new medium of film is not too surprising, because film, more than any other form of mass communication and art, can make people dream and fantasize about force and strength, historical and actual identity. There is something mysterious about this cinematic process engendered by the new aesthetic methods which enabled people to dream of being strong and good, stronger and better than the real social conditions allowed them to be. Such a perception is not restricted only to the Italian audience, but applies also to viewers all over the world who go and see these mythological Italian films. With the appearance of force and glory, cinema serves to compensate for different types of deficiencies and to mend the splits and abysses within individuals and in society.

IV.

Why not develop the idea synthesized in the formula "From Cabiria to Mussolini" and take this expression, which until now has only been used as an aphorism, in a more serious way? Even avoiding a repetition of the problematic methodological choice of Kracauer[7] (a teleologic structure built *a posteriori* on the basis of material chosen ad hoc) this kind of questioning offers the possibility of giving a positive answer for the Italian historical film. In our case we will not find an authoritarian and irrational structure of the Germans at the basis of the films, but the torn identity and national inferiority complex of the Italians. An analysis of the films would be made easier by the possibility of doing without the category of "collective unconscious" in favor of an analytical treatment of ideology which was present from 1870 until the end of Fascism. In this area we find a surprisingly coherent line on issues like Italian colonialism and imperialism, insinuating the old Roman Empire, irredentism, and interventionism.[8] Behind these "solutions" lies the attempt to hide the above-mentioned weaknesses with the creation of historical myths, while the grandeur of real historical events remains, for the most part, rather modest. Gaetano Salvemini describes the spiritual atmosphere of the Italian intelligentsia from 1870 to the First World War:

> There was the Roman Empire disease: the memory and the nostalgia of the grandeur of the Roman Empire together with an anxious yearning to carry out impossible exploits which created a sense of delusion and bitterness and led the men to demean themselves. Italy was oppressed by its past.[. . .] Absurd expectations and a constant process of self debasement are poisons which lead to persecution mania and making huge mistakes. Instead of comparing their present and their immediate past and becoming aware of the steps their countrymen were taking with heroic and silent efforts the men of the Italian intelligentsia judged the present conditions following a scale based on memories of past grandeur and impossible dreams of supremacy (Salvemini 1961, 320).[9]

The new Fascism was strengthened by the creation of myths because it could link to the ideology already present in the previous period—to the mythical dimension of the "peplum." Mussolini, a peerless rhetorician—Salvemini described his genius of propaganda as surpassing Potemkin by far (Salvemini 1967, 263)—gave the following definition of myth in 1922:

> Myth is a creed, it is a passion. It doesn't need to be reality. It creates reality in the sense that it gives it a drive and that it becomes hope, faith, courage. Our myth is the nation, our myth is the greatness of the nation![10]

The propagandistic formation of Fascist mythology refers above all to the historical periods mentioned above and starts from there, in a sort of reverse projection of this presumably glorious *Ur-Zeit* [primeval times] into its mythical order scheme for the future: the "New Italy" will form the "New Order" with the "New Man" who will provide the "organic" basis for the "New Greatness" of the Italian nation, of the future "Empire." Mussolini himself is transformed into a mythical figure by the cult of the *DUCE*, of *DUX*, or of *M*. (These icons correspond to his self-potrayal in the media iconography, but it would be an error to think that Mussolini himself created his own myth: it was produced by the intelligentsia of Fascism, on a large ideological and mythological basis, the foundations of which go back far beyond 1922). His role is the figure of a strong virile man who is a good and brave hero, a versatile sportsman and also a fan of modern technology (car and airplane pilot), soldier and general, or a diligent worker (farmer, bricklayer, miner, or ship builder). The main role, however, is that of the well-versed and all-informed intellectual, the genius man—synonym of the nation and highest incarnation of the Latin race: in a word the new Caesar and Augustus in one (of the "new civilization" and of the new third Roman Empire). At the same time he remains the "man of the people," "home-people" like Napoleon. Mussolini in this way adds new myths to old ones in order to direct himself toward modernity and modernization: "In five years Rome must appear wonderful to all the peoples of the world: vast, ordered, powerful as it was during the time of the first Empire of Augustus."[11] This process is based on old myths which have to be reactualized by new ones.[12] Congruent are German statements of the "superman" Mussolini, who expressed that "thirty centuries of history allow us to look at some doctrines beyond the Alps with a regal sense of pity."[13]

The "believe, obey, fight" motto of Fascism celebrates itself in martial forms with the required remembrance of the greatness of ancient Rome. Mussolini, on the balcony of Palazzo Venezia on the anniversary of the Empire, 9 May 1937, proclaimed in front of more than half a million of enthusiastic listeners that Italy was on the point of "completing in African soil the thousand year Italian mission to bring work and civilisation to the world."[14] There are many modernization processes of Italian society which Fascism managed to carry out and which must be taken into consideration. They are, however, far less significant than what was suggested by the mythology and propaganda.

This projective procedure can be observed also, for example, in the successful cinematic images of men and bodies, for example, the strong, muscle bound men, the *forzuti*, among the most famous: Maciste, the old-new heroes of individual and collective strength (the virility of Mussolini is part of this framework, just like Italian machismo in general).[15] Looking at divas or the female counterparts of the *forzuti*, mainly present in the second major genre of the tens, the melodrama in aristocratic-bourgeois salons, one should rather ask oneself if there is any other spectator disposition to be absorbed by the viewer, given the backward and repressive sexual ethics of Italian society. Far more interesting are the socially and sexually strong women like Cleopatra, Messalina, or the Amazons, present in the peplum films of the 50s and 60s, conveying a far more complex inner psychology.[16] At the very least they can be linked to male schizophrenic visions of woman as femme fatale/whore, in contrast to which Cabiria (with her sisters in the tens) is an innocent lamb ready to be sacrificed, waiting to be saved by a strong and good man, and to be liberated as a woman thanks to her future husband in the Roman happy ending (it is basically the old mythology of pure love and of the corresponding idealistic relationship).

V.

Until now I have tried to avoid a definition of the word myth in order to not fall into one of many traps represented by very common but very controversial definitions of the term. The intentional schematic statement of Roland Barthes ("Le mythe est une parole") (Barthes 1957, 193) might be too general, even though it suggests a new modern use of the word, in which the system of communication and discourse determines the quality of the message as a myth. At the same time the old oppositional scheme between the logical or teleological interpretation of history and rational thoughts on the one side and myth on the other is obsolete. Nor do I want to uphold an opposition between myth versus modernity or the present. If, however, myth as "the opposite of reason" can have a basic function for the existence of the individual, then I can still see valid aspects of these old definitions. On the one hand, I think that the significations of the world, interpreted in the light of the old mythical thinking, are surviving like attempts to capture "world" apart from the attempts of "logos." This also applies to the "new myths" of modernity, which are a sort of secularization of the old myths, by which ideas, people, and events are raised to an iconographic symbolic level with a great captivating power. In this sense, the myth of the cinema does not exist, but myths in cinema do, because they are cinematographic creations of mythical formations which already exist. The common functions of these definitions of myth are important for specific purposes: mastering oppressive contradictions with an order in mythical form; establishing a world order of a symbolic intuitive type (often in an iconographic sense) against fear and chaos; building a "unity" in place of what seems to be "torn apart."

From this perspective the difference between the Italian peplum of the 1910s and those of the 50s and 60s is clearly visible, just as the difference between the Italian *Schaulust* and that of the international audiences of the peplum in the silent period is: one is confronted with different phases and forms of the creation and function of myths. In the 1950s and 1960s, the presentation of old (quoted) myths and mythologies is presented playfully; it is a show which captivates because it is presented in the cinema. Its psychological function, along with the effect of the pleasures of the eye—*Augenlust,* which is obtained by the film technique—is described as typical for the genre; that is a powerful infantile hypomania—without a special national(istic) reinforcement. This will have to be specified for singular cases, but is significant for the worldwide success of the old Italian peplum. What determined the success of the novels of Bulwer-Lytton or Sienkiewicz in the nineteenth century was that the world was joined to a mythological dimension, touching on old universal archetypical mythologies of catastrophe, *finis mundi,* or the suffering history of a tribe or religious community. Yet, returning to the 1950s and 1960s, in the media game of quoting myths the strong men, for example, are joined by strong women; the rituals of battle and power are choreographed in a transparent and media-conscious way. This is also true for the organization of the representation of the foreign and the own, of good and bad and of the past. It is the evidence of medial scene settings which opens the way to a lighthearted treatment of imagined adventures of courage and force.

The situation was different for the Italian public before 1918 (and in the 1920s and during Fascism in general) with regard to peplum films. The old myths evoked here, one could call them "origin myths," narrate the origin and the strengthening of the tribe or the nation. What belongs to the distant past seems to be big, good, and beautiful and offers the possibility of projection to the difficult present. This is not confined to the content of old myths but also involves the modes of thinking of this type of collective historical fantasy. Simple expressions like "our history" or "our past," which indicate the antique strength in a mythical sense, are put into effect as significant markers. A similar process can be observed, even though in a less explicit way, with regard to the spread of Germanic myths in Germany until the Weimar Republic, which provided fertile ground for nationalistic tendencies.

V I .

As only a small part of these findings can be deciphered in the films, one has to turn to the cultural context of the social formation and their imaginations about history. Earlier, I suggested how myths served to overcome social contradictions. It is important to note, however, that one can observe an imminent rupture during this process of mythicizing: the old myths with their premodern representations and iconographies (fantasies and ingenuous tales of the actions of presumed ancestors, of their heroes and the highlights of their culture) serve to overcome problems and deficiencies on the path to the modern world. In the almost magic symbolic images of the old peplum, premodern forces were used to exorcize the dangers of the modern present. The strong men and saviors—Maciste, Hercules, Ursus, Samson, and Saetta—present a premodern muscular strength in an almost grotesque manner; they do not have the dynamism or flexibility of modern man (for example the agility of the sportsman).[17] The weakness of the viewers is projected onto these static figures like the weak national identity onto the glorious time in antiquity. This illustrates the ineffectiveness of myths as remedy, doomed to failure in real history.

We can therefore interpret the Italian peplum of the 1910s as mythological films, as films with old mythological stories which create a regression to hypomanic infantile power in a special manner; but they are also films, and that is more interesting, which in the context of the Italian culture are part of a project to construct history through the nationalistic image of national identity. I have already mentioned the intelligentia's inclination toward the past; The model of school learning and the everyday collection of anecdotes related to history, in which Roman antiquity acts as history of the contemporary nation and as national mythology, had a comparable impact.[18] This context of a myth-based definition of Italian nationality—almost an escape into the past and into mythology—shows an incredible coherence and continuity until the end of Fascism, although many historians and film historians do not want to admit this. Perhaps the irrelevance of Italian cinema in the 1920s and its lack of connection to the modernity of international cinema have something to do with this continuity and with its fixation on old genres and styles of representation. The peplum is the ideological path-breaker to Fascism, a contingent way from Cabiria to Mussolini. However, Fascism, on its way to modernity (in propaganda very tricky but in reality very obstructed), discovers the cinema as a real media power only in the 1930s.

VII.

These notes on the Italian historical-monumental films lead to some general methodological considerations. Popular cinema, as part of the modern mass media, favors the creation of myths that, in part, offer the possibility of mending historical deficiencies of identity and identification both on an individual and collective level. This aspect links them to the formation of stereotypes and renders them available for usage as propaganda instruments, in which films and genres adopt, support, and modify ideological and psychosocial dispositions. The peplum films are box office successes, a mere popular cinema for the majority of society, the less educated and subaltern. At this point, the issue of Kracauer's scheme arises again: we are confronted not only with the problem of how to define categories more precisely (like "collective unconscious," "myth," and "national identity"), but above all with the problem of providing a series of methodological frameworks for a clearer analysis of the relations between the film text and the historical cultural context. We have to ask, for example, whether the films contain, construct, and/or negotiate processes of national, individual, and collective identity or if they only present possibilities of personal identification. Can identity, in the period of modernity, be captured and fixed as an entity, or is that possible only in a mythological dimension? Where and how do film signs produce meaning and what kind of meaning is this? How important is the cinema as a social and ideological institution?

There is yet another aspect which must be reflected on in relation to popular culture. I doubt what others take for a fact, that an institutionalized official culture or ideology is always opposed or resisted by individuals as an act of a prosaic liberation. On the other hand, it seems clear that central moments of the actual *Lebensgefühl* (feeling of life) of the audience must be represented in popular films, which encourages positive aspects and weakens the negative elements of life experience. I also have some doubts that this need could be fully satisfied in the old peplum by mere *Schaulust* and psychological regression. Rather, I would think that the unifying function of the old myths could be experienced on an individual level, not only to find direction and security as a solution to the problems of individual and collective identity, but also more directly as an antidote to social unease and a repressive hierarchy of values— apart from the not-to-be-forgotten element of entertainment as a strong distraction from difficult situations in real life.

Worth considering in connection with this is the ironic voice of the viewer as the producer of the meanings of a film. How do we evaluate the reception of the film from the viewpoint of the audience—not during the experience of the films themselves, but in terms of their impact on practical everyday life. This approach fundamentally deviates from the philologist's relation with a film text (based on seeing the film as a work of art), but instead refers to the cultural context by paying attention to the everyday culture and consciousness of individuals. Developments in the apparatus-theories, which relate the symbolic system of the film to technical aspects of filmmaking, the situation in the movie theatre, and the psychic elaboration of the viewer (in terms of the Freudian "psychic apparatus"), contributed to a better understanding of the subjective perception of the film in the cinema. In connection with this, the findings concerning the specific reception of the peplum films could possibly have a more generalized validity: as a regressive type of thinking with a hypomanic tendency to fantasized ego-strength in which the viewer finds himself in a virtual subject situation which allows him to mix external and internal images in his own composition of meanings. The glance in itself becomes megalomaniacal: the viewer sees everything and constructs everything. What counts is not so much the external references of the film's images as the internal reality of his psychic experience. The identification with the camera and with the characters or the actors, established by the film theories mentioned above, seems to be integrated and subjected to the processes of psychic elaboration of repressed, actual, and past conflicts of the viewer. In this sense, cinema in general and the peplum in particular act in the same way as the old myths do: they console and help cope with the hostile present.

Notions like "*dispositif*" or "discourse formation" set up a link with social and media contexts, a link which could be specified by the various elements of the notion of ideology. Yet, this approach also continues to base analysis on the film text and, at best, merely enriches the explorations with scarce information on reception, which is mainly taken from reviews. To talk about the effects of the film or of the cinema on this thin material basis seems, at first sight, useless, but this approach is nevertheless practiced frequently.[19] In contrast to this, I prefer to situate my analysis in a context-related perspective. However, this kind of "soft" analysis, which explores the cultural practice of film viewing and its integration into everyday culture, is restricted due to the scarcity of available sources and a still rather underdeveloped methodology, not to mention the specific research problems faced in the investigation of historical contexts and reception processes.

To avoid any misunderstandings I would therefore like to emphasize that in this essay I am not proposing answers, but rather considering how the birth of the peplum in Italy could possibly be explained. This question seems a starting point for opening up more general questions: How can the creation of a film genre be explained; what is popular culture and popular cinema; what are the relations of popular culture, myth, and cultural/national identity; can identity be fixed at all in the context of modernity and postmodernity or should we speak of various layers of identifications? Elsewhere and apart from this contribution on a specific cinematic genre, I have also tried to develop some thoughts about contexts in which possibly contradictory interests and intentions of film producers and audiences are at work. This is a seemingly minor question, yet worthy of further study within historiographic research on cinema, as it opens up broader channels for cinema theory.

[Translation assistance: N. Poltorak / A. Volk]

NOTES

1. The first real colossal and worldwide success with this title was Enrico Guazzoni's *Quo Vadis?*, produced in 1912, with more than two hours of projection time. The Paris premiere was performed at the Gaumont-Palace, the largest movie theater in the world, with an original music composition by Jean Noguès and a choir of 150 persons. In London the presentation was done in the huge Albert Hall, used as a cinema; at New York the Broadway theater Astor was transformed into a cinema and opened with a triumphant performance of this film (which meant that cinema had finally entered Broadway). In Berlin the film opened at the brand new Cines-Kinotheater at the Nollendorfplatz.

2. Jasset, "Retour au réalisme," *Ciné-Journal,* 21 Oct.–25 Nov. 1911; quoted in M. Lapierre, *Anthologie du cinéma,* Paris, 1946, 89.

3. Salt is speaking about the *Cabiria* movement as "tracking shots" on nearly static scenes, which then will be imitated in Scandinavia and the U.S. For the "movements" in Cabiria see, more recently, E. Dagrada, A. Gaudreault, T. Gunning, "Lo spazio mobile del montaggio e del carrello in Cabiria."

4. Mitry consequently (especially for the first peplum films) speaks of illustration instead of narration.

5. The German Malwine Rennert writes in her review in "Bild und Film" about *Cabiria:* "This film drama in its wideness and depth is equivalent to the Greek drama." Quoted in Diederichs, *Anfänge deutscher Filmkritik,* Stuttgart, 1986, 109.

6. Needless to mention other colonial failures like in Tunisia and Egypt in 1881-82, Dogali in 1887, or China in 1899.

7. I am referring to Siegfried Kracauer's famous *From Caligari to Hitler* (© 1947), Princeton, 1966.

8. Even if it is necessary to consider the economic productive causes and the autonomous mechanisms that explain the evolution of a genre, it nevertheless seems amazing that there is a high concentration of colossals about Roman history exactly in the years from 1912 to 1914, which is right after the conquest of Libya and the first decision to follow an interventionist policy. For the ideological background of the historical monumental films above all see G. P. 1993, 160 ff. In a lot of American peplum films, in contrast to the Italian films, being Roman is seen in a negative light; see Quargnolo, 1963.

9. Salvemini, but also other writers up to Gramsci, expressed themselves with even more force, in relation to the discussion on the "questione meridionale," on the problem of the southern intellectuals who are not only overrepresented in state administration but also have an important role in the communication of culture and ideology. (The notion of the "intellectual" refers to those active on a medium level in the mediation of culture such as teachers, professors, priests, lawyers, employees, etc.)

10. *Opera Omnia di Benito Mussolini,* ed. E. and D. Susmel, vol. XVIII, Florence, 1956, 457 (from "Il discorso di Napoli," Naples, Teatro San Carlo, October 24, 1922).

11. *Opera Omnia di Benito Mussolini,* vol. XXII, 48 (Rome, Campidoglio, 31 December 1925, during the taking of the oath of the first governor of the Urbe, F. Cremonesi).

12. With reference to this point one ought to reevaluate the contribution of Marinetti and the Italian futurism movement to the celebration of force and heroism in a modernist context.

13. *Opera omnia di Benito Mussolini,* vol. XXVI, 318. Mussolini claims to have read Nietzsche in German when he was young. Regarding the Italian image of the 'superman,' see the contribution of D'Annunzio above all.

14. *Opera omnia di Benito Mussolini,* vol. XXVIII, 171.

15. For the relationship between the *forzuti* of Italian silent films, Mussolini, and the Fascist movement, see Brunetta, 1979, 88 ff., M. Dall'Asta, 1992. See also Renzi, 1992 and A. Farassino, "Maciste e il paradigma divistico," in Bertetto, *Cabiria e il suo tempo.* The conclusion that is suggested by Antonio Costa (relating to the work of Dall'Asta) seems to be very interesting: "Indeed one can consider the mythology of the Forzuti to be a popular version of the Dannunzian myth of the superman." A. Costa, "Dante, D'Annunzio, Pirandello," in Renzi, *Sperduto nel buio,* 64.

16. For an analysis of the peplum in the fifties see also M. Lagny, "Popular Taste: The Peplum," in *Popular European Cinema,* ed. R. Dyer and G. Vincendeau.

17. The static muscle bound man is made an object of caricature in a certain way in the figure of Za-la-Mort in the serial *I topi grigi* by Emilio Ghione, also for the effect of the background made up of poor environment presented in a very realistic way. Ghione also had had experience with a historical (nationalistic) film and, after 1922, he quickly transformed himself and became a Fascist militant. I cannot follow the formal analogy of Renzi who sees "a 'double' of the young Mussolini" in the character of Za-la-Mort; see Renzi, "Il Duce, ultimo divo," in his *Sperduto nel buio,* 134.

18. In an article which announces the Neapolitan première of *Cabiria* (planned for the Teatro S. Carlo and then carried out in the Teatro Mercadante) one finds as a secondary but absolutely undouted notion the following lines in the description of the plot: "Silent and tragic synthesis of the most glorious period of our history." (*La Cine-Fono,* La rivista fono-cinematografica, VIII, no. 278 (1914), 15–16; the article is signed by Keraban). This corresponds to the common idea of history. Also, famous writer Matilde Serao talks of the film in *Il Giorno* in her elegant eulogy of *Cabiria:* "And all the most indifferent, most sceptical, the biggest grumblers, will have to admire, will admire what poetic greatness, will extend the measures of a normal showing and make *Cabiria* something exceptional: like a wise union, like a vast union of a graceful and tender story of pure love, of a powerful history of passions, together with the highest

events of the epic battle between Rome and Carthage. Those terrible epic wars, from which heroic names have exalted our youth from Attilio Regolo to Scipione l'Africano, to Caio Duilio and in which the names of two soldiers of Carthage, Amilcare Barca and Annibale his son, who was called the sword of Carthage, awoke such admiration in us." Quoted in *La Cine-Fono* 280 (1914), 49.

19. Thus the study of contemporary reviews of the historical-monumental films of 1913–1914 hardly provides any direct illumination for my thesis. Looking at *Cabiria* I have analyzed the Italian film magazines of the period (in which the reviews of major newspapers are often reprinted). They have in common the satisfaction to finally be able to celebrate these films and cinematography in general as an "Art" ("new artistic film," "let us shout out the word 'Art' in a loud voice," "Cinematography is a new form of Art"), using D'Annunzio and the high-class audience and the *mise-en-scène* of the cinema event itself as legitimation. There is no nationalistic use of history, but there are a lot of references, on the other hand, about the "natural" link of current Italian history with Roman antiquity, which evidently should be obvious and normal for all Italians. For our arguments on the use of myths therefore, the field of analytic reference is the context of the reception, the cultural climate which promotes the formulation of identity processes and the construction of a national history. In this kind of *soft historiography of culture* this also applies to the film text: the formal organization and the manner of thinking linked to the plots are far more interesting than the direct, manifest content of the film. What the (lingustically and visually bombastic) inter-titles of D'Annunzio say and *how* they do it, can be even more interesting if compared with his contemporary colonialist and interventionist arguments or his later pamphlets for Fiume. For example, "Dalmatia belongs to Italy by divine and human right: for the grace of God who styled the earthly figures so that each lineage would recognize his destiny carved in his features. [. . .] Who could ever give value to the force of the barbarians against the law of Rome?" Quoted in D. Mack Smith, *Storia d'Italia 1861–1958*, vol. II, Bari, 1965, 505 ff.

REFERENCES

Barthes, Roland. *Mythologies*. Paris, Éditions du Seuil 1957.

Brunetta, Gian Piero. "Problèmes de la fascisation du cinéma italien dans les années 20." *Les Cahiers de la Cinémathèque* 26–27 (1979), 87–97.

———. *Storia del cinema italiano. Il cinema muto 1895–1929*, vol. 1. Roma, Editori riuniti 1993.

Costa, Antonio. "Dante, D'Annunzio, Pirandello." In *Sperduto nel buio. Il cinema muto italiano e il suo tempo (1905–1930)*. Edited by R. Renzi. Bologna, Capelli 1991.

Dagrada, Elena, André Gaudreault, and Tom Gunning. "Lo spazio mobile del montaggio e del carrello in Cabiria." In *Cabiria e il suo tempo*. Edited by P. Bertetto and G. Rondolino. Milano, Il castoro 1998.

Dall'Asta, Monica. *Un cinéma musclé*. Crisnée, Editions Yellow Now 1992.

Diederichs, Helmut. *Anfänge deutscher Filmkritik*. Stuttgart, Fischer und Wiedleroither 1986.

Dyer, Richard, and Ginette Vincendeau, eds. *Popular European Cinema*. London, New York, Routledge 1992.

Farassino, Alberto, and Tatti Sanguineti, eds. *Gli uomini forti.* Milano, Mazzotta 1983.

———. "Maciste e il paradigma divistico." In *Cabiria e il suo tempo.* Edited by P. Bertetto and G. Rondolino. Milano, Il castoro 1998.

Lapierre, Marcel. *Anthologie du cinéma.* Paris, La Nouvelle Editions, 1946.

Mitry, Jean. *Histoire du cinéma,* vol. 1, 1895–1914, Paris, Éditions universitaires 1967.

Mussolini, Benito. *Opera omnia di Benito Mussolini.* Firenze, La Fenice 1956 (vols. XVIII, XXII, XXVI, XXVIII).

Quargnolo, Mario. "Le due Rome nel vecchio cinema." *Bianco e nero,* a. XXIV, no. 3 (1963), 24.

Renzi, Renzo, ed. *Il cinema dei dittatori.* Bologna, Gratis 1992.

Salt, Barry. *Film Style and Technology: History and Analysis.* London, Starword 1983.

———. "The Early Development of Film Form." In *Film before Griffith.* Edited by J. L. Fell. Berkeley, Los Angeles, London, Univ. of California Pr. 1983.

———. "Un'analisi stilistica del primo cinema italiano." In *Sperduto nel buio. Il cinema muto italiano e il suo tempo (1905–1930).* Edited by R. Renzi. Bologna, Capelli 1991.

Salvemini, Gaetano. "Lezioni di Harvard: L'Italia dal 1919 al 1929." In *Opere di Gaetano Salvemini, VI: Scritti sul Fascismo,* vol. 1. Milano, Feltrinelli editore 1961.

———. *Preludio alla seconda guerra mondiale.* Milano, Feltrinelli editore 1967.

Schenk, Irmbert. "Die Anfänge des italienischen Monumentalfilms." In *Fischer-Filmgeschichte,* vol. 1. Edited by H. Korte and W. Faulstich. Frankfurt a. M., Fischer TB 1994.

———. *Der italienische Historienfilm von 1905 bis 1914,* Bremen, Univ. Bremen 1991.

Turconi, Davide. "I film storici italiani e la critica americana dal 1910 alla fine del muto." In *Bianco e Nero,* a. XXIV, nos. 1–2 (1963), 43 f.

Their Master's Voice?
The Coverage of Intifada II on
Israeli Television

TAMAR LIEBES

September 11 has transformed the world and caused me to rethink this essay. I was going to present a local case study—the Israeli case—in order to analyze the transformation undergone by media between the time of the first Intifada (one decade ago) and the present (ongoing) one. I argue that the transformation in the Israeli media environment during the 1990s, from national media, "ours," to a more globalized, commercial model, and the Israeli acknowledgment that the other side—the Palestinians—have a legitimate point of view, had a major impact. Whereas in Intifada I the media were mostly Israeli and mostly kept out, in the present military struggle they became a central actor. The media, local and foreign, all but dictate military strategy and the local and global images of the war have become arbitrators in a struggle in which neither side can win.

After September 11, 2001, my local case refused to stay local, and I have come to see it as a metaphor for global change. One decade ago, when Israel, equipped with rubber bullets, was fighting Palestinians armed with rocks and Molotov bottles, the U.S. was fighting the Iraqi army in the Gulf with M15s and smart bombs (Liebes 1997). The two wars (a thousand years apart in terms of military technology) still had some things in common. In both, the two sides were not equal, the fighting zone could be sealed off, the media at home were committed to the national mission, managed by the government and the military (at least as long as the fighting continued), and the phenomenon of television transmitting across borders was yet in the bud (with CNN joining the Schwarzkopf briefings, with networks such as *BBC World* and *Al Jezeera* and *Abu Dabi* yet to be born. The few exceptions of getting a glimpse of what "we" do to the other side, in the Gulf and in the Intifada, caused an outcry in public opinion at home. Recall Peter Arnet's broadcast from the Baghdad bunker, and the one-of cases in which telescopic cameras of the BBC and ABC captured pictures of Israeli soldiers beating up Palestinian prisoners. In the U.S., Arnet caused a fierce debate about the bombing (and about the legitimacy of screening what may well be enemy propaganda). In Israel a number of officers and soldiers were court-marshalled for what was labelled "deviant" acts.

In hindsight, TV's shift from marginality in Intifada I a decade ago to becoming a central actor in the second round in the fall of 2000, may be seen as a miniature demonstration of the dramatic change undergone by world media. I propose to first examine the Israeli case, and then look at the much larger mirror image of this switch in the two American wars, parallel in time—the first fought under the umbrella of tame media sounding their master's voice, to the 2001 War against Terror fought in the constant glare of omnipresent images, on redundant channels, fiercely competing over viewers, constraining their former masters to play by the new rules.

A dual comparison along time, and from an insider's and outsider's perspective, will be useful for pointing out the positive and the negative potential of the new globalized media during times of war.

The first round of the Palestinian Intifada, at the end of the 1980s, marked the coming of age of the first Palestinian generation born after Israeli occupation (following the Six Day War of 1967). The daily humiliation the Palestinians suffered under an occupying army erupted in mass, often violent, demonstrations (Schift and Ya'ari 1990), viewed by Israelis on the single public television channel. TV's coverage of Intifada I did the job of rallying the Israeli public around the way in which the conflict was handled, making sure there would be no suffering of any dissonance about which side was right. The conditions for the containment of the violent struggle were easy. TV's schedule was never interrupted for anything less than a surprise attack (such as the Yom Kippur War). The lack of equipment made it difficult to broadcast from the field, and almost impossible to broadcast live, and the military had control over the "fighting zone," keeping Israeli and foreign correspondents out. The only glimpse of the action was provided by the channel's evening news, and the reports were short, tightly edited, with low key framing (*unrest in the territories,* was the lame caption for the first five months of rioting).

Skirmishes between rioters and the military on TV showed Palestinians only as a threatening mob seen from a distance. Palestinian fighters were demonized as an anonymous mass of wild, shadowy figures. Their faces covered with *kafias* to hide their identity, they looked disorganized, hysterical, wild—brandishing flags, shouting abuse, hurling rocks, and lighting fires.

The portrayal of the human damage to the Palestinians was excised out of the frame. Cumulative accounts of the death toll were rare; Palestinian victims often remained nameless, "hit by fire" of unspecified Israeli army origin. There were far fewer casualties on the Israeli side, but the killings, the suffering, the funerals, the relatives in hospitals, belonged to "our" side only. Voice was given only to authority figures on the Israeli side—mostly military commanders in the field or in the studio, interviewed following the day's event.

Geographically and physically contained, the Intifada riots, did not cause an existential breakage within the Israeli collective. Public debate on TV could be limited to the tactical level of 'which means would be most effective' (Hallin 1997). Coverage hardly ever dug deep into the roots of the uprising, or into the self-inflicted damage of conquering another people. Thus, public TV had the attention of Israelis, but failed to use its position as the society's shared arena to show the daily suffering and humiliation that led to the violence or to frame the large policy issues raised by the Palestinian uprising.

Since the first Intifada, Israeli society has undergone major changes. For one, with the Oslo agreements, Israelis have come to accept that the two sides have legitimate points of view. Mainstream society has become hedonistic and individualistic, and a deep longing for "normalization" set in, apparent in the competing start-ups and an increase of people dropping out of military reserve duty. One indication is the dramatic decrease in the level of TV news viewings—from about sixty to seventy percent of Israelis watching the daily evening news in the beginning of the 90s to ten to twenty percent by the summer of 2001 (Liebes 2002).[1]

Intifada II followed Israeli Prime Minister Ehud Barak's failure to achieve a peace settlement in Camp David in the summer of 2000. This time around the Palestinians defined themselves as a movement of liberation, and the struggle took the shape of a guerrilla war of the kind that Israel is somewhat familiar with from the struggle of the Zionist-Jewish community, via its military underground movements against the British Mandatory government.

Censorship and restricted access were no longer options, as the violence could not be sealed off, and the home front was no less risky or volatile than the military front. The 1990s media revolution in Israel transformed the one channel monopoly into an environment of a multiplicity of mostly commercial channels that cross national borders. The implications are that Israelis acquired access, via cable satellite and internet, to the news of major international channels, and that Israel's privatized TV channels adopted global practices. Third, domestic TV channels are now better equipped to transmit from the various scenes of action, live and in parallel.

In this new environment, TV is less directly dependent on government, and more aware of the viewers' new capacity to zap among an abundance of channels offering alternative coverage of what goes on in the fighting, in the form of an escape into another melodrama, slightly less close to the skin. The Palestinian have their own TV channel and the Israeli government cannot control channels such as *Al Jazeera* and *Abu Dabi*, modeled after CNN, and providing massive support to the Palestinians, which also offer Israeli Arabs a new model for (Pan Arab) identity (Ajami 2001).

This multiple bubbling chaotic media scene enables public figures to maneuver among conflicting identities by conveying different messages to different target audiences. They also create confrontations over identities among channels. As nobody can stop unauthorized viewers from overhearing (or overwatching), editors can present and confront politicians with their own words, directed to the enemy. In an incident demonstrating this swift change of identity to fit in with the target audience, Israeli *Channel Two*'s evening news taped and aired an interview shown that afternoon on *Abu Dabi* television, in which Taleb A Sana, an Israeli Knesset member, representing Israel's Bedouin community, talked about a terrorist attack on Israelis in a Tel Aviv street earlier that day. On their own evening news, the Israeli public saw A-Sana expressing "our" support for the attack. Called to accountability by the Israeli anchor (less than two hours after his appearance on the *Abu Dabi* channel), the issue focused on identity. *Channel Two*'s anchor responded to A-Sana's "*we (support)*" with: "Mr. A Sana, you said 'we.' First of all, I don't know who 'we' is?" and the woman co-anchor reinforces the question with, "Perhaps you should really tell us who IS this 'we'?" (meaning, "do you regard the Israeli Arab community as Israelis or as Arabs, identifying with the terrorists who shoot Israelis")? And the answer in this case is—depends on the channel, depends on the target audience. (In *The War against Terror* this becomes quite common). The question which followed—"(Or) Did you think we will not see you?"—touches on the illusive qualities of the new media environment, in which segmented channels targeting a specific population constitute an invitation for identity shifts (all the more so in conflict). At the same time, these channels are not insular, and therefore accessible to anyone who cares to watch. In this (virtual) reality, playing around with identities becomes a dangerous game.

Geared by the year 2000 to addressing viewers as individuals seeking entertainment, not to a public with collective concerns, Intifada II presented Israeli TV with the task of taking over a collective in crisis. Unlike former wars, for Israelis it was a struggle with no mission and with no heroes to rally around. Left was only the shared empathy with the suffering—mostly that of the Israeli victims and their families, but also with the Palestinians. Following terrorist attacks, Israelis get to know the victims, are shown the family photo albums, and hear once again that "only if" ("she/he/they . . . had not taken that bus . . . , driven at that moment . . . , come home earlier . . ."). The killing is seen as a strike of fate, not as something that could have been prevented. At the same time, as the two sides were killing each other during the first year of the Intifada, Palestinian voices were frequently heard on radio and TV (to increasing protest of the government, the military, and some ordinary people), and a number of Palestinian leaders became well known figures. Palestinian Israeli reporters (Suleiman A shafi, Majdi Hallabi)[2] covered the Palestinian side (showing the suffering and the damage after Israeli attacks, and on daily life). This time around the Palestinians had a presence in the Israeli public space.

A look at the way in which external media (mainly American) portrayed the first and second Intifada shows that, in Intifada I, the need to tell a "balanced" and human story resulted in greater attention to the weak, the underdog.

After a skirmish, the reporter went home with the Palestinians, not the Israelis; the cumulative toll of Palestinian deaths was a characteristic opening line in many American items on the Intifada; American TV personalized the Palestinians, by showing the human consequences on their side and looking for activists to present the conflict from their point of view. The David and Goliath frame was chosen (reversing the one-time image of the state of Israel at the 1948 war as David overcoming the Arab Goliath).

In the second Intifada, external media could not be separated easily from the Israeli media as they are interconnected, and as, on the whole, the practices of the Israeli media are not that different form those of the world media. Yet, global media's overall correct framing of the Palestinians as underdogs created a selection process for producers not to deviate from that perception, that is, from what audiences were supposedly looking for.

In former wars, the claim that TV's framing of war played an important part related to national media sensing a budding change in public opinion and reinforcing it (Alexander 1981; Hallin 1997). In the present context, the electronic media, in countries which played the role of observer, not participant, (and who cater to their own publics), that is, the U.S. and Europe, are upgraded from spectator only to arbitrator.

Looking at the world through telescopic lenses, world media has the potential of showing any specific (violent) event as "proof" or "evidence" that—the war, the violence, not reaching a ceasefire—is "our" fault. And it is sufficient for political leaders to *believe* that public opinion is impressed (or taken in) by certain images, for the images to influence policy. Thus, the idea that public opinion "does not tolerate" a certain behavior can bring about international intervention (by the UN, or the U.S., or NATO), regardless of whether or not it is the case. As the decision to intervene in a local conflict depends increasingly on TV images, the choice of images becomes particularly significant; and the more gruel the image, the higher the chance of taking action.

It should be emphasized that it is also important that such a potential exists as it ensures that participants in ongoing conflicts exercise some kind of self-control. And in the long run, ensuring that the cost in human damage to the other side remains a strategic consideration is important for the sake of the countries (Israel in the Intifada, the U.S. in September 11) which are at war.

Media representation is of particular significance in the case of the Palestinian-Israeli struggle, as it is one in which no side can win on the ground, and in which there can be no total surrender. Winning in this case means scoring points in international public opinion. Contrary to wars such as the Gulf or the Falkland, in which the perpetrators managed to control the media, the Palestinian-Israeli war is one step further in a line of local wars in which media play a crucial role. There is no clear target on the ground, there is no way of keeping the media away, and thus (until September 11) the battle over El Aksa enters into world media. And as in the cases of the starving children in Somalia, or the suffering of refugees in Cossovo, TV around the world shows personalized pictures of death, injury, human brutality, and suffering, their naked self-explanatory images sending an emotional, universally understood message, excised out of any relevant sequence of events, or of any political context. Having shaped the political game to be compatible with the way in which media conceive their viewers, they are now shaping war itself to arouse the involvement of the global TV audiences.

If winning equals winning the battle over international public opinion, and if public opinion equals television, then television equals images of trampled-on humanity and/or inhuman brutality on the little screen. The result of this equation is that the most popular depictions of Intifada II from day one (on front page news, TV, and cyberspace) made it look like a war of murdered children and (better yet?) babies.

Out of the daily coverage, only very few images "take," that is, conquer the world, as they are purchased by channels the globe over, and repeatedly recycled. The power of such metonymic representations, turned into symbols, lies in their telling a story that ostensibly needs no words, in their immediately recognizable molested humanity, and/or in their brutalizing inhumanity. Even if the truism that a picture is worth a thousand words does not always hold (Michael Schudson claims that American public opinion took as long to shift to opposing the war in Vietnam as it had taken to turn against the war in Korea), these are the instances in which pictures are most effective. And their self-explanatory quality is particularly useful for viewers who are ignorant of the context.

In the fall of 2000, two images, one from each side, competed for the status of the emblematic horror of Intifada II. One depicted the dying moments of Muhammad A-Dura, a child caught with his father in an exchange of fire between Palestinians and Israeli soldiers at Netzarim Junction (close to Gaza) on October 1. There is no evidence in the picture as to which side the killers came from, and the results of an investigation conducted by the military were inconclusive,[3] but the child is presumed to have been killed by Israeli soldiers. The runner-up (the "Israeli answer" in terms of presenting its own plight to the world), is an image taken from the lynching of two Israeli soldiers in a Palestinian police station in Ramalla (on October 12), less than two weeks following the Dura killing. The fragment shown by the camera is of a body being tossed out of a second floor window and being molested by the mob waiting underneath.

A-Dura's image has turned into giant journalistic scoop. Like anything that makes it in the hype-world of media, it was being shown everywhere in no time, its glory lasting for days, even longer. It was fitted into news promos, becoming familiar to TV viewers the world over, and providing the answer to "Who's The Cruelest Of Them all?" The lynching of the two Israelis was a dud.

Why? Aesthetically (if you forgive the term), in terms of the immediate appeal to viewers, the Dura story provided a complete, coherent, sequence of the visual images that encapsulated the human tragedy, in comparison to the few segmented and blurred images from which the lynching had to be reconstructed. The effect of the lynching was also reduced by the Israeli military (still not fully aware of the relative importance of the battle of images compared to the battle on the ground), hurrying to retaliate, leaving only a narrow "window of opportunity" for the lynching pictures released to penetrate into the global screens. Sure enough, the footage of the Israeli reprisal, that is, the bombing of Gaza, took over world screens before the lynching had time to sink in.

But the deeper reasons for the incontestable power of the Dura image are the ways in which it fits with the expectation of world public that (correctly) sees the Palestinians as the underdog. I should add that the Israeli media assumed that the Israeli audience would be similarly moved. Israeli TV repeated the pictures, interviewed Dura's father in the hospital, and Israel's most popular daily (*Yediot Aharonot*) chose to bring together Dura's parents with the parents of a girl killed in a terrorist attack in Tel Aviv for the central story of the Independence Day issue.

The victory of the Dura image over the lynching is not necessarily obvious. It could be argued that the evocative power of the lynching images is enhanced as audiences see the falling body through the eyes of the gleeful mob. In addition, it is not 'closed' (i.e., not 'pornographic'), in the sense of Barthes's (1980) argument about photographs of that kind (in which, he claims, the horror has been all laid out for us by the photographer). In this case the image has a certain ambiguity, provided by the background of the man in the window, in which blurred dark figures are insinuated. A psychoanalytic analysis would posit that this uncertainty, with its demand that viewers complete the picture in their imagination, moves the look away from the voyeuristic pornographic attractions to awed and disturbed curiosity (Kampf 2001).

Why then did the lynching of the two Israeli soldiers not resonate with viewers, in spite of the evidence that (unlike in the case of Dura) the killing was intentional and, in spite of the grueling mass celebration following the murder, in which the participants immersed their hands in the blood? The answer is simple—the atrocity was carried out by the weak side. As Toni Morisson tells us, "lynch" is an act carried out by the stronger group—the whites reinstate order after the rape of a white woman by a black man. The same act carried out by the oppressed group would be seen as a legitimate act.

Regardless of the inherent power of the images, which viewer and researcher can judge for themselves, both are only partially aware of the extent to which the battle over rival images is conducted not only upfront but also behind the scenes. The framing of Muhammad A-Dura's killing as evidence of the Israeli army's brutality was challenged by Israeli spokespersons after it was shown. Israeli officials responded by accusing the Palestinians of "sending children to the front in order to cynically use their death for propaganda." It may have been a poor defence. But it was said publicly, and its validity could therefore be considered and challenged (NBC correspondent Martin Fletcher reported about calls to parents on Palestinian TV news to take their children away from the toys to become *shaheeds* in battle). The Palestinian attempts to contain the damage of the lynching were conducted behind the scenes, before the images were ever aired. To prevent the transmission and airing of the pictures, Palestinians censored the video footage taken by foreign reporters, not hesitating to threaten, even with death, professionals who are doing their job (Barnea 2000). The pictures of the lynching were aired only due to the insistence of an Israeli crew member, working for Italian TV, who shamed RAI into showing them (by using the argument of the need to "balance" the Dura story). While, in the treatment of local and foreign reporters, Israel is generally committed to the norms practiced in western countries, the Palestinians have no qualms about twisting their arm. At the same time, they also understand how global TV works and exploit the readiness of countries all over the world to show pictures of extreme human brutality or suffering. But, in addition to the fear of Palestinian revenge, The RAI editor was reluctant to air the lynching because he catered to the overwhelming support of Italian public opinion for the Palestinian cause. This is another clue to the argument that editors try to show publics only what is expected to reinforce their existing attitudes. In other words, no dissonant notes, only news they already know.

It should be noted, then, that the RAI example raises questions about global images on TV. It demonstrates that behind the airing of what looks like authentic, human images, seemingly speaking for themselves, there may be a process of selection and editing which has little to do with professional decisions. Under the guise of reporting the conflict as they see it, TV producers may prefer not to expose or challenge countries that censor their transmission, ending up offering a one-sided coverage of war. Moreover, their coverage of conflict may be constrained by the sympathies they ascribe to their public, causing a reluctance to let in any dissonant notes.

An examination of the part played by Israeli media in the first and second Intifada highlights central attributes that are found in the much larger phenomenon of the performance of U.S. media during the Gulf War vis-à-vis their performance a decade later in the campaign against terror. These twin comparisons of media at war, in a tiny state and in the world's super power, at two points in time, demonstrate how the pendulum has swung. The national U.S. media of the Gulf, overloyal and subservient, were kept out of the field and spoon fed with official briefings that were self-serving, inaccurate, sometimes wishful, and often wrong. By the time Bin Laden struck, they had turned into a more neutral, more independent, more commercialized media, operating in a multichannel, international environment, uncertain about whether and how to adapt their routine practices to the besieged post-Twins U.S.

The military strategy of the U.S. in the Gulf War, and of Britain in the Falkland, two countries at war far away from home, included keeping the media out. (In hindsight, American journalists publicly deplored their uncritical acceptance of the military briefs.) Once the Gulf War started, the American networks excised the Iraqi enemy out of the picture, except for Saddam Hussein

as its evil symbol. The Gulf War briefings of air attacks in the form of computer games, devoid of human consequences, had the effect of sanitizing the
technology of destruction. American TV adopted the President's rhetoric of a
just war, fought on moral grounds, with Saddam Hussein as present-day
Hitler, demonized by the emphasis on the horrible weapons and elite units he
was keeping in reserve for some mythical showdown. Following their government's line, Americans *inflated* the Iraqi threat, just as Israeli television, following their official line during Intifada I, *minimized* the Palestinian threat.

On its face, the War against Terror should have mobilized national solidarity in the U.S. and in the West far beyond the emotional support that
Operation Desert Storm enlisted, but in the new media environment enlisting
support is not automatic. The tension between what the government considers
its strategic needs and the practices taken for granted by media keeps popping
up. The stress shows time and again in cases such as the government's resorting to childish excuses to stop the broadcasting of Bin Laden's tapes. The first,
you recall, was aired as soon as it hit the channels and given the royal treatment of (unpaid) advertising—no editing, no adversarial questioning, a privilege no American politician could expect. The tension between administration
and the media showed also in the Pentagon's suggestion to CNN to give less
extensive coverage to the suffering of Afganistanis. Or in the White House
turning to Hollywood to start a public relations campaign in answer to what
was considered Bin Laden's effective media campaign.

Unlike at the time of the first Intifada and the Gulf War in 1991, the second Intifada and war in Afganistan in 2001 have to take account of the new
global media environment (in which CNN transmits live, around the clock,
from everywhere, getting pictures from *Al Jazeera* and *Abu Dabi*), and of the
new norms, which include listening to the other side and showing the suffering of the enemy's innocent victims. The new constraints have caused coverage
of "our" war to become more reflexive and less one-sided, and the knowledge
that images of human damage on the other side would filter through has a
direct impact on the war strategy (recall the food delivered for the Afganistanis by American planes or the Israeli military giving soldiers cameras so as to
counteract Palestinian allegations).

In conclusion, the media's role in the first days after September 11 has
called into question the traditional role of media, following a surprise military
attack on "our" nation. When an enemy strikes, media is expected to bring
home the immediate news but also to switch from its routine tasks in order to
take charge of the country's emotional state. Following a collective trauma,
media become a transitional object everybody turns to provide ontological
security (Silverstone 1994). They serve as links to the imagined community,
gathering the nation for an electronic town meeting to reaffirm "our" collective
identity, to reassure us that "we" are united, that justice is on our side and that
we will overcome. This is the moment to remind us (dare I say that?) of our
patriotic feelings.

Once the initial shock has been overcome, once the ritual mourning has provided closure, once some of the belief in ourselves is restored, media may return to the job of asking the difficult questions, challenging policymakers and giving voice to a broad spectrum of opinions, provocative as they may sound. But what was taken for granted in former wars is now being challenged. Today's media, globalized and commercial, represent themselves as neutral and independent, a self-image which is opposed to the idea of a committed national media.

The present media climate, however, has freed critics from day one to announce that the attacks were "our fault." The religious right (Gerry Falwell) attributes the attacks to abortions (just like Ultra Orthodox Rabbis in Israel attribute Palestinian killings to girls serving in the army). Sophisticated left wing critics (and media scholars), did not wait for the missing to be declared dead before calling the Bin Laden attack an opportunity for media to peep through the cracks into the way the system really works, and to understand where we went wrong.

The latter criticism is a variation on the (insightful) model offered by sociologists Molotch and Lester (1974), according to whom accidents or scandals are the moments in which the political establishment loses control, and thereby provides cracks in the routinely opaque system. Adopting this approach to the attack on the Twin Towers means that, in the hours in which everyone was waiting to see whether the U.S. was going to disappear, the media should have taken the opportunity to point to the failures in the system. Were the Twins constructed against the instructions of the building code? Were the fire brigade officers trained to guard property, not lives? (One would have preferred not to call it "an attack," but "revenge.") And the U.S. striking back became a good example of exploiting the opportunity for conquering oil fields.

This media critique may be seen as evidence of the contradiction between commercialized global media and war, as a situation that calls for invoking collective identities and catering to collective, national needs. It fails to realize that restraint on these first days when Americans' belief in the safety and stability of their world was shattered does not threaten media with a loss of independence. The tasks of delivering essential information and reaffirming a shared identity precede the need for investigative reporting. But the necessary rhetoric of reminding the public that it is ultimately a war between good and evil, between progressive and regressive forces, welcomed by the more nationalist groups (the settlers in Israel would finally, for a brief period, experience media which is not hostile), gets the left, always more cosmopolitan, to start worrying.

NOTES

1. This article analyzes media practices during the first year of the second Intifada—fall 2000 to summer 2001.

2. A-Shafi is a Palestinian married to an Israeli Bedouin woman, Halabi—an Israeli belonging to the Druze community, and referred to as Palestinian as Israeli Arab citizens now identify themselves as Palestinians.

3. On April 2002, German TV aired an investigative report providing evidence to counter the allegations that Israeli soldiers were responsible.

REFERENCES

Ajami, Fuad. "What the Muslim World is Watching: A Close Reading of Al Jazeera." *The New York Times Magazine*, 18 November 2001.

Alexander, Jeffrey, "The Mass News Media in Systemic, Historical and Comparative Perspective," In *Mass Media and Social Change*. Edited by E. Katz and T. Szecsko. Beverly Hills, Calif., Sage 1981, 17–51.

Barnea, Nachum, "The Lynch Test." *Ha'ayin Hashvi'it* 29 (2000), 4–5.

Barthes, Roland. *La Chambre Claire*. Paris, Gallimard le Seuil 1980.

Hallin, Dan. "The Media and War," In *International Media Research*. Edited by J. Corner, P. Schlesinger, and R. Silverstone. London, New York, Routledge 1997.

Kampf, Zohar. "Crime and Punishment: Television's Story of the Rammalla Lynching from the Perspective of an Israeli Viewer." Department of Communication and Journalism, The Hebrew University, 2001.

Liebes, Tamar. *Reporting the Arab-Israeli conflict: How Hegemony Works.*" London, New York, Routledge 1997.

———. *American Dreams, Hebrew Subtitles: Globalization at the Receiving End.* Cresskill, N.J. Hampton Press, 2002.

Molotch, Harvey and Marilyn Lester. "News as Purposive Behaviour." *American Sociological Review* 3 (1974), 101–12.

Schiff, Ze'ev and Ehud Ya'ari. *Intifada: The Palestinian Uprising—Israel's Third Front.* New York, Simon and Schuster 1990.

Silverstone, Roger. *Television and Everyday Life.* Chapter 1: "Television, Ontology and the Transitional Object." London, New York, Routledge 1994.

Drifted Liberties and Diffracted Identities?
Algerian Audiences and the "Parabola"

RATIBA HADJ-MOUSSA

QUESTIONS AND CONTEXTS

Something has happened. A sign of that something is the introduction of satellite television in Algeria.[1] After three decades of "monumental history" (Benslama 1995), during which dissension was covered and silenced by the signs of unanimous republican brotherhood of "specific socialism,"[2] Algerians have begun to become conscious of divisions and of the powerlessness of the rentier state. Algerians have lost their fa(r)ther orientation and do not know whether to mourn or to celebrate the loss of the far-reaching vision of a paternalist state. Television played the role of reinforcing an ideological discourse stressing unanimity. It was an easy task while no competing structures existed. However, state television has become more and more inept in ensuring hegemony. Satellite television made its appearance during the introduction of a wave of economic liberalization measures before the significant cuts imposed by the World Bank and the International Monetary Fund during the 1990s.

In the three North African countries of the Maghreb, a number of paradoxes crop up in the broadcasting sector, among which is the existence in Tunisia and Morocco of private television networks, while the official records claim the existence of a state monopoly and inversely [in Algeria] the de jure recognition but actual absence of private ownership (Mostefaoui 1995, 42). Observers refer to a process of demonopolization. For each situation, this process shapes itself differently. When *Antenne 2* in Tunisia, with its prime time terrestrial transmissions began to irritate the powers that be, the broadcaster was cut off. In Algeria, on the other hand, the lawmakers faced a *fait accompli* when mini cable networks appeared. A number of political factors, notably a favourable conjugation of forces for "democratic openness" have a *laissez-faire* beneficial for viewers.

This de facto situation was first orchestrated by the military nomenclature on the heights of Algiers, at Ryad el Feth. The development of this complex called for the enshrinement of the history of the Algerian revolution, most notably with the creation of the Moudjahid Museum and the Monument to the Martyrs and the move toward a liberalization of the regime. The commercial complex adjacent to a lower-class neighborhood was to cater to the well off. Satellite dishes were later adopted by the middle class located in towns and in semirural regions. The prohibitive prices of the first "parabolas," as Algerians call the satellite dishes, created a new phenomenon. The interested parties collectively financed the installation of the devices. Although at the end of the 1990s the purchase of satellite dishes was being done more and more on an individual basis, the phenomenon remained a collective one in two ways: because of the significant number of "subscribers" and because of the massive and seminal presence of collective ownership and management of dishes.

Satellite television raises several questions: what type of modernity does it produce? What are its effects on public space? What connections does it create between interior and exterior spaces? How does it effect the relations between the sexes? How does it inscribe viewer identification? Something other than a history, the task at hand is an anthropological one. The answers to these questions call for a reinvented anthropology focused upon understanding multiple articulations of Algerian society.

I intend to approach these questions through a reflection on the point where satellite television impinges upon shared spaces, such as the neighborhood, and through a consideration of its various impacts upon gendered actors in order to understand the effect of viewing practices on the meaning and importance of the political in a society that has no tradition of a democratic past. Here, I find an inspiring model in the recent work on civil society in nonoccidental contexts (Hann and Dunn 1996), which demonstrate that the notion of civil society needs to be rethought in the light of local realities, such as religion, which would thereby displace received notions of the political (Hann and Dunn, 1996). According to Buchowski, anthropologists have contributed to the enlargement of the notion of the civil society which would now rest upon considerations of groups that are not "necessarily overtly political" (1996, 81). Another suggestive current flows from research on what Lucas calls "citizenship from below" (Lucas 1989; Neveu 1999a). This research was conducted in the context of democratic societies (notably France). However, it was centered on the practices of marginalized actors such as workers, the unemployed, or immigrants. How does the political get expressed in contexts of loss of voice, "when it is deployed outside the moments and instances and modalities considered as political" (Neveu 1999b, 564)? Lucas extends this thinking further and claims that "there is no longer any civil society, there are civil stakes" and that stakeholders mediate between society and political society (1985, 251).

> These areas of research and lines of questioning are interesting because they
> contribute an alternative perspective that challenges the vertical aspect of the

structures often assigned to the political. If the State is an important figure of the political, it is not the only one, and it is not the one and "only source of rights" (Lucas 1985, 249).

The examples collected in this research are akin to the situation I am aiming to describe here in that the Algerian political system is often depicted as a authoritarian patrimonial system that has inserted its tentacles so deeply into society that one asks oneself if there is indeed such a thing as Algerian society or if all there is now is the State, a swaggering procurer, a vile seducer of a society that has ceased to exist. The argument can be carried further. If the State is to be located at the opposite pole in relation to society, then a completely executed divorce would find them back to back running in parallel and never meeting. I believe that to divest oneself of the burden of "l'esprit d'État" (Bourdieu 1994) is to think about events and entities differently and also to allow them to resonate differently. In other words, such an approach will not allow us to foreclose the field of investigation and limit it to the concept of State power and conceive of daily practices as springboards that also lead to the political. Feminist theory has, for quite some time, cast a critical eye upon the divisions between public and private space and has demonstrated that these divisions, as creations of bourgeois regimes, have been reduplicated in theories of public space, the theorizing of Habermas among others (Fraser 1989; Landes 1995). Although these feminist theories do recognize the validity of the concept of a normative dimension in regards to public space as suggested by Habermas, they underscore the exclusion of women from public spaces as a constituent of bourgeois public space. This means that the space for intellectual exchange and deliberation is constructed by way of a space made absent but certainly not made to disappear. Moreover, what is one to do with the case of the private sphere engendered by television or of the public spaces it may generate? A number of authors address the difficulty of maintaining these separations, not only because television has served to spearhead the creation of a sense of belonging and national cohesion (Morley 2000, 107; Martin-Barbero 1993), but also because the private sphere is restructured by the advent of television. Indeed, as Dahlgren has written,

> [. . .] while most viewing still takes place at home, which is traditionally seen as a private space, this domestic site of 'mediated publicness' is where talk about public matters may begin (Dahlgren 1995, 18).

Does this mean that "home" is no longer a private space? By virtue of the introduction of a public instrument, does the domestic sphere come to occupy a place no long in parallel with the "outside," but a place articulated in relation to the "outside" that is connected to the "outside" in various fashions? In particular, does "mediated publicness" in the context of nondemocratic situations create, not so much television publics which are, as D. Dayan (2001) demonstrates, "almost publics," as create publics that are poised for potential action?

Only partial and open-ended answers can be given to these questions. The answers can not be definitive. The first reason is because television is not the only territory upon which publicness materializes itself; the second, because the response from the actors is not a political response, in the sense of a considered response reflecting a set of demands and aimed toward the transformation of institutions.

As Lucas and Neveu note in the case of citizenship, A. Querrien notes in "L'art des centres et des banlieux" that public space is not a given:

> that community does not prefigure public space and does not presuppose agreement as implied by theories of representation, community proposes such an agreement [. . .] Public space is a practice consciously selected, a matter of options. It is a practice of self recognition and affirmation in the context of a field of possibilities where the guidelines are not yet establish but will begin to be marked (Querrien 1991, 91, my translation).

For Querrien, the Soviet queue lines represent a minimal public space because of the different actions that emerge from them over the course of time (mutual aide, collective decision making, surveillance) (Ibid.). Such an approach, which anchors public space less in deliberation and more in action, allows us to consider the introduction of satellite television in Algeria as a moment when a minimal public space came to be and out of which emerged constitutive moments.

THE STAKES OF PUBLIC SPACE

I have demonstrated elsewhere (Hadj-Moussa 1996, 2003) that Algerians have experienced a dramatic expansion of satellite television since its introduction at the beginning of the 1980s. I have also described how entire neighborhoods have become "dished [*parabolés*]" due to the organizing efforts of viewers grouped as collectives. Many observers have remarked on the rush on the part of Algerians to participate in these collectives, all the while appearing to be indifferent to the problems in their immediate surroundings. Of course, one can see here a consumer phenomenon, but it is one that is accompanied by a desire for change. This desire is evident in the debates and discussions that led up to the decision to hook up a satellite dish. These decisions are influenced by differences in cultural capital, most notably the access to schooling, as well as the relations between the sexes and the rural versus urban roots of the viewers. To the extent that the cities and neighborhoods are composed of individuals with differing class allegiances, the spirited debates over the installation of satellite dishes, not to mention the choice of which stations to view, refigure, in a sense, the diversity of social ties.

> In the beginning it was very difficult because there were people for and against. In the city, we are experienced; we know Europe; we have traveled. I

regularly visit a friend who is a teacher living in the small town of El Kolea. There the problem is very serious. It is a town where bureaucrats, teachers, workers, and farmers live side by side. When they came together to elect six representatives of which the treasurer—these are informal neighborhood associations—some of them were in opposition. They held that there were depictions that should not be viewed in a family setting. Later, the representatives of various buildings came together to discuss the satisfaction or dissatisfaction of the subscribers [. . .] Those that had been opposed came around to asking to be hooked up. One of the organizers, an ex-*moudjahid*, rather excitedly told them a few home truths: "When we asked you to participate, you refused saying that it was *harem* [forbidden], not to be done, that we should be viewing obscene depictions. And now, like us you want to hook up but you want it before any other building! You're not even men! You are pushed by your wives. Your wives have seen what is happening elsewhere and they pushed you to hook up . . . Where I live, in the city, it is not the same. We are better organized. There are more intellectually-minded people, more people with jobs" (Djamel, 51 years old).

In other words, even if everyone has access to satellite television, that access is organized along different lines. Viewing practices depend on social position and they serve to distinguish members of the television audience from one another. When viewers intent on increasing their choices and intent on entertainment (I will return to this theme) bring their organizing efforts to bear on the acquisition and management of a satellite dish, without a predetermined political will to organize themselves collectively, they create new spaces and opportunities to reinterpret and critique everyday practices and the political system. The success of satellite television is based on the repudiation of national television, which is deemed to be "obsolete" and is perceived as the house organ of the ruling class. This is true all over the Maghreb. In organizing themselves collectively, viewers create a "minimal public space" (Querrien 1991) which becomes a vital venture for the visibility of forces at work and for the capture of physical spaces.

Thus, thanks to satellite television, Algerians during the 1980s saw members of the political opposition living in Europe as well as the leaders of the Front Islamique du Salut (FIS, the Islamist Front of Salvation). With access to national television denied after October 1988,[3] the FIS, which already had a popular power base, was pushed toward the use of satellite television. However, it is true that in and of itself the broadcasting of these oppositional voices would be politically insignificant if other means of communication did not support and reinforce these moves. I here limit my remarks to the FIS. Other opposition parties at the time hardly had any grassroots support. In this battle over public space the FIS had access to neither television nor radio. It turned its efforts toward mosques and partially toward schools. The FIS used means already in place, such as the amplified loudspeakers installed in the mosques during the period of "specific socialism." These devices had already reshaped the physical boundaries of neighborhoods and had shifted focus onto other places, such as homes and houses. The preaching of the official *imans* progressively became linked to those of the FIS and at times even cannibalized by the *imans* close to the FIS in their the preaching. During Friday evening prayer services, sermons could be heard everywhere; they reached into even the tiny, tiny corners. As well, audio cassettes played an important role in the propagation of the FIS ideology. These cassette tapes contained prayers but mostly sermons that came, for the most part, from Egypt. These tapes were distributed by authorized dealers on market days. The FIS also derived a great deal of its support from charitable work that often operated out of mosques. This appropriation of the technical apparatus of communication, which in the past had been the prerogative of the governing powers and which constituted a means of "effecting the materialization of the power of the mosques on the population" (Benkheira 1985, 144), became a tactic accessible to the FIS. When it was granted legal party status, the FIS was critical of the unacceptable imitations of French society offered by *Radio Chaine III* (the only network broadcasting in French) and cast doubt on the Algerian pedigree of its announcers (Al Hafnaf et al. 1991, 237) but was not critical of satellite television.

A certain qualitative transformation occurred between the period when satellite television was utilized (though critiqued) and the moment when it came to represent nothing but the other, the incommensurably different. This passage from the "justification by ends" to the "justification of values" (Labat 1994, 66) became quite remarkable after the suspension of elections in February 1992, which were predicted to result in victory to the FIS. With the decimation of the ranks of the Islamicists, the constriction of speech, and the changing tone of international media undermining their ideological position, the Islamicist groups and their supporters transformed themselves into ardent defenders of morality, challenging the *taghout* (i.e., the satellite dishes). Having recently surfaced in the discourse, *taghout* is an Arabic term designating the idols which must be attacked according to traditional interpretations of the Koran.

The more fervent protesters tried to convince the population that the satellite dishes were a satanic technology because they incited splits in the Algerian family. Satellite dishes were seen as vehicles for immorality and the corruption of youth. Youth gangs identified with the FIS and intimidated subscribers to divest themselves of their dishes.

> Slim: In 1993, "they" took away the dish [*habssouhalna*]. The emir was passing through. He found the leader and told him "we give you two or three days to make the dish disappear." "Their"[4] emir, himself, who is well-know in the neighborhood, came. Sometimes, "they" send their soldiers who then say, "Remove the dish. We have been sent."

Ratiba: Do they come armed?

   Slim: Yes, they come armed, but they address you very politely [*belakliya*]. They do not show their weapons. They hide them but you can still see them. They say to you, "Remove the dish. Our leader asks you to do so. But this order does not come from us. It comes from God." Which is to say that religion does not tolerate this *fsad* [depravity]. This is their perception [of the dish]. You have to follow their orders ... If you dare to oppose them, they come back and they kill you.

Why this prohibition? Is it to justify the reproduction of an Islamic morality or is it aimed at the appropriation of public space that is in control of a political discourse? To answer the question we must consider the two, political discourse and public space, as indissoluble. Several authors have already noted that the political programme of the FIS was defined by morals and essentially inflected toward questions of morality. I want to try sketching out here some tentative responses which rely upon the eminently political interpretations of some of this study's participants. I want to show that something has shifted, that something is germinating. We need to understand this shift and this germinating seed in order not to fall back upon the negative and the disappointing. Such a negative interpretation would only see the "people as hostage,"[5] hear only silence, perceive only resignation, and notice only the obstacles to thinking, if not the very impossibility of imagining an alternative.

   I, myself, believe that the dish bothers them [the Islamicists] not only because there are films that we should not view in a family context but also because they do not want us to know what is happening elsewhere. Everyone knows that our television supports the State, supports the government. It bothers them but less [than the satellite dish]. But when there are assassination attempts, the foreign media such as MBC [Middle East Broadcasting Corporation] or other networks show us what is really happening. Now [1996] France is anti-FIS and anti-terrorist, so now is the moment they prohibit satellite television. We are not supposed to see that France has captured certain people [terrorists and their supporters]. They want us blind and deaf, they want us to seal our borders. . . . But they have [video] cassettes (Hayet, 35 years old).

Another informant explained to me that "the current system put in place by the governing powers is so absurd, so immoral, so boring" that it did not represent a serious contender for the Islamists. Once the former, lacking any credibility, is eliminated:

   there remain two types of social directions. Either the direction of the Islamists—and they were spreading propaganda in the mosques, in the neighborhoods, where they organized everything—or it is the direction of Western culture which comes to Algerians via satellite dishes. Thus, if you wish, in parentheses, the number one enemy to defeat, is the satellite dish. Which amounts to cutting off entire sections of Algerian society [from Western influence]. It is above all youth [which are targeted by this strategy]. They are not interested by my mother or me for that matter. It is mainly the age group of 18 to 25 year old who are hesitating between embracing the culture of the Islamists or that served up by television on a daily basis. It is truly a war and the stakes are very important to the Islamists. They needed to cut that line. Obviously they need to demonize the dish (Omar, 35 years old).

RESISTANCE AND RETORTS

Aware that they were poorly informed and indoctrinated day in and day out, Algerian viewers en masse turned toward satellite television. It is a dual-purpose move: it is a turning away from national television and away from Islamist prohibitions. They are literally boycotting Algerian television. They do so not only because it is less fascinating but also because they do not perceive it to be a "public good." They say, "It belongs to four or five persons" and by that they mean it is in the hands of a clique. In other words, Algerian television does not offer them representations of themselves nor does it take into account their "culture."

> Réda: All day our [national] television network broadcasts Egyptian films and shows that . . .
>
> Rafik: They want to push Algerian culture [Réda: No, hold on], they want to replace our culture by another so-called culture, they want our culture to incorporate other ideas.
>
> Réda: That is our television wants to impose upon us here in Algeria an arabo-islamism [. . .] Television is mobilized to erase all traces of Algerian culture! However normally its role is not to transform us into [copies of the] French or others, but to make us Algerians.
>
> Ratiba: Which means?
>
> Reda: Our culture, our traditions, our arts and our music.

This erasure of the quotidian is also experienced as a forgetting. It is as if people's lives did not count for much in the face of State security or simply in the face of a tradition of secret holding which has a long history in Algeria. In 1996, a bomb exploded in the neighborhood of a small town where I was conducting research. The explosion left several dead and wounded. Everyone was waiting for television to run a story. There was general disappointment when the people noticed that the news was not reported on the national television broadcast, but TF1, A2, Canal Plus and MBC each devoted air time to the event.

> Normally in other countries, a news cast is used to show what is happening in that country but not in Algeria. The bomb, for example. There would have

> been human interest stories, accounts of the casualties, if only to provide some comfort to the relatives and [they] would not have waited for two days before printing a story (Adel, 24 years old).

In the face of such an information blockade, satellite television becomes fundamental, especially when the State's television network, in order to shield the populace from the Islamist influence, tries to outdo them. For example, from the outset, Algerian television has started and ended its programming day with the national anthem. At the beginning of the day the anthem is followed by a recitation of a passage from the Koran and it is preceded by such a recitation at the close of programming. On Fridays, national television broadcasts the sermons associated with midafternoon prayers. Although this does not perturb viewer sensibilities, it is nevertheless perceived as an instrumentalization of Islam by the State.

> Before ENTV [entreprise nationale de la télévision] used to run the religious program at a specific time, that is at 2 o'clock in the afternoon. Now, in the middle of a program, they switch to the call to prayer. Even in the midst of a sport broadcast, just as one team is scoring! (Youcef, 26 years old)

I have indicated above that satellite dishes were in various cities prohibited in a number of neighborhoods, and the prohibition was often supported by the force of arms. At the height of the prohibition, between 1993 and 1995, certain subscribers had to dismantle the dishes very often because there was no dissuasive counterforce, such as the police, the army, or the gendarmerie, whose presence would have discouraged incursions by armed groups. The satellite collectives at first obeyed the commands to dismantle the devices but as time wore on they invented tactics of resistance. For people who individually owned a satellite dish the response was less direct.

> A section of the FIS had already threatened us. We had to remove the dishes. Personally, I hid mine. I moved it from the top terrace and placed it on the bottom terrace. They are treacherous. They wait to kill you until you are leaving work or they surprise you right at work. You have to play the game. They can not impose the prohibition unless this country adopts a totalitarian regime like that of Iran. And even then, there are ways (Hammoud, 46 years old).

For those that collectively own and manage a dish, the tactics vary:

> Let me tell you about what happened in neighborhood.[6] The residents had set up a satellite dish. The FIS came and took it away. For a period of eight months, they had no dish. Can you imagine?! As you know, satellite dishes have become necessary in Algeria. The residents of that town were afraid but at the end of a few months they were *disgusted* ["*dégoutés*" said in French], so they reinstalled the dish. Each person took up a piece. One picked up the receiving head, another the scoop [laughter]. I swear I'm not exaggerating.

What that meant was "we are all linked to the installation." Just think that if I install a satellite dish they will come *directly* [*"dirext"* said in French] to beat me or kill me. But with one hundred, three hundred persons each holding some part? If they come back and ask who installed the dish? We can say that half or even the whole the neighborhood [*"cites"* in French] had a hand in it. Those gentlemen will not kill us all (Bakir, 22 years old).

Can one call such actions practices of resistance? Yes, if we adopt the point of view of the actors. According to them, if satellite television were to be regulated by the authorities, or simply prohibited either by the authorities or by the Islamists, the actors would in "one way or another" react together, collectively. Furthermore, it is not only the young that are ready to defend this communication option. The not so young are also adamant. They too declare that they will fight and demonstrate. According to Réda, if such a situation is "possible" it cannot come about without struggle,

> we would have to be already dead, because I for one would not let them remove the dish and paint me with a beard [me mettre à la barbe] . . .

> Rafik: Me, I would burn down the mosque. I tell you if they took away the dish I would go to the mosque and burn it down!

DIFFICULT BORDERS

In a way, a war of signs exists and the contours of its profile are not clearly identified (we will come back to this). However, there are very discernible attempts on both sides to mark space. As a physical object, the satellite dish also occupies a certain space and its quite visible presence plays a role in collective and individual affirmation. Indeed, the struggle over satellite dishes is at once concrete and symbolic and this struggle sometimes, as we have seen, places in very violent opposition the mosque and the satellite dish as object. Without doubt, this confrontation is considerably paradoxical and is played out over a significant range of multiple dimensions.

The family and the neighborhood represent the theatre where affiliations and disaffiliations are produced, and at times this entails the rejection of "strangers" and "nonconformists." The forms of affiliation offered by the neighborhood or the *houma* constitute the site par excellence for the acting out of masculinity, in particular for the unemployed who develop a sense of owning the neighborhood, not only its roadways but also its persons, notably young women. At the same time, the *houma* is an urban space which absorbs the ruralness of its inhabitants. It reshapes itself and reinvents itself in newer and larger ensembles that cover populations with different origins and different familial allegiances. Already during the 1960s, P. Bourdieu (1964) spoke of uprooting in reference to the Algerian family. However, the tragic destructuration to which the Algerian family has been subjected has also loosened its confines. A similar phenomenon is applicable in the case of the *houma*. It is no longer the simple reconstitution of village space or of the extended family. The *houma* also mobilizes heterogeneous practices notable for their mercantile and individualistic aspects. The spirit of solidarity, which apparently existed once upon a time in the *houma* and knitted together its members, is now disparaged by the implacable rule of cash transactions: one no longer helps those that are less wealthy to get connected and signal pirating is discouraged. Satellite television has also spawned a host of new practices. It becomes a source of knowledge and a site of social interaction. However, it also becomes, for young people in the cultural desert of daily life, an attraction, an attraction that turns young men away from the *houma*. Although the *houma* remains an important support in the lives of the television viewers, its contours are reshaped by television viewing. Television is a source of fascination:

> There are in the neighborhood those who no longer go out! At home twenty-four hours a day! They come up for air and plunge back into watching television. Twenty-four hours! Especially at the beginning.

When one is "disgusted" by the *houma,* one abandons it for television and vice versa. However the *houma* always assumes its function. As an intermediary space, it favors exchange. It is the place where one

> talks about all sorts of things, trades anecdotes, discusses sporting events and current affairs, [. . .] talks about what is happening elsewhere and what is being hidden from us here.

In determining the nature of the link between *houma* and television, the family also plays a central role. Families are not monads cut off from one another due to the conveyance role played by women and due to the effects of satellite television on the behavior of men outside the home. Notwithstanding the degree to which the return of men to the domestic sphere is still highly codified and only partial, however significant and meaningful the return may be, it has not been provoked by satellite television alone. This phenomenon is an adjustment to a new reality which, it seems to me, derives from fundamental and structural changes in the Algerian family. These changes herald new questions that touch upon the neopatrimonial State and upon the nature of tradition, constructions since forever in the Maghreb associated with the family. It is my hypothesis that the family, just like the *houma*, constitutes a locus of sociality, and it is through this sociological and anthropological reality that public space comes to be. Researchers that focus on the neopatrimonial State, with its closed networks of patrons and clients, do take into account the elites and their already constituted intermediaries. These researchers, however, lose sight of the informal networks in which the family comes to play a welfare function. The family as relay or point of mediation plays a capital role in the translation work between neighborhood, city, and household. Satellite television makes its *entrée* through the household. This insertion takes on specific modalities. There is a price to pay both by and to the family which is a mediating instance. Cohen and Arato believe that the inclusion of the family in the discourse on civil society is fundamental (Cohen and Arato, 1992). However, they associate its inclusion with a condition which, to my mind, can vitiate the thrust of their proposal. According to them, the family serves civil society and contributes ultimately to "the development of civic virtue and responsibility with respect to the polity;" furthermore, the family must be grounded in "egalitarian terms" (Embirbayer and Meyer 1999, 186). Although cast in *a priori* terms, this proposition can prove to be useful in that it reminds us of the importance of the links between the family and other social groupings and does so without situating the family in a space either before or after, but in-between.

The second problem is the connotations and implicit meanings that attend the Algerian (and Maghrebian) family when it is dressed up with the adjective traditional. This is a move that partakes of the larger debate surrounding the pairing of tradition and modernity. In a recent study on nuptial arrangements, Kateb observes, in the case of this most central (if there ever was one) focal point, "the slow and inevitable evolution towards a matrimonial system based upon the free choice of partners encountered by chance," although one's family of origin remains the determining factor in strategies for family building (Kateb 2001, 89). When one considers the profound upheaval that the Maghrebian family and, in particular, the Algerian family has experienced (Bourdieu 1964; Kerrou and Kharoufi 1994) due to effects of colonialism and the direct-action programs of the independent States, one can really ask just where this traditional family is. It seems more important to pay attention to the complexity of actual practices without being troubled as to a practice's status as traditional or without being worried about how it conforms to norms of modernity, norms which are themselves complex and fluid.

This longish digression has allowed us to set the stage for a consideration of the possible conditions that have favored the adoption of satellite television by the family unit whose bearings have been redefined. As we have seen, one of the most important changes has been the retreat of men toward the household. It is worth noting that this return is inflected by strategies which can appear to be quite disorienting, in all senses of the term, for the foreign observer. Upon an initial consideration, it appears that the retreat of the men is a breach of custom. Such is the strength of the sexual division of space. And so numerous arrangements are set up to make this apparent breach of custom palatable. These arrangements between the gendered parties at times require consensus and, at other times, the submission of one or the other party. The common vision and familial perspective are codified by what the parties themselves call "custom and tradition," which prescribe for mixed sex groupings and for cross-generational groupings, including groupings of the same sex, a certain propriety (in what is shown and seen). For those who are well off and possess the necessary space, the solution appears to be the purchase of several television sets, one for viewing national programming, the other for satellite transmissions. In certain cases, men and women can view the same shows (including variety shows) but do so separately in order to escape the unexpected appearance on screen of a naked body or an embarrassing scene. One also finds improvised arrangements such as turn over, where one group watches while the other sleeps (an arrangement found even among brothers of the same generation), or one simply finds a frenzied use of zapping. There are also the borderline cases where women are ejected from the room where the television viewing takes place (or they leave of their own accord).

> I have a cousin on my mother's side who was with 'them' [the FIS] and he owned a satellite dish. He watches sporting events all by himself. Certainly not with his daughters! He closes the door (Naima, 23 years old).

But the force of numbers affects the balance of power and leads to situations of "applied cleverness."

> At my grandmother's there has to be three or four women in the room where the television is. My cousin tells me that when she is alone, he [her brother] has the upper hand. However, just before he arrives home, she calls us, my sister, a neighbor and myself, so that he leaves when he sees us all there (Naima, 23 years old).

But the matter is not so simple. This play of permission and prohibition, this staging of modesty and propriety, this performance violating women's space, evident in these arrangements, are counterbalanced by a new type of relation that is based upon knowing the unacceptable. The covertness of this knowing, or rather its elusiveness, is key, providing passing indications of how the father-son relation and the mother-son relation have been dislocated by the actualization of the unacceptable (such as viewing pornographic films at home) and by the tolerance demonstrated toward the actualization of the unacceptable. Such practices assert the power of men but, at the same time, render the relation between generations brittle as they undermine the sacredness of the home.

Several authors (Bekkar 1998; Mostefaoui 1995; Madani 1995) have pointed out the adjustments provoked by national and satellite television. I will not dwell upon their findings. I want to concentrate here upon certain aspects of these adjustments which seem to describe and reproduce a division found elsewhere in society, and which relate to the place of language and its use. How are policies relating to language reflected in ways of seeing? How are these policies translated into a gendered context? And how is such a translation expressed in [the construction of] public space?

GENDER OR LANGUAGE?

Many authors (Gallissot 2000, 100; Labat 1995), in order to explain the civil war and the predicament of the Algerian [political] system, invoke the split that has emerged between the camp favoring Arabic acculturation, neglected by a system that has failed to integrate them, and the camp favoring French acculturation, which the system has continued to serve and benefit. It is claimed that this would be one of the reasons that the proponents of Arabic acculturation have embraced Islam. How does the advent of satellite television affect the segmentation of these groupings? It is in fact gender that accounts for this polarization and challenges any explanation based on the language of schooling which, since the 1970s, has been in Arabic.

When asked about satellite television viewing choices, the majority of men interviewed clearly indicate that they prefer women, and especially their sisters, to watch national television or the other Arab networks (MBC—owned by Saudi interests and broadcasting out of London—and ART—Arab Radio & Television). The main reason given for limiting the feminine sex to these choices is that the Arab networks, unlike the foreign networks, respect decency and decorum. Thus, if we take the case of MBC, it appears that it attracts only a small number of men,[7] including those whose educational background is Arabic. Apart from its news and sportscasting, MBC is ranked with the national network:

> Yes, I know that Algerian women just love Egyptian movies, but me, I don't like them. Always the same storylines of rich business men and their lovers. That is all there is on MBC. What's its merit? Nothing. Women like it because there is fashion news and Egyptian movies. There are about two movies a day and the rest is Syrian music. It is just like our [national] television except that the newscasts are better (Tarek, 20 years old).

No doubt, for Algerian women[8] MBC's appeal stems in part in from the romantic ideology displayed in those never-ending Middle Eastern soap operas, but also from what P. Bourdieu calls the "paradox of the *doxa*" which consists in neither defying nor questioning the status quo (Bourdieu 1998, 7). This "paradoxical submission" is not always expressed in forms that are easily objectified or open to objectification [and hence critique]. It is incorporated in such a fashion that it becomes natural for both men and women. It comes to belong to the order of nature. I have cited Bourdieu—not because I totally agree with the framework of his analysis of masculine domination, which seems to me to be entirely situated by him in the realm of substantial and formal domination and leaves no room for opposition, subterfuge, and novel practices—but because his framework allows us to understand how micro-practices stemming from everyday life can be read in the greater context, a social structure, and how actors justify what is imposed upon them (women[9]) and what they (men) impose.

Let us begin by stressing that women do not only watch MBC but that it is expected that they concentrate on this particular network and that they do report a preference for this network in the context of the real and possible "danger" presented by images broadcast by Western networks. After all, and despite everything, they say "we are [at heart] Arab" or "we are Muslim," and they cannot be exposed to situations that will "corrupt our soul." Alongside these controls exists another kind of generalized appropriation by the men of the television sets linked to satellite dishes. As soon as the men come home, we find either people watching national television as a mixed group or we find, as we have seen, women being asked to leave. "I have a nephew. He's twenty years old. At 9 o'clock he settles in and asks us to leave" (Djohra, 44 years old). This selective appropriation of the object is not solely focused on the prohibited (what is, by a kind of understatement, referred to as "scenes") but also extends to the conductors of knowledge—in the form of documentaries, game shows—that operate through the French language. All things considered, satellite television has filled the vacuum left by the shortcomings and deficiencies of the school system.

> You were asking me questions about satellite television. Well. It teaches us French. [Through it] we learn French. I swear, I sometimes watch a movie with a dictionary beside me. If a word is used, let us say *"avare,"* I immediately look up its meaning and learn that it is a *masmar* [a nail in Algerian Arab] or in classical Arabic, *el bakhil.* We are learning the language! There was a show the other day called *La route de la fortune,* it was a language-focused show. We learn a lot that way. And when the show is boring or uninteresting, we still learn French! (Hafid, 20 years old)

However, Hafid, who was educated in Arabic, would never ever want his sisters to be exposed to satellite television and he believes that they should wear the *hidjab* because it is a duty (*fard*) for Muslim women.

Thus, upon an initial reading, satellite television is perceived as essentially (in regards to euro-programming) as a man's television, conspicuously open to the other, the foreign, certainly a conduit for images of naked bodies but also of debate, polemic, critique, or, simply put, "democratic modernity." Women are partially confined to the déjà vu of the Arab networks. Women maintain the "umbilical cord" link with Arabness, with Islam, and with Algerian values. The introduction of satellite television reveals to us, in this first instance of interpretation, a dominant configuration explicitly at work in political discourse in which women are the very incarnation of Arab and Muslim values in Algeria.

The advent of the satellite dish in the space of the household, like the coming of the factory into Algerian space previously, is greeted with a sense that it should not affect the established order, which is essentially reducible to the prohibition against women occupying public space and taking up a voice. In a sense, by this prohibition targeting women, male viewers, be they Francophone or Arab speakers, situate themselves near the centre of Islamist discourse. The practices elicited by satellite television enter into a serial relationship with those practices emanating from other sites of expression and abet the production of a discourse that regards women as having very little to contribute. It is less a question of [Arab or French] language than a question of the formation in public space of a hegemonic and uniform discourse. As evidence of the stakes involved, let us take the case of the Arab networks, in particular *El Djazira*[10] and MBC. The two networks differ on a number of points. Broadcasting from Qatar since 1996, *El Djazira* has distinguished itself through its political reporting, which has provoked the ire of more than one Arab regime.[11] Ever since the second Palestinian uprising (October 2000), *El Djazira*'s audience has grown throughout the Arab world. It has captured the loyalty of numerous viewers, among Algerian men in particular, because of its news reports. Unlike the [viewing of] Western networks, watching *El Djazira* can include women and can be conducted in public. For example, in the summer of 2001 in Algeria, I found myself in a household appliance store. A television set was on and tuned to *El Djazira* to a show where an ex-officer of the Algerian secret service, now living in Europe, was being interviewed. The September 11 attacks on the World Trade Center in New York have accentuated this phenomenon, which still remains essentially masculine. Thus, it is along political lines that the divide between men and women is established.[12]

I concede that to fully lay out this interpretation I would have to highlight the dynamic nature of these practices in such a fashion as to nuance the structure of domination so that the analysis could account for the singularity of an emerging voice, albeit a merely muttering voice for the moment. Would it be the case that, as in the past, women, like the cohorts who were educated in Arabic, have been overlooked? Will women be able to break away from the "symbolic violence" (Bourdieu) imposed upon them by the brotherhood (it is very often brothers who impose interdictions[13] and affirm their own voices)? My response to these questions will entertain two types of argument which show the complexity of the distinctions invoked to separate men and women. The first relates to the question of "modernity," which coincides with viewing practices, and the second, to television genres. The two arguments are inseparable.

Several female scholars[14] conducting research in the field (Mankekar 1999; Abu-Lughod 1995) have demonstrated that television is an instrument of modernity to which women easily subscribe. Abu-Lughod thus criticizes the Egyptian novelist N. Mahfouz who grows nostalgic in remarking the passage of cafe gatherings which are being replaced by television. She notes in particular that he

> forgets that this older form of entertainment, with the imaginary non-local worlds it conjured up, was only available to men [. . .] Television give women, the young, and the rural as much access as urban me to stories of other worlds (op. cit. 191).

Television allows women (especially those that do not work outside the home) to link up with public space and opens new horizons.

> We have seen women sell their jewelry in order to acquire a satellite dish. They were ready. [Interviewer: ready for what?] because with television one can escape the gloominess of the everyday; so when they turn it on, they see things, they see people thinking (Hakima, 46 years old).

The examples presented by satellite television "force national television to broach taboo questions such as AIDS" and women are discovering the existence of a self or at least daring to name the existence of such a self, like this young woman who said to me in a statement that was probably intended to express a will for individuation,

> You know, there was a woman psychologist on MBC who said that we Arabs do not feel it when our psyche *el nifs* is not well. We are only concerned by our physical organs.

The Brazilian, Mexican and even Arab soap operas that are broadcast on satellite and national television reveal hidden realities that are censored in everyday life, realities such as incest, amorous liaisons, marriages based on love, and "strong women that prod men into conformance" (Abla, 38 years old).

In order to determine the extent of these disturbances, we need to take the term diversion in both the sense of entertaining distraction and in the sense of detour, deviation, and variation. Indeed, it is not men alone that seek diversion and who take up critical positions vis-à-vis national television. In fact, if women prefer Egyptian to Algerian films,

> it is not because of the content but how it is shown, with what setting, with what clothes, with what manner of speaking.[15] Women can go to Egypt without any problem. They know the language. You know women love what is *matmoum* [concise, precise and condensed] (Naima, 23 years old).

Foreign soap operas give access to the different, access to that which women will manipulate, embroider, and integrate into their daily lives.

If it is undeniably true that political reporting occupies a prominent place in viewing habits, especially the habits of men, pure entertainment is also highly valued, especially since television is, for all practical purposes, that only cultural space available. The civil war is not the only cause of such a void, it began to be felt when the implementation of policies favored the profit motive to the detriment of social and cultural wealth. But is entertaining diversion to be considered solely as an outlet for the multiple frustrations induced by daily life? Recent studies question the undertheorized dichotomy between information and entertainment, especially if the dichotomy is considered from the perspective of the construction of meaning by viewers and in light of the fusion of traditional genres into what is now referred to as "infotainment" (Dahlgren 1991, 18–19; Miège 1995). Genres that were once considered minor, such as the talk show, are now at the centre of lively discussion. Several authors consider the talk show as a particular form of counterdiscourse which is part of public life (Shattuc 1999). Morley writes:

One can argue that the rise of the talk show, with its carnavalesque and dialogic qualities, in which a range of voices clamours for expression [. . .], has rather to be seen as part of the long-term process in which the voices of those who were historically drowned out by the patriarchal and imperialist meta-narratives of modernism and finally allowed to speak in public (Morely 2000, 117).

IDENTITIES

Identity is without a doubt one of the finest lenses through which to view the complexity of shifting alliances introduced by satellite television, since it reveals to us the status of the public space in question. What does satellite television bring to the problematic of identity? Certainly it is not a globalizing apparatus that determines in and of itself people's allegiances. As we saw, satellite television is instrumentalized and repositioned by the various individual players and political factions (Chouikha 1995). Thus, it is difficult in the case of Algeria to circumvent how history has been elaborated in the context of memory work and has come to occupy public space. This construction has obliterated the multiplicity of memories and has led to the recognition solely of the historic role of the FLN (National Liberation Front) through a process of mythologizing verging on fossilization. This process has largely depended upon television. It is from that history that viewers seek diversion. They turn away from that history because it neither represents "the truth" which it censures nor does it represent what informants refer to as "Algerian culture."

> Before then [1988], it was the government's newspaper, it was the newspaper that worked for the ruling power, *El Moudjahid.* Television was the FLN television and it was from sun up to sun down indoctrination. [But] they didn't succeed! (Mourad, 46 years old)

> There is too much censuring on our [national] television, which is itself too pro-FLN [. . .] I'm telling you the truth, I, myself do not watch it not even for newscasts. We have had enough. We know they will begin with the president and his entourage, his *smala.* 25 minutes of that! (Hayet, 36 years old)

Monumental history, ossified history, no longer seems to have a grip on people's imaginations, whereas emerging and parallel histories are giving everyone the right to examine history. "[. . .] there is a nationalist sentiment. It is innate. It is not the FLN that fostered it. It is a sentiment that is ingrained in every Algerian. No matter how very happy they (*emigres*) are in France, when summer comes, they know that it is their country."

What of these modes of belonging to "Algerian culture;" what is their basis? In a country where the history of the quotidian or, more exactly, the life of people does not signify to the same extent as the grandiose past and present of the FLN, "Algerian culture" is in the examples offered by television identified with the "daily life of the people," with "their dress, their songs, their art," identified, that is, with a reality that is tied to a given territory. This is not to say that it is no longer that "kaleidoscope of instable identities and transpositions" (Morley 2000, 10). The relation to place and territory is correlative to identification. However, this correlation, as many authors have indicated (Gupta and Ferguson 1997; Malkki 1992), should not be essentialized. If, as Massey maintains,

> the definition of the specificity of the local place cannot be made through counter position against what lies outside; rather it must be precisely made through the particularity of the interrelations with the outside, then, the correlation between identity and territory should be thought of through "an extroverted notion of identity of place" (Massey 1994, 117).

The processes of identification are also inflected by the Other, by the external world. Such is the example of language. In order to come to terms with colonialism, the Arab language became, "against others," the national language (Benrabah 1999, 101); French, Algerian, Arabic, and the Berber tongues were banished once again from the nation.

However, the informants do not challenge the status of the Arab language because, as they say, "we need a language" and "we cannot allow speakers on television to say *el vilou* instead of bicycle or *el cartable* [satchel] or *l'icoole* [school]." However, the official language should not be the only one to rule the airways. Paradoxically, informants are seeking less to boost the vernacular than education reform (even among Kabyle informants and despite the Kabyle crisis). Overall, the Arab language is not placed in opposition to the other languages[16] which have, despite all, remained vibrant but in opposition to French. "The Arab language is not a scientific language," nor is it "a technical language;" it is not a language opening on to the world. The satellite dish compensates for this lack and brings Algerians closer to France, their "neighbor." An essential ambivalence, even a "kaleidoscope of instable identities" appears vis-à-vis France, the Other par excellence, the Other which is not solely an insurmountable difference, but also an alter ego. This not a case of "partial identities" (Dahomay 2000, 103) which surface when a framework for social organization is absent or inadequate, be it the State, the family, or the clan. It is rather an ambivalence that is rooted in a strong and dual sense of belonging. Even if Algeria, through its direct-action programs, has relegated the French language to the margins, France too has played a great role in the Algerian turn toward Arabicization and Islamicist currents.

> It is the visa that botched it for people in Algeria [. . .] In imposing the visa, France pushed Algerians to go elsewhere [. . .] the Europeans perforce outlined new directions. Young people fell back upon the Middle East, Syria, Egypt, the Sudan [. . .] "They" brought us customs from Afghanistan, from the Sudan. We were not used to these customs (Djamel, 51 years old).

France is an alter ego, a mirror for Algerians who almost obsessively ask themselves "how [France] is speaking about us, what it sees in us" while "we know about every political event that takes place in France." However, this mirror function is not only operative at the level of comparisons between France and Algeria, it is also a function that is concerned with the international visibility of the Algerian drama. It is through the mediation of images disseminated from France that Algeria becomes visible. But it is a problematic visibility since the gaze from France is judged negatively. France "knows nothing about Algeria" and its claims are in vain.

> I was telling you earlier that they [the French media] indulge from time to time in spreading disinformation. We have been enemies for 130 years. That cannot be erased simply in a week or in a few years. Time needs to run its course. It's normal! They will visit a polling station where there are only two chaps but will not go to the one with 10,000 people (Hammoud).

Besides the fact that viewers prove themselves capable of establishing a distance indicative of their critical capacities (Hadj-Moussa 2003) they also point toward "that other great repressed thought of the twentieth century in France [. . .] which if for sure, that of colonialism and notably the war in Algeria" (Le Monde 4-6-2002). "The deep connection" between Algeria and France, discussed by Grand Guillaume (1995), corresponds to a buried memory and to a sensing of events finding, with difficulty, its objective correlatives. However, this long and difficult process of imbuing material traces with meaning, this process of memory work, has begun. It has begun with the opening in France of the issue of torture. It is an issue that has been commented upon by the Algerian press and widely picked up by the French networks. This opening up of the issue without a doubt contributed to the coming forward of Algerians tortured under Le Pen during the war (Le Monde 03-06-2002) to bear witness and to respond to the images coming from elsewhere and to allow the French to avoid falling for the line set by the FLN.

France, "our saboteur"[17] is also a model. Despite "the gaps in its memory [. . .] its unhealthy connection the [dark] zones of its past" (Le Monde, 03-06-2002), and despite the "presentness" of its past, France is the example through which a political identification is possible. Whereas cultural identification is ambiguous and oscillates between the poles of repulsion and attraction, political identification is elected most often. I have discussed elsewhere the possibilities created by satellite television and have insisted on the opportunities it presents for political education and on the openings satellite television creates in the national public space by linking this space with other secular public spaces. To watch satellite television is to project other people's experiences onto one's own. France is like the thread leading out of the labyrinth and it represents the possibility of imagining a democratic future, a future which the Algerians glimpsed in a flash between 1988 and 1992.

I see France. It is an exemplary country for me. It is the country that has strengthened itself through its democratic traditions. It is a country where laws exist and no one can escape the law, whether they are a general or a president. We saw [on screen] ministers placed in prison, we saw the police take a CEO into detention. That doesn't happen in our country. Here it is might over right. So it is France that gives the example in this domain. The law applies to all equally. [. . .] Presently, the presidential advisor is the son of a *flen*.[18] The minute those guys graduate from the ENA [Ecole nationale d'administration] they are automatically sent abroad as ambassadors whereas the sons of the losers who first of all face a challenge getting into the ENA find themselves as paper pushers [in some corner of a regional bureaucracy] in a *daira* or a *willaya*. And the son of Ali Kafi[19] is a counsellor! What a wretched individual, straight out of university, first degree in hand, all shiny and new, without any background, without any experience, and he becomes advisor to the prime minister. The [Algerian] media picked up the story. We found out thanks to the media, by the way, thanks to *Liberté* in particular (Hammoud).

CONCLUSION

Satellite television and its massive adoption in Algeria[20] corresponds to what Bayat calls the "quiet encroachment of the ordinary" in his study of social change movements in the Middle East and North Africa. He thinks that these movements should be considered as "grassroots non-movements" in that they do not manage to create lasting mobilizations. Bayat associates the activism of these movements with what he calls the "quiet encroachment of the ordinary," (Bayat 2002, 19) which he believes has a significant impact on the possibilities for social change:

> This quiet activism challenges many fundamental state prerogatives, including the meaning of 'order,' control of public space, and the meaning of 'urban' (Ibid., 120).

It seems to me that such practices can be considered as close to the experience of viewing satellite television. Indeed, the notion of "'quiet encroachment' describes the silent, protracted, and pervasive advancement of ordinary people on the propertied and powerful in a quest for survival and improvement of their lives." Although Bayat's examples relate to the social (access to water, electricity, and property) rather than the cultural, it seems to me that the Algerians have produced this "encroachment" in adopting and fighting for the right to access entertainment and ways of opening onto the world. Satellite television has favored the production of knowledge over the hegemonic distillations offered by national television. It also deeply plays a role in the emergence of subject positions and individuality, if only by the choices it encourages. However, satellite television does not represent the totality of public space whose various "relay" components (Querrien 1991) rely on other modes of expression, such as the press which, despite all its shortcomings and despite censorship, is playing an essential role in the opening of public space in Algeria. The press is one of "those rare successes derived from the democratization of the regime" (Kreamer 2001, 83). It too is grounded in civil society[21] and on the transformations of the family notably the changes in the relations between men and women and the redefinition of common spaces (the household) and spaces previously marked as male domains (the street, the *houma*). Fundamental questions are raised by the emergence of satellite television: is it fruitless to think in the case of a constrained political space such as Algeria's that any instance, where there is an attempt at singular and novel expression, is either insignificant or a mark of political disorder because the expression is not mediated through a representative?

NOTES

1. One of the participants to this research used a proverb to suggest an analogy between the "parabola" [satellite dish] and travel: "*Li majel mayahrafech ergjel*" [Without travel there is no knowing of people]. This research consisted of a series of interviews that I conducted between 1994 and 2001 in Algeria in the context of my research on the use of satellite television. I am grateful to the men and women who trusted me and granted me these interviews during difficult times (particularly 1994 and 1996) when, as they report, "we trust[ed] no one." I wish to signal here my appreciation for the trust placed in me.

2. I am here relying on the meaning of "brotherhood" which links men together and on the use of the term "brother" to refer to those who fought in the war of independence (1954–62). Specific socialism is the ideology that held that the Algerian regime, between 1965 and 1978, was socialist and Muslim.

3. October 1988 is a key moment in Algerian political life. Massive riots protesting against a two-tier society, injustice, and growing poverty, were followed by a new constitution (1989) which established freedom of association and allowed multiparty activity.

4. The possessive pronoun is often used to mark a distance between the locutor and armed groups, the Islamists and/or the State.

5. The expression is part of the title of a book on Algeria by the group Reporters sans Frontières.

6. X is a new neighborhood where one finds in close proximity a number of villas and urban development. This neighborhood was well known in this little town on the outskirts of Algiers as existing practically out of the control of the authorities because armed groups (associated by the people with the FIS) ruled. These armed groups prohibited satellite dishes and, under the threat of executing their fathers, forced adolescent women to wear the *hidjab*.

7. All the young men that were interviewed received their schooling in Arabic. A number of them hardly speak French, though they do understand it well.

8. It is evident that this is a generalization. There are women, even among those that do not work outside the home, who do not like MBC. However, most of the women who do not like this network received their schooling in French.

9. It does happen that women will quite consciously impose upon themselves a rule, as is the case of one of the women interviewed who indicated that, after inadvertantly viewing a risky scene, she cleansed herself again with ritual ablutions.

10. The Qatar-based network positioned itself from the outset (1996) as a rival to MBC, especially in terms of political reporting. Because of its links with the ultra conservative power base of Ryad, MBC has been shaken by the irreverent and critical tone of *El Djazira*. As a number of oppositional parties from different Arab countries have found a voice through *El Djazira*, the network's broadcasts have become a reference point for viewers in Arab countries and viewers throughout the Arab diaspora. It became famous during the U.S. invasion of Iraq in 1998 when it covered "Operation Desert Storm" and its reputation was affirmed when, during the second Palestinian uprising, *El Djazira* filled the void left by CNN's refusal to cover the Intifada and its reputation was again boosted recently with coverage of the U.S. war against Afghanistan.

11. The network has received more than four hundred official complaints from Arab regimes (Hirst, 2001) while the Americans through Secretary of State, Colin Powell, have asked Sheik Hamad ben Klifa el Thani to put pressure on the network's journalists (Al Quds Al Arabi 2001).

12. It is during such times of crisis that one can note this type of fall-back behavior. During the Gulf War, Algerian television gained high praise from viewers who found CNN and the French networks to be very biased to the point of disseminating disinformation.

13. The source of the interdiction is an important fact to consider. It is to be correlated with what F. Colonna describes in reference to the spread of riots in Algeria which are "extraordinarily juvenile and masculine in character" (Colonna 1996, 46).

14. I am grateful to Aline Tauzin who reminded me of the importance of this line of argumentation.

15. Such emphasis on the form of presentation echoes the work of Mankekar on Indian television and references the interpretative position of women who simultaneously identify with characters (and yet such an identification requires an emotion, *baav*, which everyone can claim to possess) and critique the programs. Mankekar further indicates that "Neither they nor I saw a contradiction between these two divergent modes of viewing" (*op. cit.* 26).

16. Algerian television now includes in its programming newscasts in the Berber tongue of Kabylia.

17. It is in such terms that one of the informants relates her experience of French television: "I like French newscasts because they refer to us. When my brother is watching the newscasts, I ask him to call me if they are talking about Algeria. But we know that when something is happening in Algeria, 'they' always open with 'we are being sabotaged'" (Abla, 38 years old).

18. A *flen* is an Algerian term referring to a person with power and ranking over others.

19. A. Kafi was the president of the powerful National Organization of *Moudjahidin* [fighters]. Following the assassination of President Boudiaf in June 1992, he became the President of the High State Commission.

20. In 1999, 80 % of households possessing television sets had access to satellite transmissions. This is the highest degree of saturation in North Africa and the Middle East. In Western Europe the rate is 48.5 % (Sakr 2001, 114).

21. It may seem problematic to speak of civil society in the case of Algeria. If one is to believe the authors who insist on the iron grip of the regime, civil society is but a shadow whose existence would depend upon the State and its infrastructure; other authors, in contradistinction, recognize the existence of civil society despite its being fresh and weak (Zoubir and Bouandel 1998, 18).

REFERENCES

Abu-Lughod, L. "The Object of Soap Opera: Egyptian Television and the Cultural Politics of Modernity." In *Worlds Apart. Modernity Through the Prism of the Local.* Edited by D. Milner. London, New York, Routledge 1995, 190–210.

Al Quds Al Arabi. "Critiques d'al Jazira: la liberté d'expression menacée." Éditorial, trad. Pierre Vanier. Medea.be (dossiers spéciaux): Bruxelles (http://www.medea.be/) 2001.

Al-Ahnaf, M., B. Botiveau, and F. Frégosi. *L'Algérie par ses islamistes.* Paris, Karthala, 1991.

Bayat, A. "Activism and Social Developement in the Middle East." *International Journal of Middle East Studies.* 34 (2002), 1–28.

Beaugé, F. "Quatre nouveau témoins accusent Jean-Marie Le Pen de torture." *Le Monde Interactif,* 3 juin 2002. *www.le Monde.fr.*

Bekkar, R. "Écoute et regards: la télévision et les transformations spatiales en Algérie." In *Miroirs maghrébins. Itinéraires de soi et paysages de rencontre.* Edited by S. Osman. Paris, CNRS 1998, 177–185.

Benkheira, M. H. "Ivrognerie, religiosité et sport dans une ville algérienne (Oran) 1962–1983." *Archives de sciences sociales des religions* 59, no. 1 (1985), 131–51.

Benrabah, M. *Langue et pouvoir en Algérie. Histoire d'un traumatisme linguistique.* Paris, Séguier 1999.

Benslama, F. "La cause identitaire." *Intersignes* 10 (1995), 47–66.

Bourdieu, P. and A. Sayad. *Le Déracinement, la crise de l'agriculture traditionelle en Algérie.* Paris, Minuit 1964.

———. *Raisons pratiques. Sur la Théorie de l'action,* Paris, Seuil 1994.

———. *La domination masculine.* Paris, Seuil 1998.

Buchowski, M. "The Shifting Meanings of Civil and Civic Society in Poland." In *Civil Society. Challenging Western Models.* Edited by Ch. Hann and E. Dunn. London, New York, Routledge 1996, 77–98.

Chouikha, L. "Le patrimoine familial dans le Ramadhan 'télévisuel.' Le cas des familles 'modernes' de Tunis." *Communication* 16, no. 2 (1995), 105–30.

Cohen, J. and A. Arato. *Civil Society and Political Theory.* Massachussetts, MIT 1992.

Colonna, F. "Sur le passage de l'émeute à l'attentat collectif (1978–1996)." *Monde arabe Maghreb Machrek* 154 (1996), 40–47.

Dahlgren, P. "Introduction." In *Communication and the Citizenship. Journalism and the Public Sphere*. Edited by P. Dahlgren and C. Parks. London, New York, Routledge 1991, 1–24.

———. *Television and the Public Sphere. Citizenship, Democracy and the Media*. London, Thousand Oaks, New Delhi, Sage 1995.

Dahomay, J. "Identité Culturelle et identité politique: Le cas antillais." *Revue de philosophie et de sciences sociales*, no. 1 (2000), 99–108.

Dayan, D. "The Peculiar Public of Television." *Media, Culture and Society* 23 (2001), 743–65.

Dictionnaire Historique de la langue francaise. Paris, Le Robert 1992.

Emirbayer, M. and M. Sheller. "Publics in History." *Theory and Society* 28 (1999), 145–97.

Fraser, N. *Unruly Practices: Power, Discourse, and Gender in Contemporary Social Theory*. Minneapolis, Univ. of Minnesota Pr. 1989.

Galissot, R. *Le Maghreb de traverse*. Paris, Bouchène 2000.

Granguillaume, G. "Être chez soi et hors de soi." *Intersignes* 10 (1995), 79–88.

Gupta, A. and J. Ferguson. "Culture, Power, Place: Ethnography at the End of an Era." In *Culture, Power, Place. Explorations in Critical Anthropology*. Edited by A. Gupta and J. Ferguson. Durham, London, Duke Univ. Pr. 1997, 1–29.

Hadj-Moussa, R. "New Media, Community, and Politics in Algeria." In *Media, Culture and Society*. 45 no. 4 (2003), 451–468.

———. "Les antennes célestes, les généraux-apparatchiks, les émirs et le peuple. L'espace public en question." *Anthropologie et sociétés* 20, no. 2 (1996), 129–155.

Hann, Ch. and E. Dunn, eds. *Civil Society. Challenging Western Models*. London, Routledge 1996.

Hirst, D. "Al -Djazira une chaîne libre au Proche-Orient. La télévision arabe qui dérange," *www.monde-diplomatique.fr*, August 2001.

Kateb, K. *La fin du mariage tradionnel en Algérie? (1978–1998) Une exigence d'égalité des sexes*. Paris, Bouchène 2001.

Kerrou, M. and M. Kharoufi. "Maghreb. Familles, valeurs et changements sociaux." *Monde arabe Maghreb Machrek* 144 (1994), 26–39.

Kreamer, G. "Presse francophone et arabophone en Algérie." *Monde arabe Maghreb Machre* 173 (2001), 73–83.

Labat, S. *Les islamistes algériens. Entre les urnes et le maquis*. Paris, Seuil 1995.

———. "Islamismes et islamistes en Algérie. Un nouveau militantisme." In *Exils et Royaumes. Les appartenances au monde arabo-musulman aujourd'hui*. Edited by G. Kepel. Paris, 1994, 42–67.

Landes, J. B. "The Public and the Private Sphere: A Feminist Reconsideration." In *Feminists Read Habermas. Gendering the Subject of Discourse*. Edited by J. Meehan. London, New York, Routledge 1995, 91–116.

"Le Pen et l'Algérie." *Le Monde Interactif*, 4 juin 2002. *www.le Monde.fr*.

Lucas, Ph. "Après la citoyenneté les mutli-citoyennetés." *Cahiers internationaux de Sociologie*, LXXIX (1985), 252–86.

————. "Citoyens d'en bas. Contribution à une anthropologie de la contemporanéité." *Cahiers internationaux de sociologie*, LXXXV (1989), 276–99.

Madani, L. "Modalités et usages de la réception télévisée par satellite en Algérie." *NAQD* [Critiques], nos. 8/9 (1995), 31–51.

Malkki, L. "National Geographic: The Rooting of Peoples and the Territorialization of National Identity Among Scholars and Refugees." *Cultural Anthropology* 7, no. 1 (1992), 24–44.

Mankekar, P. *Screening Culture, Viewing Politics. An Ethnography of Television, Womanhood, and Nation in Postcolonial India.* Durham, London, Duke Univ. Pr. 1999.

Martin-Barbero, J. *Communication, Culture and Hegemony.* London, Sage 1993.

Massey D. "Double Articulation. A Place in the World." In *Displacements. Cultural Identities in Question.* Edited by A. Bammer, Bloomington and Indianapolis: Indiana Univ. Pr. 1994, 110–21.

Miège, B. "L'espace public: Au-delà de la sphère politique." *Hermès*, nos. 17–18 (1995), 49–61.

Morley, D. *Home Territories. Media, Mobility and Identity.* London, New York, Routledge 2000.

Mostefaoui, B. *La télévision française au Maghreb. Structures, stratégies et enjeux.* Paris, L'Harmattan 1995.

Neveu, C., ed. *Espace public et engagement politique. Enjeux et logiques de la citoyenneté locale.* Paris, L'Harmattan 1999a.

————. "L'anthropologue, le citoyen et l'habitant. Le rapport au politique dans une ville du Nord." *Ethnologie française*, no. 4 (1999b), 559–67.

Querrien A. "Un art des centres et des banlieux." *Hermès* 10 (1991), 85–93.

Sakr, N. *Satellite Realms: Transnational Television. Globalization and the Middle East.* London, New York, I.B. Taurus 2001.

Shattuc, J. M. "The Oprahication of America. Talk Shows and the Public Sphere." In *Television, History, and American Culture. Feminist Critical Essays.* Edited by M. B. Haralovich and L. Rabinovitz. Durham, London, Duke Univ. Pr. 1999, 168–80.

Zoubir, Y.-H. and Y. Bouandel. "The question of Human Rights in Algeria: An Analytical Approach." *The Journal of Algerian Studies* 3 (1998), 1–18.

The Right to Be Different:
Photographic Discourse and
Cultural Identity in Hungary

PETER BRAUN

I.

What has happened in Europe since the internal collapse of the Soviet Union is remarkable. Who would have been able to predict that a mere fifteen years afterwards, three former Soviet Republics—Estonia, Latvia, and Lithuania—and four former "brother states" under Communist rule—Poland, the Czech and Slovak Republics, and Hungary—would become members of the European Union? As soon as the former "Eastern Bloc" had disintegrated, voices in these countries were raised that set the goal of a "return to Europe." These countries' political accomplishments since then have been impressive. In all of them, economic reforms were carried out quickly and political institutions have stabilized. Although different governments have come and gone, the political course set in all of them has remained unscathed. Not least importantly, their populations have actively supported this transformative course, despite the hard times and the sacrifices that it brought about. Now, with their accession into the European Union on May 1st, 2004, they have been rewarded for their patience and the political division of Europe into two blocks has finally been overcome. Nevertheless, it is legitimate to inquire into the condition of cultural identity in these countries.

Eastern European history has, in the twentieth century, been formed by radical change and upheaval to a much greater extent than that of Western Europe (Schlögel 2001 and 2002). States disappeared, nations were pulled apart, borders redrawn in the interest of foreign powers. Some of the European Union's new members once belonged to the Habsburg monarchy. After this multiethnic empire collapsed during World War I, new nation states were built, all of which were, in turn, confronted with many ethnic minority populations. Two decades later, the German National Socialists occupied the countries of Eastern Europe. They were followed by Soviet troops, so that the horrors and criminal deeds of World War II were followed by the terror of Communist dictatorship. The Iron Curtain abruptly cut Eastern European countries off from developments in the West. This agonizing experience of powerlessness and of being controlled by other forces has spawned a reserved nationalism since 1989. However, it has, from the beginning, been character-ized by a pledge of loyalty to Europe. This has forced official cultural policy to strike a difficult balance between national and European, between global and local concerns. On the one hand, initiatives encouraging or even reviving local customs and practices have found support, such as traditional music and dances. On the other hand, large representative exhibitions have celebrated these countries' Latin and Christian inheritance and emphasized those ele-ments of history and culture that the West could understand as symbols of membership to its cultural circle.

However, this background information sets just the beginning for an investi-gation of cultural identity in Eastern Europe. Current theoretical reflection on the term culture has demonstrated that we must leave behind all essential-ist notions of unity and homogeneity. To the contrary, culture is no longer conceived of as a static structure, but instead as a network of dynamic, as well as conflictual, discursive practices in which competing interpretations and the claims to power associated with them come into contact with one another. These discourses are staged in various media, making it of primary impor-tance for any analysis of these processes to determine which groups hold the institutional power over them. Seen in this way, "cultural identity," too, can no longer be conceived of as a given we grow into like hand-me-downs from our older siblings. Cultural identity is also consistently undergoing change and for this reason must repeatedly be renegotiated within certain social groups by means of discursive processes supported by the media. Thus, it is continu-ally being reinvented, reconquered, altered, and lost again. Cultural studies, too, must take account of Clifford Geertz' conclusion that the "world (is) in pieces" (Geertz 2000, 218–63).

On the basis of this understanding of culture, created on the most part within the discipline of Cultural Studies, I would like to treat the situation in Hungary after 1989 and redirect our attention away from official cultural policy and its symbols to the country's periphery. In this way, an institution enters our line of vision that has played a marginal and ambivalent role within the discursive fab-ric concerning Hungary's cultural identity. I am speaking of the *Department for Cultural and Visual Anthropology* (Kulturális és Vizuális Antropológia Tanszék), founded in 1992 at the University of Miskolc, an industrial city located in the northeast of the country, not far from the border to the Slovak Republic, to Ukraine, and to Romania. This chapter is the result of six months of research at the *Department for Cultural and Visual Anthropology*.[1] During my stay I became familiar with the development of this young institute and learned more about its founder, Ernő Kunt, who died under tragic circumstances in 1994 at the early age of 46. To begin with, I will sketch the discursive background and intellectual history that led to the Institute's founding, as well as the political context. I will then present examples of Ernő Kunt's work, which centered on the photographic medium. Finally, his own photographic practice will be framed as a dialogue with his scholarly research, a process that led him to develop an exhibition concept for his photography that consciously attempted to influence the discursive processes concerning Hungarian cultural identity. This concept bears definite signs of resistance against the official, politically determined discourse on a new national cultural identity and offers an alternative that attempts to account for the centuries-old multiethnic history of Eastern Central Europe.

II.

When, between 1989 and 1990, Communist rule in Hungary collapsed, a new scholarly discourse came into use: Cultural Anthropology. This was a counter-discourse directed against previous empirical cultural research under the name of Ethnography. The latter studied the cultural heritage of Hungary's peasants in a positivistic manner and under the primacy of 'material culture.' Of course it had had to accommodate itself to official ideology as well as pass up nationalistic tendencies in favor of seeing an originary form of communism in the old peasant traditions. The new discourse was meant to introduce a complex, interdisciplinary form of cultural research that would open new perspectives on the current condition of culture beyond all ideological premises. From the start, this counterdiscourse also directed itself against the nationalism that was sprouting up everywhere and the glorification of Hungarian history in the second half of the nineteenth and at the start of the twentieth century as a national "golden era." Indeed, the focus of this new field of study intended not to limit itself to Hungary, but to integrate neighboring countries such as Romania, the Slovak Republic, Ukraine, Slovenia, and Croatia, among others. All of these countries have strong ethnic Hungarian minorities that are caught between assimilation and the preservation of their own language and traditions—people who speak multiple languages and have hybrid identities.

In terms of institutional structures, the periphery proved to be more flexible in its reception of this approach than did Budapest. The cultural-anthropological discourse was anchored above all at the Universities of Pécs and Miskolc. At the time, Peter Niedermüller was teaching in Pécs at the Institute for Communication Studies; in Miskolc, Ernő Kunt was commissioned to establish a new chair, which led to the founding of the *Department for Cultural and Visual Anthropology*. Both maintained close contacts with WAC (Workshop for Anthropology and Communication), a research institute located in Miercurea-Ciuc, Romania but not associated with any university. At the Institute a number of scholars, headed by Zoltán Biró, had come together to study the Eastern region of the Carpathian basin, where Hungarian traditions are still very much alive.[2]

A conference held at the University of Miskolc on the 6th and 7th of November, 1992 can be regarded as the founding act through which the new cultural anthropological discourse took shape in public. It was dedicated to the topic of "The Dilemma of Complex Cultural Studies in Today's Hungary." Peter Niedermüller contributed by far the most extensive paper, which provides a systematic overview of the development in the social sciences, putting a special emphasis on Sociology and Cultural Anthropology in both English and German language scholarship. Against this background he can take a decisive stance against traditional Hungarian cultural research and identify a significant and extensive task for Cultural Anthropology in the Eastern Central Europe cultural region (Niedermüller 1993). While this strictly scholarly contribution serves to create the means by which dialogue could be entered into with the international social scientific research community, Ernő Kunt's paper prefers an essayistic tone and attempts to verbalize the challenges presented by the new cultural studies from a personal point of view. The text reflects the two years he spent attempting to establish his new institute and give it a contemporary profile (Kunt 1993).

Because I will analyze examples of Ernő Kunt's scholarly photographic works at a later juncture, I would now like to examine this paper in greater detail. The text starts surprisingly:

> I have been visiting the graveyards of the Eastern Carpathians from Löcsé to Kolosvár, from Munkács to Brassó—as I have done for decades. I hope I will be able to consider things more calmly from here and be a better judge of them. Above all, I am concerned with culture: how do you explore it, how do you teach it? In the face of gravestones and remembrances, I have been asking myself how to contemplate culture in an appropriate way: not to confuse important and unimportant matters, to perceive the present but to see the future as well. [...] I roam between the graves, listing the names, recalling the lives—in an attempt to understand them. Because I have always been convinced that any valid future must be based on a credible past (Kunt 1993, 111).

The opening of the text appears less surprising if you know the intellectual biography of Ernő Kunt. After finishing his studies in Hungarian Literature and Ethnology, he was employed at the Ottó Herman Museum in Miskolc in 1974. The director of this museum, which maintains both natural history and ethnological collections, was interested in improving the reputation of his house and increased emphasis on field research, to which end he cooperated with a number of young scholars. Thus, in 1976, Kunt received a ten-month grant to study in Finland. During his stay in Helsinki and Jyväskylä, the interests that were to shape his future sharpened: he focused on the entirety of human knowledge and rituals connected to death and on Visual Anthropology. In addition, he received training in creative photography at the Art School of Helsinki. In 1979, he finished his Ph.D. with a thesis on the graveyards of Aggtelek, a mountainous region close to the Slovak border. Many publications on the subject of cemeteries, burials, and cultural imaginations hereafter followed, all of which were summed up in *The Last Metamorphosis,* published in 1987 (Kunt 1987). A few years before, in 1981, he had brought out a book—or, better, a pamphlet—in which he criticized modern societies for not providing culturally appropriate ways to cope with mortality and death. For him, culture represented the fundamental means through which the members of a community or society face death and which enables the relatives of the deceased to live on and to keep the community functional. Although his book broke several taboos at once—among them that surrounding suicide—it was published despite difficulties with the censors and caused a great deal of public debate (Kunt 1981).

Indeed, above and beyond its ties to its author's intellectual biography, the essay's introductory passage contains a number of important elements. It develops a mapping of the Eastern Central European cultural region to which the new Cultural Anthropology was meant to dedicate itself. Löcsé, the old Hungarian name of the city and Levoča, the actual Slovakian one, is located in what is now the Slovak Republic; Kolosvàr is now located in Rumania, as is Brasso (Cluj and Brassov in Rumanian, respectively). Munkács is a Transcarpathian city in the Ukraine known as Munkaçevo in the Ukrainian language, a center of Chassidic Judaism in the nineteenth century. Although these places last lay within Hungarian borders before 1919, they remain home to strong Hungarian-speaking minority populations. The Hungarian people have coined the term Trianon to designate the cultural trauma resulting from the dissolution of the Austro-Hungarian empire after the town near Paris where World War I victors made their decision to draw new borders in 1919. Implied in the essay is the message that the people living in a region in which the borders of four countries come together, with its multiple traditions and languages, will have to overcome this Trianon trauma. This can by no means be achieved through a revisionist reestablishment of the pre-war physical borders of the countries involved. Instead, a more appropriate solution lies in developing an understanding of basic differences and valid knowledge about each other. Building on the diversity of the people and the region, a new consciousness and mixed hybrid identity can be formed in this part of Europe.

As of this point, the essay as a whole is carried by its author's decisive orientation to the future. In order to fulfill this ambition, he must identify the contours of this future culture to the extent that they can be drawn from today's perspective. This is just what Kunt undertakes by means of a number of approaches, showing himself to have attained an astonishingly advanced level for Hungary in 1992. Indeed, he unfolds the central paradigms discussed within Cultural Studies. He first mentions the interplay between the global and the local that, on the one hand—from a superficial perspective—is said to lead in the future to a uniform world culture, while on the other, local cultures and subcultures are said to gain profile as an opposing camp to globalization that promises familiarity and recognition. Secondly, he directs our attention to the growing significance of technical media apparatuses by means of which information has already become a new and powerful factor in the forming of society and culture.

At the end of the essay, the cemetery motif reappears, but is now centered on a specific location, the cemetery of Hazsongàrd, a district of Cluj. Cluj, or Kolosvár, had long been a center of Transylvanian culture and the site of many famous Hungarian's graves. While roaming the graveyards, Ernő Kunt questions if all his ideas can really be accomplished. He finds a mute answer in the grave of the Hungarian-Jewish scholar Sámuel Brassai, who lived from 1800 to 1897. In the course of his century-spanning lifetime, he was a journalist, a librarian, and a university professor with a vast variety of interests—a poly-historian who achieved an all-encompassing education. He was also the teacher of another famous intellectual, Ottó Herman, who was born close to Miskolc in Lillafüred and who established the cultural research of this area.

> I walk to the grave of Sámuel Brassai, the one with the statue. The way he perceived himself has always been very valuable to me. It is possible to know a lot of things but still to question this knowledge constantly, it is possible to recognize personal talents and to enhance them—in order to form your own personality. And yet he insists that I listen to his quiet warning: to learn few things thoroughly and slowly and to teach in the same manner (Kunt 1993, 128).

III.

In the following, I would like to turn to those of Ernő Kunt's works that are centered around the discipline of photography and analyze them in respect to the heterogeneous discourses on a new Hungarian cultural identity. Their specific nature stems from the many years Ernő Kunt spent in research and exhibition design at the Ottó Herman Museum before he became an academic. During this period, he brought a Department for Visual Anthropology into being at the museum, the main purpose of which was to establish a collection of historical and contemporary photography. Thus, Ernő Kunt's work combines a theoretical approach to the photographic medium, which includes the issues of adequate documentation, archival preservation, analysis, and presentation with the practical experience of cataloging private collections and organizing exhibitions and—not least significantly—his own photographic practice. All the while, these spheres of activity remained in close dialogue with one another.[3]

In 1979, Ernő Kunt opened his first exhibition for the Ottó Herman Museum, entitled *Azok a gyerekek*. It was based on materials from the estate of a pioneer of ethnographic photography in Hungary, Kálmán Kóris (1878–1967). In the exhibition catalogue Ernő Kunt writes:

> The exhibition shows the life of peasant children of a Hungarian Village in North Hungary, Mezőkövesd, through photographs taken in 1904–1905. Kálmán Kóris, who was 26 years old at that time, made them on 13x18 cm glass negatives. Kóris, due to his many-sided interests, has left us photo-documents of great value from a time when ethnographic photography had just begun. His sociological and ethnographic knowledge is a guarantee for the authenticity and inner richness of the photos, his technical interest ensures the good technical quality of the plates, while his art school training made a sensitive visual composition possible. The organizer of the exhibition wishes to show the life of peasant children before the two World Wars to the adults and children of our time by means of these photographs, as well as the enlargement and offcut of some details (Kunt 1979).

The manner in which Ernő Kunt proceeded in this exhibition is to be assessed as an attempt to analyze old photographs as ethnographic sources. To the extent that the exhibition itself can be reconstructed on the basis of the catalogue, its concept lies in creating a balance between cultural-historical contextualization by means of text and the aesthetic presentation of the photographs. Kálmán Kóris's photographs were presented in their original form, but at the same time enlargements of selected details were used that altered the original compositions. In this way, Kunt accentuated elements that had been of little importance in the original composition. In doing so, he made what he discovered in the photographs visible to his audience. Furthermore, the catalogue text's description of the qualities to be found in Kálmán Kóris's photographs could just as well be Ernő Kunt describing himself. They put into words the very expectations that he had for his own photographs and that he tried to realize in his photographic practice.

During his years at the Ottó Herman Museum in the 1980s, Ernő Kunt's research was dedicated to one question in particular: how did the peasants incorporate the urban, bourgeois medium of photography into their own rural culture? On the basis of John Collier's method (Collier and Collier 1986), he developed a complex research practice, which he elucidated in a number of theoretical articles (Kunt 1986; Hägele 2001). Even though it represents an exact copy of the image it captures, according to Kunt, photography nevertheless more or less obscures the object of its interest. This makes it important to conduct accompanying interviews with those who make use of the photographs and to not only ask them for information about the image, but also to record everything they can verbally associate with the photograph. Only then can we cast light upon the hidden, invisible layers buried in photographs; only thus can we learn about the visual culture of the people making daily use of the photographs. Therefore, a further step in the process of analysis must lie in giving these people a camera to work with themselves and asking them to photograph their own life-worlds—this method is known today as "substitutive field research," although it is still seldom put into practice.

Based upon his analysis of many associative interviews with peasants in Hungary, the Slovak Republic, and in Romania, Ernő Kunt was able to gain many important insights into their unique perception of photography as a visual medium. The results made it obvious that this medium had not simply been adopted, but rather that an active process of acquisition had occurred, leading to its integration into the pre-existing visual culture. Only through this active adaptation could photography claim a place within this visual culture. For representations of expressions of individuality and personal identity of this sort were entirely unprecedented. As a result, schematized and typified signs of membership to one of the sexes, an age group, a particular village, or a local region, that is, those signs and codes that create the collective, not the individual dimension of human culture, were emphasized in both the interviews and the photographs. This was also reflected in the manner in which the photographs were used and displayed in individual households. Even today, photographs are seldom hung on the walls in isolation from other decorative elements; instead, they are integrated into collages of Christmas cards, religious homilies, newspaper clippings, small figures, and other objects, such as mirrors, that have been arranged according to aesthetic criteria. It follows that, even today, photography is not implemented as a representation of individual identity. Instead, what is of primary importance are the social relations, emotional sympathy, and religious values that can only be created through such 'life collages.' The peasants who design and continually expand upon these 'life collages' clearly associate aesthetic capacity with an individual interpretation of their lives and recognize that the ensemble hanging on their walls is its valid visual representation (Kunt 1997).

In the second half of the 1980s and during the great political changes that followed for Hungary, Kunt began to use the research he had conducted over the years to create programmatic exhibitions of his own photographic works. These exhibitions were thematically centered on his explorations of graveyards and concepts of the hereafter. Their venues were variable—sometimes they were held in galleries, sometimes in ethnographic museums. Just as was the case in Ernő Kunt's first exhibition, their concepts, although always flexible, once again attempted to achieve a balance between contextualization and aesthetic presentation. The first of these exhibitions were held in the Galéria Budapest and the Ethnographic Museum Schloss Kittsee in Austria. For each of these, an accompanying catalogue was published, entitled *A mulandóság szobrai* or *Statuen der Vergänglichkeit* (Sculptures of Transitoriness), respectively. The preface summarizes in a precise fashion what was most important to Ernő Kunt:

The wooden grave carvings in Hungary are nothing other than the experience of death put into an aesthetic form. Everything the people sense and understand of death, the dead and of the hereafter is integrated in these aesthetic forms. [...] The carvings not only fulfill the purpose to commemorate the dead. Their beauty is rooted in a deeper sphere. [...] We must grasp the sensual quality of the carvings which maintains a visual reality of its own (Kunt 1985, 5).

Taking the exhibition's context into account, one could say that it reverses Cultural Studies' research program in respect to photography. If the latter aims to reveal the hidden aspects of photography through associative interviews, then the exhibition initiates a movement in the opposite direction. Through contextualizing photo essays and accompanying text, the observer is meant to gather information about the production and the ritual use of wooden grave carvings, about their history and their local variations, about the meaning of their ornaments and much more. However, all this is merely intended to lead the observer to the genuine visual essence of the grave carvings that is accessible in the photographs. The observer is meant to gain access to these visual representations and, on this basis, to engage in an aesthetic experience that is no longer possible in our everyday way of encountering cemeteries.[4]

If we consider the political and cultural situation in which Hungary found itself at the time of the exhibitions, the photographs take on a significance that reaches far beyond their professed concept of presentation.[5] If we proceed from Ernő Kunt's research and the conclusions he drew from it, and, further, if we consider his programmatic 1992 essay, then, in many ways, the photographs in the exhibition and the discourse that they legitimize reflect and develop the search for a new—however fragile and temporary—cultural identity in Hungary.

Seen in themselves, the motifs in the photographs, the wooden grave carvings, refer above all to a cultural practice from northeastern Hungary and the neighboring Carpathian basin that has roots reaching back to the pre-Christian era. These were rediscovered by the Reformers of the seventeenth century and employed to differentiate themselves from the Catholics and other religious groups. Against the background of a dominant discourse that emphasizes Hungary's deep Western heritage as a product of its early Christianization and its long Catholic tradition, these photographs make claims on a right to difference. Moreover, they can be read as a plainer, alternative ornamental style, which harmonizes with natural cycles and stands in opposition to the pomp of Catholicism. In articulating this right to difference, the discourse situated in the photographs creates an additional cartography. For, in opposition to the revisionist discourse of a number of right-wing parties calling for the reestablishment of Hungary Major within borders that in 1919 extended to the eastern foothills of the Carpathians, these images posit an inescapably heterogeneous Eastern Central European cultural region that takes into account a multiethnic history that is hundreds of years old. Not only the spatial, but also the temporal coordinates have been redrawn in this alternative cartography. Challenging the future-oriented new beginning that is often felt to be the means to shake off the hated socialist past, these photographs remind us—like a modern *memento mori*—of the taboo fact that modern life, too, will someday pass. At the same time, they seek their base of reference in the multifaceted traditions and histories that are only to be found off the beaten track of those urban centers and golden eras that have left their traces in the layers of cultural memory. Finally, as objects concretized in a particular media, the photographs represent a counterdiscourse. They express themselves in an antiquated medium from the nineteenth century as a reaction to the challenges of the present. Surely the decision to employ photography as a medium also indicates what was economically feasible in this situation and could be put to productive use in cultural research. However, at the same time, they refer—as photographs—to the growing importance of the visual media and reflect critically on this change. Through their use of the slower and more contemplative rhythm that is inherent to photography, they represent for the observer, not only a school of seeing—at the same time, they invite the observer to engage with that process of negotiation through which a sense of understanding for one's own culture must continually be regained.

Admittedly, this discourse is a marginal one, an institutionally weak voice from the periphery. Nonetheless, the photographs and the concept behind the exhibitions in which they were shown clearly indicate the existence of a counterdiscourse and are rooted in knowledge won through research in the field of Visual Anthropology. Although the exhibitions of Ernő Kunt were limited to the period of the political change in Hungary when there was a strong sense of a new era about to dawn, the scholars who are involved in the Institute today still keep faith with the ideas of its founder. Even today they try to initiate counterdiscourses through their scientific and public work—for example by giving a new meaning to the process of acculturation—and to strengthen the positive effects of the long multiethnic history of Middle East Europe.

NOTES

1. I would like to offer my heartfelt thanks to the present director of the Institute, Prof. József Kotics, as well as to, representative for all the other colleagues I met there, Dr. Gábor Biczó and Dr. Zoltán Ilyés for the friendly welcome I received, their openness for my research interests, and the intensive introduction to Eastern Europe as a cultural region which they provided me.

2. Since 1993, WAC has published an Annual Bulletin in English entitled *Experiments*. It can be ordered from the following address: WAC, 4100 Miercurea-Ciuc, P.O. Box 81, Romania.

3. Ernő Kunt's highly developed sensitivity for the visual has its roots in his biography. He was influenced by his father, Ernő Kunt sen., who was an art teacher

and successful painter. From the beginning, the field of the visual possessed a natural quality for him. For Ernő Kunt, the visual opened its own gate of access to the cultural sphere, convincing him that he had to find a visual reaction to culture's visual phenomena. Although Ernő Kunt was also an active painter, he found his true medium in photography.

4. During my research, I was able to speak to Orsolya Danó. She was among the first twenty students to be accepted to the Institute for its first academic year, 1993/94. According to Danó, in his lectures on visual anthropolgy, Ernő Kunt developed shamanism as a model for the discipline. As do shamans, visual anthropology mediates between the visible world of everyday life and a hidden, invisible world that it makes accessible for human experience and enacts in the immediate present.

5. The Institute's staff continues to develop a concept, which lies queer to the patterns of reception in Art and in Ethnographic Museums. A catalogue accompanying one of its exhibitions offers an overview of the most recent research situated in between photography and cultural studies: Bán, *Körüliert Képek.*

REFERENCES

Bán, András, ed. *Körüliert Képek. Fényképezés és Kultúrakutatás.* Miskolc, Miskolci Gáleria 1999.

Collier Jr., John and Malcolm Collier. *Visual Anthropology: Photography as a Research Method,* Revised and expanded edition. Albuquerque, Univ. of New Mexico Pr., 1986.

Geertz, Clifford. "The World in Pieces: Culture and Politics at the End of the Century." In *Available Light. Anthropological Reflections on Philosophical Topics.* Edited by Clifford Geertz. Princeton, Princeton Univ. Pr. 2000, 218–63.

Hägele, Ulrich. "Visual Folklore. Zur Rezeption und Methodik der Fotografie in der Volkskunde." In *Methoden der Volkskunde.* Edited by Silke Götsch and Albrecht Lehmann. Berlin, Reimer 2001, 277–300.

Kunt, Ernő. *Azok a gyerekek* (Children without childhood). Unpaginated, Miskolc: Ottó Herman Museum, 1979.

———. *A halál türkrében* (In the face of death). Budapest, Magretö Könyvkadó 1981.

———. Statuen der Vergänglichkeit. Volkskunst ungarischer Dorffriedhöfe, Eine Fotoausstellung von Ernő Kunt. Ethnographisches Museum Schloss Kittsee, 1985.

———. *Az utolsó átváltozás* (The last metamorphosis). Budapest, Gondolat Könyvkiadó 1987.

———. "Fotografie und Kulturforschung." *Fotogeschichte* 6 (1986), 13–33.

———. *Photo-Anthropology. The Role of Photography in Cultural Research.* Edited by András Bán and Mária Kunt, Miskolc, KVAT füzetek 3, 1997.

Kunt, Ernő and Zsuzsa Szarvas, eds. *A Komplex Kultúrakutatás Dilemmai A Mai Magyarországon* (Dilemmas of the Complex Cultural Research in Today's Hungary). Miskolc, KVAT füzetek 1, 1993.

Niedermüller, Peter. "Empirikus kultúrakutatás avagy az antropológia esélyei Kelet-Európában (Empirical cultural research or the chances of anthropology in East

Europe)." In *A komplex kultúrakutatás dilemmái a mai Magyarországon* (Dilemmas of the complex cultural research in today's Hungary), edited by Ernő Kunt and Zsusza Szarvas, Miskolc, KVAT füzetek 1, 1993: 27–85.

Schlögl, Karl. *Promenade in Jalta und andere Städtebilder.* München, Carl Hanser 2001.

———. *Die Mitte liegt ostwärts. Europa im Übergang.* München, Carl Hanser 2002.

Contributors

ALEIDA ASSMANN

Studied English language and literature in Heidelberg and Tuebingen. 1992–93 Fellow at the Institute for Cultural Studies, Essen; since 1993 Professor for English literature and literary studies at the University of Constance. 1995: Member of the research group "Historische Sinnbildung" (Jörn Rüsen, ZiF, University of Bielefeld); 1998/99 Fellow at the "Wissenschaftskolleg," Berlin; 1999: Research Award for Humanities, Philip-Morris-Foundation. Research interests: writing and memory, historical anthropology of the media. Publications: *Die Legitimität der Fiktion* (1980), *Arbeit am nationalen Gedächtnis. Eine kurze Geschichte der deutschen Bildungsidee* (1993), *Zeit und Tradition* (1999), *Erinnerungsräume* (1999), with Ute Frevert *Geschichtsvergessenheit / Geschichtsversessenheit. Über den Umgang mit deutschen Vergangenheiten seit 1945* (1999). Editor: *Weisheit* (1990), *Kultur als Lebenswelt und Monument* (1991), *Mnemosyne* (1991), *Texte und Lektüren* (1996).

PETER BRAUN

Associate Professor for German Literature and Media Studies at the University of Constance. He studied German Literature, Cultural Anthropology and Art History at the University of Hamburg. He also attended the Documentary Class of the Art School of Hamburg. His Ph.D. thesis deals with the photography of Leonore Mau and the literary works of Hubert Fichte, who together explored African-American cultures for more than fifteen years. The book entitled *Die doppelte Dokumentation* (Doubled Documentation) was published in 1997. He has published articles in the fields of documentary film, literature, and cultural studies. His latest book, *Schattenspiele* (Shadow Plays), will come out in 2006. He spent several months as a guest lecturer at the University of Prague, Czech Republic in 1996 and at the University of Miskolc, Hungary in 2001.

MIRIAM BUTT

Miriam Butt is Professor of Theoretical and Computational Linguistics at the University of Constance. Her interests include morphology, syntax, historical linguistics, and sociolinguistics. She has authored, coauthored and coedited several books on morphosyntax, semantics, historical linguistics, and computational linguistics: *The Structure of Complex Predicates in Urdu, A Grammar Writer's Cookbook, Theoretical Perspectives on Word Order Issues, The Projection of Arguments, Time over Matter, Argument Realization, Nominals: Inside and Out.*

Arif Dirlik

Knight Professor of Social Science at the University of Oregon. He is the author of many works on China, the Pacific, and theoretical issues of cultural studies and globalization. His most recent book-length works are *Kuaguo ziben shidaide houzhimin piping* (Postcolonial Criticism in the Age of Transnational Capital, in Chinese) and *Marxism in the Chinese Revolution.*

Wimal Dissanayake

Professor in the Department of Comparative Literature at the University of Hong Kong and member of the Graduate Faculty at the University of Hawaii. He is the author and editor of over thirty books on cinema, communication, and cultural studies published in the U.S. and U.K. Among his books are *Melodrama and Asian Cinema* (Cambridge University Press), *Colonialism and Nationalism in Asian Cinema* (Indiana University Press), and *Global/Local* (Duke University Press). He is the founding editor of the "East West Film Journal" and a general editor of a series of books on Hong Kong cinema to be published by the University of Hong Kong Press. In 1995, he was invited to give the distinguished Wei Lung Professorial lecture at the Chinese University of Hong Kong.

Natascha (Vittinghoff) Gentz

Junior Professor, Sinology, Frankfurt University. M.A. 1994 on Contemporary Chinese Historical Drama, Ph.D. 1998 on the History of Modern Journalism in nineteenth-century China at Heidelberg University. 1999–2001 Research Fellow in a VW-Project on the Transfer of Scientific Knowledge in nineteenth-century China at Goettingen University. Currently engaged in a research project on the Invention of Chinese Tragedy in Drama Theory and Theatrical Practice. Publications: *Mapping Meanings. The Field of New Learning in Late Qing China,* ed. (2004); *Die Anfänge des Journalismus in China 1860–1911* (2002), *Geschichte der Partei entwunden, eine semiotische Analyse des Dramas Jiang Qing und ihre Ehemänner von Sha Yexin (1992)* (1995). Articles on Modern Chinese Literature and Journalism and Cultural History in Late Imperial China.

Ratiba Hadj-Moussa

Assistant Professor of Sociology and associated with the Joint Graduate Programme in Communication & Culture (York and Ryerson University). Her recent research projects revolve around the issue of public space and new media technologies in the Maghreb, in which she tries to think the specificity of the political in non-Western contexts, and the issue of cultural identities and media as they are elaborated by first generation Muslim women in Canada. Recent Publications: 1994: *Le corps, l'histoire, le territoire: les rapports femme-homme dans le cinéma algérien* (Body, History, Territory: Gender Relations in Algerian Cinema). Books edited: 1996 K. Fall, R. Hadj-Moussa and D. Siméoni, *Les convergences culturelles dans les sociétés pluriethniques* (Cultural Convergences in Multiethnic Societies), F. Lorrigio, R. Hadj-Moussa and M. Peressini (Eds.); *The Mediterranean Rediscovered*, Ottawa-Hull, Canadian Museum of Civilizations, (forthcoming). Articles: 2002: "Between the Cultural Imperative and the Desire for Political Emancipation: What is at Stake in Gender Relations in the Arab World," Blackwell Companion to Gender Studies, Ph. Essed, D. Grossberg, A. Kobayashi (Eds.); 2000: "Indétermination, appartenance et identification: penser l'identité" (Indetermination, Belonging and Identification: Thinking Identity. Produire l'identité, produire la culture ? (Producing Identiy, Producing culture?), A. Fortin (Ed.), 1999: Reprint of "The Locus of Tensions: Gender in Algerian Cinema," African Cinema: Post- Colonial and Feminist Readings, K. Harrow (Ed.).

Roger Hillman

Has taught at the A.N.U. since 1979, originally entirely in German Studies, but then convened the new Film Studies Program from its first year in 1995 till last year. Relevant publications include the coedited volume *Fields of Vision* (UCAL Press). Current research interests include the overlap of music and cinema in identity issues.

Stefan Kramer

Associate Professor of Media Studies at the University of Constance, Germany; Associate Research Fellow at the Institute of Chinese and Korean Studies, University of Tuebingen, Germany; Publications on Media Culture, Cultural Media Theory, Intercultural Communication, Cinema and Television Culture and East Asian Media Cultures; among them: *Schattenbilder* (Dortmund 1996), *Geschichte des chinesischen Films* (Stuttgart, Weimar 1997, Korean Edition: Seoul 2000), *Bilder aus dem Reich des Drachen* (with Hu-Chong Kramer, Bad Honnef 2002), *Vom Eigenen und Fremden* (Bielefeld 2004).

Tamar Liebes

Chair of the Dept. of Communication and Journalism at the Hebrew University of Jerusalem. She has written about the way in which globalized culture infiltrates into local cultures. More lately she has been interested in electronic journalistic genres, as the new site of public discourse, in times of peace and of war (*Reporting the Arab Israeli Conflict: How Hegemony Works*, Routledge; *American Dreams, Hebrew Subtitles: Globalization from the Receiving End*, Hampton Press 2003). She has collaborated on comparative research with European and American colleagues. She has written about media globalism and cultural identity (Liebes and Katz: *The Export of Meaning: Cross Cultural Reading of Dallas*, 1993), and on media genres (soap opera, news, political talkshows, live broadcasts) with a special interest in the reporting of conflict.

Irmbert Schenk

Professor for Media Studies at the University of Bremen. Publications on the History of Italian Literature and Theatre in the 20th Century, Media Studies, and Media Pedagogy. Scholarly Interests: Film History (Germany, Italy, Silent Film), Film Reception, Intermediality.

Michael C. Stone

B.A. Anthropology, Amherst College; M.A. Latin American Studies, Stanford University; Ph.D. Cultural Anthropology, University of Texas at Austin; at present Executive Director of the Program in Latin American Studies, Princeton University. Field research in Central America, Jamaica and the U.S.-Mexico border region; translator of the book *Beautiful Flowers of the Maquiladora: Life Histories of Women Workers in Tijuana*, by Mexican anthropologist Norma Iglesias Prieto (University of Texas Press, 1997); current research concerns the transnational character of indigenous musics of Caribbean Central America as "world music" in the global circuits of capital. Visiting Senior Fulbright Professor (2001–2002) at the University of Constance.

Kyle Wohlmut

B.A., English Literature, University of California, Santa Cruz. Has worked in the Netherlands as a full-time translator since 1999, and is also a noted harpist with several published articles in harp journals in Europe and the United States.

Index